WE HEARD
IT WHEN
WE WERE
YOUNG

WE HEARD IT WHEN WE WERE YOUNG

Chuy Renteria

UNIVERSITY OF IOWA PRESS | IOWA CITY

University of Iowa Press, Iowa City 52242
Copyright © 2021 by Chuy Renteria
www.uipress.uiowa.edu
Printed in the United States of America

Cover design by Kimberly Glyder; text design by April Leidig

Printed on acid-free paper

Library of Congress Cataloging-in-Publication Data
Names: Renteria, Chuy, 1985– author.
Title: We Heard It When We Were Young / by Chuy Renteria.
Description: Iowa City: University of Iowa Press, [2021]
Identifiers: LCCN 2021007088 (print) | LCCN 2021007089 (ebook) |
ISBN 9781609388058 (paperback) | ISBN 9781609388065 (ebook) |
Subjects: LCSH: Renteria, Chuy, 1985—Childhood and youth. | Mexican American
youth—Iowa—West Liberty—Biography. | Children of Immigrants—Iowa—
West Liberty—Biography. | Mexican Americans—Iowa—West Liberty—Social
conditions. | West Liberty (Iowa)—Biography. | West Liberty (Iowa)—Ethnic relations.
Classification: LCC F629.W4464 R46 2021 (print) | LCC F629.W4464 (ebook) |
DDC 977.7/68—dc23
LC record available at https://lccn.loc.gov/2021007088
LC ebook record available at https://lccn.loc.gov/2021007089

To Stephanie Cromer and Carol Clark

Years ago you saw it in me,

even before I saw it myself

CONTENTS

THE TALES IN THIS BOOK reflect the author's recollection of events. Dialogue has been recreated from memory. Some events have been re-mixed and rearranged for the sake of clarity and pacing. Some names and identifying details have been changed throughout for varying reasons deemed by the author. The author maintains that the underlying spirit of the events is true. Chances are the parts that seem the most unbelievable are the most real. Just ask anyone from Wes Lib.

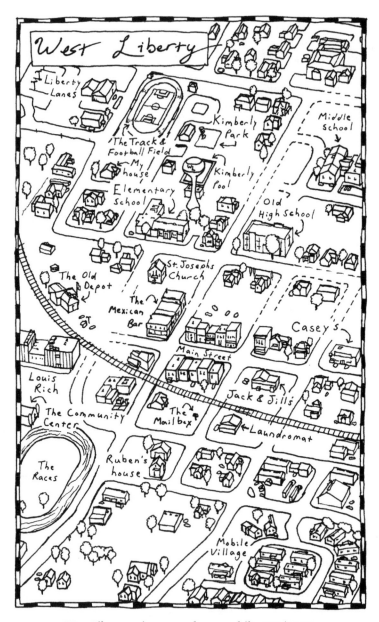

West Liberty as it appeared to me while growing up.
Illustration by Zoë Woodworth.

PROLOGUE

BY THE TIME I noticed someone was talking to me, he had repeated himself a few times. His voice invaded my thoughts, like someone turning the dial on a radio until words creep up from the static. "Hey. Little Mexican. Hey, I'm talking to you, motherfucker. You little fucking Mexican."

My daydreams of Nickelodeon shows and video games dissipated. It was the second "Mexican" that snapped me out of my thoughts. It had so much acid and hate in it, this word that was a statement of who I was. A qualifier. An identity. A thing for a man to belt out at a child walking home from school. I was confused at first. Was someone talking to me? All sense of the childhood I had known before this changed as I turned and saw the couple walking behind me.

They were high school kids. A man and a woman, for all intents and purposes. They were tall like how all high schoolers are tall when you're a kid. It was only for an instant when I turned around and saw them, but the look on the man's face has stayed with me more than twenty years later. He was blond with the fuzz of a mustache that teenaged boys try to grow as a badge of honor. His hair was long and pulled back, like a hockey player before he puts on his helmet. The woman had her arms entwined in the man's as they stepped in pace behind me. "Yeah, got your attention, huh, faggot? I'm talking to you, you little fucking spic. You goddamn wetback. Who do you think you are, walking and looking back at me like you own this sidewalk?"

I remember his eyes. The way his brows furrowed in anger as he spat out his hate. I was in fifth grade, around age ten or eleven. But I recall feeling so much younger. I remember this incident as a little boy. As an infant. I mull over this incident at night. In walks and car rides. In my memories I envision a child walking on two little legs, which I very much was, but it caught me off guard to realize I was already in fifth grade when this incident happened. Maybe I remember myself as being so young because I felt so powerless. To this day his hate distorts this memory. The memory of a child who doesn't yet know what it feels like to be dehumanized.

But it was his girlfriend who brought about the worst of it. She tightened her arms around the man. I don't remember her features, only her hands as they applied pressure to the denim sleeve of the man beside her. She said his name but I've lost it. "Come on, leave him alone," she said in a voice that wasn't so much pleading as it was singsongy annoyance that she had to temper her boyfriend. "He's only a kid."

At this time I turned away from the couple. Everything was on fire. My senses were reduced to base-level manifestations. Get out of here. Tighten your grip around the straps of your backpack and quicken your steps before things get worse. Curl up in a ball as you walk. Steel yourself for more. The man's words projected across the sidewalk, into my ears and echoing for all of time. "No, that is the goddamn point. That's when the hell they need to hear it. Don't you get it? These little spics need to hear this. They need to hear it young." And then he laughed.

I heard him say it and will never forget the words. I said nothing as I increased my distance from the couple. The woman said something; I imagine she patted him on the arm as she chastised him. A playful tease as they watched the little boy quicken his pace and cross the street toward the elementary school where he used to play Heads Up, Seven Up and cry during tornado drills. I will never forget the deliberateness in his fury. He wanted me to hear it. I write these words as a child having learned one of the great and horrible lessons of human nature. We heard it when we were young.

———————

I kept this confrontation buried deep inside me. It stayed tucked away as a lump in my throat, as an ache in my stomach. To tell my family was to somehow make it more real, to admit evil like this existed not only in our town but in the world at large. It wasn't enough to say that somewhere out there an adult could hurl slurs at a young child to deliberately tear him down. This wasn't a scene that played out in grainy black-and-white video on school projectors or in the sanitized texts of beat-up books you threw into your backpack to be forgotten by the time you got home. No, this happened right here in my hometown. To me. It was enough to make my eyes water at the very thought of it. I couldn't bear to tell my sister or my mother. I didn't know how to bring it up to my father or brother. It was my load to bear as I went through school that week. I didn't even tell my best friends. It wasn't until Thursday's catechism class when it all came out of me in a small yet pronounced fury.

We entered St. Joseph's Church the same as any other Thursday, from a nondescript side door leading down into the basement. This Thursday it all looked so drab and gray. I slunk into my brown metal chair as Mrs. Liddell closed the partition to our room. Eric clapped his hand on my back as he sat beside me. I hadn't told him about the incident by the high school, but he knew me well enough to know that something was eating at me. Ruben flanked me on the opposite side and offered us each a piece of gum. My head shake was a barely registered no as the man's words repeated in my head: "I'm talking to you, you little fucking spic. You goddamn wetback." My eyes adjusted as the lighting in the room changed from the closed partition.

Mrs. Liddell got right into the lesson for the week, saying, "Today we are going to talk about something very important. Respect. We are going to talk about respecting your elders."

"Oh, here we go," said Eric as half the class sniggered and laughed, fueled by whatever recent spat Eric had gotten into with the teachers at school.

"No, this is serious," Mrs. Liddell continued. "The entire basis of what we are doing right here and right now is based on respect. I have something to teach you, and you are, or should be, paying me that respect." This elicited another response from the class as Mrs. Liddell shot a smile at Eric. Eric blushed a bit and smiled in return, not talking back this time. "What I implore you all to do is listen to the adults in your lives. Really listen to them and show them the respect they show you. Your elders have things to teach you as long as you are willing to listen. They will show you the way."

As far as a lesson went, this was fairly average. Benign, even. Listen to your teachers, brush your teeth, don't eat too many sweets, pray before bed. Any other day I would have met it with my usual inattentiveness and longing for Nintendo sessions back home. Instead it was the first and only time I said something directly to our catechism class.

I unfurled my hand toward the buzzing fluorescent lights of the church basement.

Mrs. Liddell did a slight double take when she saw my hand in the air. "Oh, Chuy? You have something to add?" I could feel Eric and Ruben looking at each other from either side of me. Maybe they thought I was going to bring up the "masturbation is a sin" lesson from two weeks ago.

"But not all of the adults in our lives are good people. Not everyone in this town is good. Why should we listen to people like that even though they're older than us?" I said with the quiet fury of a boy pouring out trauma.

There was a shuffling in the room, an energy of not knowing how to deal with this question. It was a question uncharacteristic of me in the context of our classes. It was like the air got sucked out of the partitioned room. Mrs. Liddell stammered, "Wh-why, yes. There are bad people out in the world. This is true. But I'm talking about the adults in our community looking out for you. The ones in our church. In our town."

My eyes were welling up. I wished they weren't. I wished that they were dry and that I was free from any emotion as I responded. I wish they weren't welling up now as I write this. That the pain I experienced as a little boy didn't still hurt as a man looking back at the cruelty of the world. "No. Even in this town. There are evil people. Just because they're old doesn't mean they know anything. It just means they are older people who are evil," I said, my voice wavering.

The adult in the room full of children stopped. She looked at me and saw something. Pain or anger. Fear and questioning. The pretense of a lesson stopped then as she really looked at me. "Chuy, what happened?" And I told her and my classmates what happened. It was only a couple of blocks from where we were in the church. I told them about the high schooler and the things I heard.

"Chuy, yo, this is for real?" Eric asked as I finished my recollection.

"Yeah, of course it is," replied Ruben as his head shook like he was very slightly repeating a nod yes, a tic he has when he's really internalizing something. The usual bustle of our class was silent.

Mrs. Liddell reeled from the revelation. "And that was at the high school, you said? Here in town?" I nodded from my seat, my head turned down toward the table.

It wasn't that Mrs. Liddell didn't believe me. It was that she couldn't believe her town had the capacity for such hatred. I will never forget how she stood in the middle of the room, processing the story, trying to reconcile it with the town she once knew. Because she now had to add this extra piece to West Liberty, one that changed the sum of it from its individual parts. It changed her like it changed me, the knowledge that this hatred manifested itself in her neighbors. In the graduating seniors as they celebrated Skip Day and drove around town. It was part of the factory and homecoming parades. It was the grocery store and tractor trailers on the south side of town. It was schools and libraries. It was in the church she stood within. All of the parts of the town had to share space with the revelation of this hatred that seared itself into the soul of a little boy who played games with her son at recess. It's all I can do to keep myself from crying, the memory of this woman not being able to reconcile the town she knew with the reality before her. "I'm sorry," she said with a deflation of authority. "You're right. You're right and I'm sorry." I felt a touch on my back as one of my friends comforted me, their hand moving in little circles and swishing against the fabric of my coat.

PART ONE

WELCOME TO WEST LIBERTY

THE MANGLED OPENING guitar licks of "Angel Baby" by Rosie (real name Rosalie Méndez) and the Originals drifted from the tape deck through Ray's garage. Anyone who knows a little guitar can tell you that the player is an amateur, stiff and unsure. But to us it didn't matter. That song is a bona fide lowrider classic, enough to make it into the mix of oldies Ray had on in the background. I was a kid when my dad took me to see Ray, young enough that the memory is only a few images and sounds like those guitar licks. All I knew was that we were in "Lowrider Ray's" garage in nearby Muscatine, and that he was a big deal.

Lowrider Ray was a legend in our circles. If you were Mexican in West Liberty at the time and had even a passing interest in cars, you knew of Ray. He painted and fabricated fantastical lowrider modifications to classic cars. A *Lowrider Magazine* calendar of pinup girls adorned my dad's garage. That very magazine featured Ray in different issues, and I remember combing through one of them. In the feature, Ray was kneeling by one of his tricked-out creations, pointing out the full bar in the trunk. Its back doors opened wide to present enough libations to start any party, anywhere.

Ray had christened my dad's '52 Chevy Fleetline lowrider, applying its signature white-and-pink paint job before selling it to my dad. This was all before my time, mind you. I asked my dad, and he has it pegged that he bought it around '88 or '89. I would have been three or four at the time. Now I was old enough to come with my dad to check out Ray's latest work.

Rosie hit her falsetto on Ray's tape deck. Her vocalizations cut through the cigarette smoke that wisped throughout the stuffy garage. "Ooh ooh I love you, ooh ooh I do . . ." I was by my dad's side as Ray showed us around his garage. There were two lowriders he was currently working on, one apple green and the other cherry red, both painted as bright as one could make colors in the real world. Ray had framed snippets of his *Lowrider Magazine* features on the wall. Beside these were other photos of him, squatting and posing with the cars he built. His babies, as he called them.

Ray and my dad talked in Spanish as I followed along. Ray would sometimes break out into Spanglish, usually directed at me. He had this way of talking in English, this accent that was the opposite of my dad's. The cadence and lilt of his words flowed in a stereotypical vato accent. "Primo, mira, check this shit out," he said to me as he squatted down and pointed out some detailing on one of the cars. Like I said, I don't remember how young I was then, but I was young enough that he had to get real low. He knew I liked to draw, and he switched his beer bottle and cigarette from one hand to the other to better gesture toward the detailing. His hands were hard and calloused, like my dad's.

I remember feeling a little afraid of Ray. I was a shy, anxious kid and didn't talk much to any adult. But there was something about Ray. When he noticed I wasn't responding to how he painted the car's trim, he took a drag on his cigarette. "Mijo, go get us another Bud Light, huh?" And he patted my head before standing up with a groan. He and my dad continued their conversation in Spanish as I walked over to the mini fridge, happy to step away for a bit with a task I knew how to do. I remember my dad and tíos tasking me to go get them some beers while they were talking at parties or watching boxing matches in the living room. Sometimes my Tío Javier got so buzzed that he would give me a tip.

After I grabbed two bottles, I turned around and got a look at my dad and Ray. Besides their work ethic, manifested in their calloused hands, I regarded them as opposites. My dad had his unofficial uniform on, the same outfit he has worn throughout his day-to-day life: some type of button-up shirt, short-sleeved in the summer, long-sleeved in the winter. Slacks or muted jeans. Unassuming work shoes, worn and black, picked for their utilitarianism and comfort on the factory floor. My dad had fine, thinning hair that he parted to the side. He was light-skinned and handsome in the way that people say an older man is comfortable in his handsomeness. He looked like an older version of the dude on the Tapatío bottle. There are two real people my friends said my dad looked like while we were growing up—former Iowa Governor Terry Branstad or a Mexican Saddam Hussein, which was more a comment on my dad's perpetual mustache than anything else. Our family always thought that was funny though. We'd point out "our dad" when "he" was talking Iowa politics or Iraqi regime change on the news. My dad had a very slight potbelly, like the kind a weightlifter has. Like the one I am beginning to develop in my midthirties, which is around the same age my dad was that day in Ray's garage. His belly paunched despite the strength in his arms and hands.

Ray was shorter and rounder. He was dark, like how I got the summer I did roofing with my brother. Ray had that horseshoe-shaped male pattern baldness. But it was fine because he always wore a nice fedora. Sometimes you'd forget about his baldness because it looked like he had a full head of hair peeking out from his hat. Ray always wore sunglasses and would wear button-ups like my dad. But whereas my dad's shirts were functional, Ray's were stylish. He always matched his shirts with his Dickies or rocked them with a crisp white tee underneath. As my cousin Tony says, "They don't make them like Ray no more, man. That dude was one of the true lowriders." He had style. Not just in the way he dressed or how he carried himself but in how he articulated it in his craft. In his babies.

I have to be fair to my dad here. I would be straight-up lying if I said he didn't have style. He rocked the finest cowboy hats and boots at the bailes at the West Liberty Community Center near Louis Rich. He would wait until he went back to his hometown of Ojinaga and buy the legit stuff worth hundreds of dollars. But here's the rub. There's this question that gets thrown around in different Mexican communities in America. The question of what *kind* of Mexican are you. There are the Texas paisas and the California vatos. Both my mom and dad are from northern Mexico–southern Texas border states. We are norteños. Hell, I'd go so far as to claim another subsect I don't want to admit—we are *midwestern Mexicans*. (I bleat out "Ope" when someone bumps into me at the grocery store.) Compound this with the fact that every kid thinks their dad is a square compared to their idea of what constitutes "cool"

Me in my cowboy outfit, age seven.

Mexicanness, and Ray's lowrider oldies intrigued me. The way he talked like the hood movies my sister would watch was light-years cooler than my dad's English. My dad dressed me up in cowboy boots and hats when I was a toddler. I remember his disapproval when I got old enough to switch the Mexican radio station to pop in my brother's *Nirvana Unplugged* cassette tape.

As a young kid my admiration of Ray's style never translated to a real interest in lowriders or cars. When I was still quite young, the police arrested Ray Olivarez. According to court documents, "Raymond Olivarez pled guilty to conspiracy to distribute narcotics" in November of 1995. I can't say for certain, but it makes a lot of sense that this was how Ray was able to afford the cars he worked on. I never thought about how much it cost my dad to buy that lowrider from Ray. Growing up I'd say we were lower middle class as far as the average goes. Closer to the lower than the middle for sure. We weren't *struggling*. But I was on the free and reduced lunch program. And there were a few times when the electric company shut off our energy and we couldn't immediately pay the bill. We lit candles while my parents scrambled for cash. That car had to have cost my dad a big chunk of his resources. He sacrificed to buy this car from a man the police arrested for selling dope and put in jail for a long time. Ray's incarceration is why I only have this one scant memory of his garage. And why a bit of danger, fear, and mysterious coolness tints that memory.

It's still hard to reconcile my low-key, straight-laced dad with Ray and that car. In a way, I separated the purchase and ownership of that car from my dad. It existed as a constant in our driveway. I can't picture my dad stunting and flaunting, hitting the hydraulic switches. That car is a manifestation of when you hear stories from your parents' friends of how they used to wild-out as teenagers. You can believe it but you can't picture it in your brain, like for real for real.

So the following I pieced together from different accounts, from family members and people in the community. Juan De Dios Renteria bought Lowrider Ray's Chevy Fleetline in the eighties. My dad had heard of Ray and his cars shortly after he moved to Muscatine, Iowa, from his hometown of Ojinaga, Mexico. My dad actually grew up in this tiny little pueblo a few hours away from Ojinaga named Maijoma. Maijoma reminds me of the places Gabriel García Márquez writes of, full of lore and mystery. The last time we went to Maijoma, my dad pointed to an old stable by his childhood home. He said in Spanish, "My brother and I built that for my parents in a week."

Back in Ojinaga, he heard about work in a city called Muscatine in Iowa. He heard about this through various means. Part of it was very much word of mouth; one family goes and they tell loved ones of the opportunity. "There's inside factory jobs here. It's hard work, yeah, but it's stable. You actually get paychecks." My dad says he also saw flyers for these Iowa meatpacking factories, for places like IBP (Iowa Beef Processors) in Columbus Junction, Heinz in Muscatine, and Louis Rich in West Liberty.

Like a lot of other first-generation kids, I never knew the specifics of my parents' pilgrimage until I was older. My mom said her journey was

My parents on their wedding day.

easy but my dad had a journey fraught with sadness. She said with a smirk, side-eyeing my dad, "Él estaba un wetback. Tiene una historia llena de triste." My dad sat in his recliner and nodded. He was like a lot of other Mexican and Central American immigrants who made the trek in the late sixties and early seventies, forever changing the landscape of these sleepy Midwest towns.

Not that Muscatine was all that sleepy. Its population in 1970 was hovering around twenty-two thousand people. Mark Twain lived in Muscatine at one point in his life. Juan De Dios Renteria met Irene De La Paz in Muscatine. They were both from separate border regions in Mexico, hours apart. They each followed family to Iowa. After they had my older brother and sister, there was an accident. A space heater caught fire and their house burned down. To start anew in a quieter, smaller place, my parents moved twenty miles northwest to the "more peaceful" West Liberty.

Not too long after this move and before I was born in '85, my dad bought his lowrider from Ray in Muscatine. It's important to stress that, to me, all accounts of my dad's lowrider actually functioning are second-hand. My own personal experience with it was that it sat dormant in our

Nancy in the lowrider before my time.

driveway—except that one time Jerry and I got it to lumber up for a few moments of goofing off and posing for pictures like vatos in front of its rusted carcass.

It's also important to stress that through these accounts I learned something integral to the car's history. I learned how badass, legendary, and *Mexican* that thing was in West Liberty. My dad's lowrider was the first Mexican anything in the Muscatine County Fair Parade. This was the parade that kicked off the county fair every July, when nomadic carnies and hustlers would descend on the town, settling in a temporary spot by the West Liberty Community Center. Back in the day, the parade was like any other typical small-town parade in Iowa. A rural white affair. There was the 4-H float. Convertibles with heavy-haired pageant queens practicing their slow waves. Tractors and more tractors and heavy farm machinery. And, of course, the Shriners doing doughnuts in their tiny cars and throwing candy to us kids. My favorite part of the parade was the end, when a mass of clowns would walk through the streets. Clowns terrified my sister and I reveled in her fright. I took it as karma for all the times she beat me up.

But before my time, among the clowns, tractors, and fez-wearing

Cruising around downtown.

Shriners, there was my dad and his lowrider. He would lumber through the streets, waiting for the right moment. For the float in front of him to get some distance. Then he'd flip the hydraulic switches and make that car dance in front of the crowds. My brother and sister would laugh and relish the attention. They'd throw out candy from the back windows to kids jumping up and down, mimicking the lowrider in front of them.

Those parade rides placed my dad and his lowrider in the annals of West Liberty's history. If you were to ask older Mexicans in particular, they'd reminisce about that lowrider and the times it cruised among the country fare in the parades. Even when it nestled into its permanent home on our driveway to accumulate cobwebs and rust, they'd wax poetic about the beauty of that car lying in wait, begging for Juan and his sons to fix it up. How it shone as a beacon in our driveway by the football field and track. If you came into town from Highway 6 and turned onto Elm Street, it was one of the first landmarks you'd see. "Go past the bowling alley and track. See that bomba-ass lowrider? Yeah, then you're on the right track."

I was in a few of those parades too, when I was a baby or toddler, but too young to remember. I can imagine my dad's smile, though, like the smile he gave me when we were standing before the husk of his car one day and he said, "We can fix it if you want."

———————

The cicadas' whine was a pulse. Wave after wave reverberated through the trees with violence as we rummaged through the trunk of my dad's lowrider. It was a balmy afternoon in '93 and Jerry Sayabeth's shoes were coming up off the concrete of my driveway as he seesawed into the trunk like a toddler who needed to fold his entire body into the toy chest. Jerry hesitated. The sharp metal lip of the trunk dug into his belly as he held the jumper cable clip in his hands.

These were the cables we found in my dad's garage, among the old tires, blue barrels of scrap metal, oil-stained cardboard, and roofing shingles. We found them along the same wall as the girl-of-the-month *Lowrider Magazine* calendar. Ms. April beckoned to us in the damp garage that smelled like gasoline and sweat and rust and work. The calendar was a talking point to us ten-year-olds. We pretended like we weren't kind of scared of the poofed-up hair and high-waist swimsuits. Skirted around the fact that we hadn't gone through puberty. That we hadn't had that awkward class on "the changes" with our gym teacher Mr. Nelson, the class that culminated in him telling us we stank and giving out deodorant samples. Jerry made sure to laugh as he went to change the month and spotted the jumper cables.

"Chuy. Yo. There. There they are. Those are the cables we need for the last battery. The one to make the car jump!" he said, letting go of the calendar.

Now Jerry teetered before three ancient batteries in the trunk. I was in the driver's seat of my father's '52 Chevy Fleetline lowrider. It had a white base with pink trim. Accent lines wrapped around its bulbous body. The huge black- and gray-cushioned seats were swallowing me whole. My gaze oscillated from the control panel of hydraulic switches to Jerry in the rearview mirror.

Earlier that day we had scraped off the rust and corrosion from the batteries in the back of the lowrider. The car had been dormant long enough that we could only get it to start in spurts. We would turn the ignition and it would shake and shudder, idling for a few seconds before cutting off with a groan.

Our plan was this. In the precious seconds after I turned the ignition, Jerry would clamp our scavenged cables on the last battery. Right after, he would holler at me and I would try the hydraulic switches in a furor to see if we could get the car to jump like the cars in the music videos we watched at White Josh's house.

I was looking at the switches on the middle console. Some of them were regular-looking metal tails that clacked with satisfaction. But a few had these colorful polymer accents plugged over them, like big Jolly Ranchers with celestial detailing. This one switch in the middle looked encased in amber. It was the mosquito from Jurassic Park atop the old guy's cane, the metal switch inside lit like magic hour.

"I said! Are you ready?" Jerry called from his spot at the trunk.

"Whoops! Yeah, yeah, I'm good," I replied. "Okay, here we go, on three, two . . ."

I reached over and cranked the ignition. The car convulsed. Ancient framework ground and groaned, gears and machinery from before our time scraping against itself.

I heard Jerry make a sound loud enough that it cut through the roar of the car. It was a yelp, wingdings and symbols in comic book speech bubbles. It was surprise and panic.

"Yo . . . yo . . . holy shit, yo! Help!" Jerry said as I struggled to scooch from the seat. His panic turned to patented Jerry giggles as I rounded the corner of the lowrider. Jerry was patting the arm of his long-sleeved Adidas shirt. There were wisps of smoke coming from scorch marks on the dark blue sleeve, like an absent-minded smoker fell asleep and dropped their cigarette on select spots of Jerry's arm. I could smell the burned fabric. Jerry was smiling, his voice the embodiment of prepubescent squeal.

"Dude, you shoulda seen that shit."

"You're kidding, right? You caught fire?"

"Man, you know it! The battery sparked like crazy. I actually had to put out the sparks on the rest of the trunk. The felt lining caught fire first. I don't think it's regulation," Jerry said.

"Yeah, I think that's the point," I said while we both surveyed the damage to Jerry's favorite shirt. He actually had two shirts on, as was the style at the time. His Adidas was over an extra-large long-sleeved white tee that came close to his knees, a style he aped from the older Laotian kids at the trailer courts.

Before we internalized how bad things could have gotten, one key sound remained. It was the rumble of the lowrider. Still on and idling. Our window before its inevitable sputtering death was closing. We looked at each other, wide-eyed.

"The switches!" we said in unison. I ran back to the driver's seat as Jerry scrambled around the other side. I clambered into the car and tried the switches closest to me. Jerry opened his door and executed a perfect dive onto the passenger seat like we had seen Mr. Austin teach the JV football players. He tried the far-right switches. Our fingers worked like they were playing Nintendo. The switches clicked in rapid-fire succession, clickclickclick. We felt the car give a massive heave as our hands both reached the last switch in the middle. The amber Jurassic Park switch. I looked over at Jerry.

"Do it," he said while he propped his chin in hands, his elbows on the seat. I flipped the switch and we felt the lowrider heave and shudder, but differently from before. Jerry gripped the bottom of the seat tight as the entire body of the car lifted into the air. We whooped and hollered like it was a carnival ride at the fair, except we'd activated this car by our own design. This wasn't standing in line to ride the Zipper, waiting for a bored carnie to wave you through. This was all us.

"Try the blue one now," Jerry said. Gravity pulled our weight against the back of the seats. The front of the car stuck several feet in the air. I held the blue switch and the back of the car raised to meet the front. "Alright, alright, alright, now how do we jump?" Jerry asked himself. But before we could try any more switches, the lowrider gave one last groan.

"It's dying, man," I said. The car hissed and deflated. We were silent as it descended to the earth. Attained equilibrium.

"Dang, yo, go, go," Jerry said as he began flipping switches at random. It was over. Jerry corrected himself, sat upright in his seat. We were silent for a few minutes. An eternity in ten-year-old time. "That shit was tight though, right?" Jerry asked.

"Yeah, it was!" I replied before he even got his question out.

We both cackled with laughter for a long time. I grabbed my dad's car keys from the ignition after our laughter subsided, tracing my thumb over the lacquered scorpion on the keychain. I had stolen them from their spot hanging on the kitchen wall. Remembering I had taken them without permission sobered me up.

We both strained to slam the heavy car doors shut. Making our way to the back of the car, we closed the trunk and did that move kids do to jump up on seats that are too high—use your hands to boost yourself up, spin midjump, and land with aplomb. The paint job on the rest of the body was holding up, but the back side was developing these cancerous rust spots from facing the sun all day. By then the spots were big and melding into one another. Flecks of paint and rust chipped into the air as we plopped onto the car.

The midday sun shone bright on our faces as our conversation lulled. My family lived in a white house on Elm Street, the last house before the high school football field and track, and the sounds of a lazy afternoon in small-town Iowa came into focus as we sat. The forever and ever, never-ending locusts, loud and oppressive. Dueling lawn mowers in the distance. The coming and going of cars as they passed. Almost everyone did a variation of a wave or head nod. Some did a combination of both. Some did that move where you keep your hand on the steering wheel but acknowledge with two fingers. I lay back on the trunk and stared at the clear blue sky, swirls of gnats coming in and out of focus at will.

"Some of these people don't have nothing better to do than to just stare," Jerry said.

"Who passed by?"

"Last one was Ms. Morrison. Before that was the lady that works at True Value, in the truck. And before that was your sister's friend, Maria. Cruising," Jerry said, taking off his visor and brushing his hair from his eyes. Jerry's hair was a bowl cut with red-orange highlights. The Laotian kids at the trailer court where he lived would cut each other's hair. There was a hierarchy of who got to cut whose hair based on age and ability. I wasn't privy to those details and never asked Jerry about it. I thought his hair was cool but never something I could rock because it was a Laostha style.

I always felt average compared to my friends, Jerry in particular. He had style and was the funny guy in our group. He wore his visor backward and upside down. Baggy jeans poked from under his oversized tee. His pant legs were rolled to display his chunky K-Swiss shoes, always clean and white. In comparison I had on black gym shorts and a West Liberty Comets shirt. These were hand-me-downs from my older sister, Nancy. I ended up getting lots of her clothes, and I hated it. Not because of the look—Nancy was a tomboy and the clothes were innocuous enough—but because she loved to terrorize and beat me up. She had a mean streak and I was often on the receiving end of her wrath. This, and the fact that my wardrobe first belonged to a fourteen-year-old girl, was something I kept from my friends.

"Maybe they're looking at the car?" I asked.

"They shoulda saw it a couple minutes ago when the hydraulics were working and we had its nose up in the air," Jerry replied. "It woulda been dope if it got stuck like that. To prove to people that we did it."

I thought about how my dad would feel if he found his car in such a state. What my mom would yell at me as punishment. I changed the subject.

"Where's Ruben and Eric? They should be here by now."

"They're prolly still dealing with the aftermath of Eric and Mr. Ingles getting into it. You heard about that right?"

"Ruben was telling me at lunch that he had to calm Eric down, that he got into some . . . stuff again . . ."

"Some shit, you mean?" Jerry said.

" . . . that Eric talked back in social studies and Ruben had to step in so he didn't get into more trouble. But that's all he said."

From his perch on the lowrider Jerry pantomimed looking around so no one could hear. Jerry was our go-to recapper and relayer. He rubbed his hands together.

"Okay, so Mr. Ingles is going off talking about hot dogs and history like he usually does, right? And he starts talking about Cinco de Mayo."

"Uh-oh," I said, remembering last May and how Eric got into it with a girl at school when she wished him a happy Independence Day.

"You know it. And Ingles is going business as usual when Eric up and yells, 'That's not our Independence Day! It's just a random battle that white people use as an excuse to get drunk!'"

"What? He said that?"

"Didn't even raise his hand or nothin'."

"Whoa. I mean. I didn't even know that," I said.

"Yeah, he must've learned it from one of his brothers." Eric Maldonado was the third oldest in a family of six boys. Legend had it that his parents kept on trying for a girl and kept on having boys till his mom couldn't bear it anymore. Eric's two older brothers rubbed off on him, the same way all our older siblings influenced us, more than our parents or teachers. They were the zeitgeist. But Sergio and Junior were both bigger guys finishing high school, big and tough. Eric was one of the smallest boys in our grade. His three younger brothers were already catching up to him in size. Being the runt of the Maldonado litter gave him a Napoleon complex. If something rubbed him the wrong way, he'd be the first to escalate. "You know Eric though, little guy can't keep it in when a teacher pushes his buttons. And Mr. Ingles wasn't having it, telling Eric he was wrong. Eric kept saying, 'Let's get an encyclopedia right now and prove I'm right!' They went back and forth until Ruben jumped into the convo, trying to calm Eric down. But in the end they both got in trouble."

The sound of bike wheels on gravel cut through the air. Eric and Ruben tore through the alley by the side of my house, raced through the front yard, and slammed their brakes, fishtailing and coming onto their front tires.

"Yo, yo, nalgas!" Ruben yelled as he jumped off his bike. It rolled and slammed onto its side on the grass.

"Ah, speak of the devil and the little devil," Jerry said as he pushed off the lowrider.

Eric smiled. "Ay, man, don't push it," he said as he came over and gave me dap. Eric's notorious short fuse didn't transfer to our clique. It didn't take much for someone outside our group to say or do something that set him off. But he was always jovial with us. And we took it upon ourselves to try our best to mitigate and curb Eric's outbursts.

"You should have seen this guy going off," Ruben said as he scooped up a dormant basketball. The lowrider was opposite a USA Dream Team basketball hoop my dad set up. Our group wouldn't so much play, like my older cousin Freddy and his jock friends. But we'd practice trick shots in HORSE or lower the hoop to engineer fantastical dunks. "Jerry—all you!" Ruben said as he heaved the ball at the backboard.

Jerry ran and jumped to catch the ball midair and complete the alley-oop they had been perfecting. His fingers tipped the ball and changed its trajectory, causing it to slam into the passenger door of the lowrider. "Party foul," Jerry said as he jogged to catch the ball. The side of the car had various dents and dings from our *NBA Jam* recreations.

"Anyway," Eric said as he leaned against the lowrider, "it don't matter. I'm not scared of Mr. Ingles. And he was wrong. I'm not gonna keep my mouth shut when people don't know what they're saying."

"Yeah, we definitely know that," I said as I joined Eric to watch Jerry and Ruben botch their move, ducking out of the way when the ball came slamming into the car. "You proved that over and over . . . and over."

Ruben palmed the ball in both hands and stopped for a moment. His words came out sharp. "Yeah, fool, we know! But you forget about the Snow Bowl. Mr. Ingles ain't gonna forget that come winter."

Eric strained for a retort but couldn't think of anything to say. The Snow Bowl was a glorified recess game of flag football that Mr. Ingles orchestrated when there was enough accumulated snow on the field to emulate a Lambeau Field winter classic. Mr. Ingles was the designated quarterback for both teams, reliving some golden age of his youth. It was legendary among the fifth- and sixth-grade boys transitioning into tackle football in junior high.

Sensing the energy shift, we all stopped and waited for Ruben to continue. "You don't think Mr. Ingles talks to Mr. Austin, or shit, even the high school coaches?" Ruben's words hung in the air. Jerry and I scuffed at the pavement, averting our eyes.

Eric's words came out small. Scorned, he held onto one arm like he had gotten a booster shot. "Okay," he said.

Ruben held Eric's gaze for a moment. Until he unfurled his eyebrows and slapped the ball in his hands. "Okay, then! Jerry, let's get it." And he passed Jerry the ball to switch positions on their alley-oop attempts.

After a bit, when Jerry's laugh echoed off the garage door amid basketball bounces and crashes, I went to Eric. "Ay, man, it's all good. Mr. Ingles takes anybody that wants to play. It'll all blow over."

"Nah. Ruben was right. I messed up," Eric said while watching to see if the other guys could hear. "I shoulda thought of the team. I was right about Cinco de Mayo though."

I slapped Eric on the shoulder. "You *were* right, dude! Man, I wish I could have seen his face when you put him on blast." Eric broke into his little ladies' man smile. In contrast to his short fuse, Eric was good looking and a hit with the girls in our class. Unlike the rest of us, who were still very much awkward around girls, he rotated to another girlfriend every week. They only wished he wouldn't get so *angry* all the time.

"Yeah, I was right. Pinche Mr. Pringles. He looked more like Mr. Pringles than ever before."

"Pinche culero," I said in my best vato accent. We proceeded to call

Mr. Ingles every Spanish curse word we knew and elaborate all the ways he reminded us of the Pringles chip mascot. Unlike me, both Eric and Ruben were fluent in Spanish. I could understand most of what adults said to me, but I'd get nervous talking back. My friends would translate my English for their parents when I visited their houses. But I knew enough to blurt out Spanish curse words with my friends. Which was funny because I didn't curse in English much, a fact that led to much ribbing from my friends.

"Whoa, whoa," Ruben said to us while making a time-out sign with his hands to Jerry. "Is this true, Chuy? That you got the lowrider to jump?"

Eric's eyes lit up as he looked at me. "Nuh-uh. For real? You got that ancient thing to turn on?" he asked, turning around and backing up to look at the car as if it would start again by way of magic. "How crazy was it?"

All eyes were on me. I could already feel that this story was going to shift and morph, the way all stories out of West Liberty do. Our tale of getting the hydraulics to heave the car before sputtering out would become this story of us struggling to contain the car as it jumped and bucked. "I mean. We got it running and up. That much is tru—" I started before getting cut off by the group's excitement. Jerry began rapid-fire recapping the events, his story punctuated by exclamations from the other two.

Finally Eric said, "Dude, that's crazy. Do you think you could ever get it running again? I mean to actually be able to drive it?"

Jerry replied, "Nah, I don't think so. That thing's from the ancient times. Besides, why would you want to actually drive it? It's nice to look at but it's all show, no go."

Eric and Ruben threw their arms in the air and talked over each other in response.

"Man! You're just repeating what Da and them say. Lucky says that all the time when he's comparing other cars to ricers!" Ruben said.

"Yeah, well, it's true though. I mean, look at that thing. It's a piece of shit."

"Damn, dude, do you hear that, Chuy?" Ruben asked.

"He's talking shit about your dad, man!" Eric said while they laughed.

Jerry looked at me. "You know I'm not trying to say anything like that. You said it your—" he started. But a low adult voice interrupted in Spanish. In Spanish that was sure of itself, from an adult who knew it as their first language. It wasn't the mangled Spanglish of the playground. Sure, Ruben and Eric could speak it, and I could understand it, but even their Spanish wasn't as confident as this. This was the Spanish of the newscasters on Univision. It didn't care if you could understand or not. Or if you grew up in Iowa and oscillated between languages, bastardizing both.

"Ay, Chuy. ¿Qué están haciendo?" It was my dad, standing before us by the basketball hoop. He was in his Louis Rich work shirt. Louis Rich was the turkey processing plant on the other side of town. It's where the majority of our parents worked. The reason why West Liberty was West Liberty. The shirt was a brown button-up with his name stitched over his breast pocket: "Juan."

"Nothing. W-we were just play—nomás estamos jugando," I replied.

"¿Y las llaves?" he asked as he stretched out his hand. And in that gesture I knew he had caught us. I reached in my pocket, walked over, and handed him the keys with the scorpion keychain. The guys were already at attention and quiet at my dad's arrival, like we always got when a parent invaded our space. But at the key transfer they began searching for an escape. Ruben and Eric picked up their bikes. Jerry looked over at me as he followed, his face heavy. He was no doubt wondering if my dad had heard him disparage his car. Or if he had heard him but not understood.

"Ay, wait up, let me get on," Jerry said before jumping onto the pegs on Ruben's back tires. Ruben had installed those fat chrome pegs so a passenger could stand up while he pedaled. Jerry held onto Ruben's shoulders for stability as Ruben gave an extra effort to pedal off.

"Chuy, we got something to show you though. Meet us at the bowling alley when you're done!" Ruben said as they started their way over to Liberty Lanes. The bowling alley was up the street from my house, opposite from the track on Elm Street. I watched as they pedaled off, bursting into sound as they laughed and chided Jerry.

I yearned to be with them. There was nothing more I wanted than to be away from my dad and with my friends. Not because my dad scared me or I was going to get it. My father was a mellow guy. I don't ever recall him hitting or even yelling at me. If we upset or annoyed him he'd let us know, but my mom, the matriarch, she delivered the real corporal punishment. No, I wanted to go because at that time my friends were all that mattered. And I also knew that what was coming would be awkward and embarrassing. We got by communicating with one another in short bursts. Any longer communications stilted. Became exercises in futility.

"¿Y por qué estabas jugando con el carro?" he asked, getting a closer look as he knelt by the dents in the side of the car.

"I meant we were playing with the ball. Not the car," I replied, sounding less defensive and more annoyed than I wanted. He noticed something while looking at the front tire and I noticed a shift in his tone. "¿Comenzó?" He sprang up and looked inside the car. I looked at his reflection in the lowrider's side window as I replied.

"Y-yeah. We got it to start! We couldn't jump it but we got it up." I watched my dad's eyes as he searched the interior of the car. His head gears were grinding as his eyes darted from switch to switch. He started to speak faster now. Words cascaded out of his mouth as he noted things about the car. I couldn't quite make out the Spanish. When my dad and I talk to each other in our respective languages it's slow and methodical. To let the other person catch up. These words were too free flowing for me. There were recollections of past work he had done on the car. Things he could still do. We could do. Nosotros.

"Jerry said that it won't ever run again. That true?"

I saw my dad's reflection smile a real smile. Not a "talk to the lady at the bank for a loan smile" but a genuine one. His lips upturned underneath his mustache to show his teeth. His English was a lilt. Each sentence fragment sounded like a question. Like he wasn't sure if it should be a question. "Yeah . . . yeah, we can fix it . . . if we want to." He chuckled.

My face grew hot. There was a beat. My dad's smile dissipated as we both stood before the car. Another beat. I could feel my cheeks blush, like in many of our conversations. We stood silent as we realized we couldn't translate the words to articulate between us. The question that should have followed: *Do you want to fix it with me?*

My dad was gifted with his hands. In his bones. He had a passion for tinkering with cars and fixing up the house. Every weekday after work he would go straight to the garage and work until dinner. I suspect my dad always had a master plan when it came to the lowrider. The plan was that he and my older brother Johnny would upkeep the car. Plan B was that he and Johnny would fix it up when it fell into disrepair. Johnny shared my dad's talent for working with his hands. But his interests focused on audio equipment and speakers. He could install the audio system into the lowrider no problem, but actually fixing it up? That was never entertained.

Which left me. But I didn't share my older brother's and dad's penchant and proclivity for fixing things. I liked the software side. Video games and screens. I couldn't be bothered with the nuts and bolts. The *work* of it all. The notion of doing manual labor on a car was akin to having to mow the lawn. It didn't matter how cool the car looked. My dad began futzing with the lowrider's side mirrors. I took this opportunity to dip out and head inside our house.

Full disclosure. When it comes to my family, we don't talk. Like *really* talk. Like they do on sitcoms. I'm amazed at the idealistic ways characters deal with conflict on TV shows. If one person is feeling something, they'll corner another person and hash it out. My family, especially my dad and me, don't talk like that. Some of it's the language barrier, but some of it is plain old emotional baggage. I don't know if my ten-year-old self comprehended these emotions about my dad and his car. I thought it was about wanting to be with my friends. That's where the adventure and fun were. But I remember walking away from my dad that day and feeling guilty. Like I was in trouble with myself for some reason. What happened next with my dad cemented that feeling.

"Espérate, Chuy—wait," he said. The image of my dad before me caught me off guard. He wasn't by the lowrider anymore. He was standing by the basketball hoop with the ball in his hand. I noticed his hands as he moved them across the ball before his chest. "Want. To play?" he asked.

A beat. I had seen my dad shoot some hoops before. He was as good as I was at it, meaning he wasn't very good at all. I thought about the games at the bowling alley. About what new adventure the guys were alluding to before they rode off.

"I can't. I got to go," I said as I walked past my dad, then the lowrider. As I made my way past the gravel parking lot of the football field, I remember looking back at my dad in the driveway. My cheeks got hot and I felt that feeling again, like I had done something wrong. At the time my dad was forty, an age I couldn't comprehend. I always thought of him as an *adult* age. Like how you always think a parent is forever sixty-five years old until you look at pictures and realize how young they actually were. But I remember how he looked then when I glanced back at him. How old he looked. How sad he looked. I turned back toward the bowling alley and doubled my pace.

Here's a truth a lot of first-generation kids grow up with: they assume they're smarter than their parents. It stems from language barriers. Communication issues from parent to child. It's in the same Venn diagram of horribleness that could occur when someone in the wild talked to our parents. I recall people getting annoyed at our parents. Raising their voices as if they were talking to children. Grocery clerks or teachers, coworkers and bank associates. We internalized that young. Saw how people treated our parents like they were beneath them. I'm not proud to say it rubbed off on me.

My dad and I couldn't communicate with one another. Every time we tried, it was this stuttering, jagged mash of words. I never got to hear my dad wax poetic about his favorite band or have a nuanced discussion with his friends about politics. Mind you, these conversations did happen. My dad's shy, but when he's around people he knows and talking in the language he first learned, he can get downright loquacious. But when I was a kid and I was in the vicinity of these conversations, his words were noise. They were in Spanish. Charlie-Brown-adult vocalizations, wah-wahs with rolled Rs.

Here's another phenomenon that happens with boys and their fathers. Ask any boy how it felt the first time he realized his dad wasn't the be-all and end-all. When he became a strong teenager who could beat his aging father in sport. In physical competition. It feels terrible. It's this business of facing your own mortality in the face of the man who raised you. My dad's stilted English triggered this response in me. I learned to read young and always liked words. English words. Reading and communicating in English was me slam-dunking on my dad as a kid.

This undercurrent was flowing through ten-year-old me. It was there when I saw my dad that day and felt sorry for him. Looking back, I see how misguided that sentiment was. We all have to remember how gifted people who can communicate in a second language are. Even if they're mechanics and housekeepers. For real. I'm in awe of it. I'd say my dad has pretty good English. He still talks with a lilt and in short bursts. But it's so much better than what I can do in Spanish. Yet I can't change the perceptions I had as a kid. I can't change how I thought about my dad growing up. And I can't change the fact that I didn't jump at the chance to save that lowrider with him.

My steps crunched on the gravel of the football parking lot. I passed the track and football field. In a couple years we'd be playing games for the town under Friday night lights. But back then we saw the field as the place with the big blue high-jump mat. We'd stage Royal Rumble and Wrestlemania matches on the mat. King of the Mountain, where the last person standing after throwing everyone else off was the winner.

I walked past the mat and by the home bleachers. When we were younger, we'd found out that you could squeeze under the walkway leading up to the bleachers, that it created this tunnel no one would know you were in. We hung out in the tunnel a few times, just to say we did. After the third or fourth time, the luster of secrecy started to wear off. The fifth time we squeezed into the tunnel with a flashlight, Jerry found some shit in the corner. "Dude, I think that's from a person," he called out to us. We scrambled out from beneath the bleachers, never going back again.

I cut across Elm Street, away from the football field and toward Liberty Lanes. Smoke billowed out the door as I pulled it open. The air inside was stale and muggy, the carpet a blotchy brownish-red. There was a large mirror on the right side of the entrance hall that sat opposite the arcade. I always guessed it was a two-way mirror for the owners to be able to keep watch. So they could keep an eye on all the Mexicans and Asians playing games while the white people bowled. Okay, okay. That's not completely fair. We all bowled back then; it wasn't only the white people. Race came secondary to having another activity in town. I still think the mirror was two-way, though.

I spotted Jerry's dyed hair in the mirror, by the all-in-one Nintendo arcade cabinet. Eric and Ruben were playing a game of pool beside him. Eric saw me first. "There he is, guys," he called out.

Jerry continued button-mashing, bouncing his ninja up a wall in a game of *Ninja Gaiden*. The game selection at Liberty Lanes paled in comparison to ones like Aladdin's Castle in Iowa City. But we had to take what we could get in town. Jerry's eyes, shaded by his visor, never strayed from the action. "Dang, dude, took you long enough. Did you get it bad from your dad?"

Ruben hunched over the pool table, lining up his shot. His eyes darted up to meet mine at Jerry's question. "Nah, nothing like that," I replied. "I had to make sure I had enough quarters so we could play."

The cue ball rocketed toward the eight ball with a snap. The two collided and the eight ball zoomed into the corner pocket. "Well, you can save them. You wanna see what I was talking about or what?" Ruben said as he lobbed his pool cue onto the table. Eric's face twitched, as if he thought to protest that Ruben didn't call his shot, but he stayed silent and went to throw away the remains of his cold fries.

"What's this big thing you want to show me? You gotta keep it a secret?" I asked. Jerry slapped the cabinet's joystick as he cursed.

Ruben, already making his way past me and out the door, said over his shoulder, "Let's go. And do you really want me to tell you? Or do you want to see it for yourself? It's worth it, dude, for real. I'm telling you." He pushed open the door, taking a breath of fresh air. As Jerry hopped onto the pegs of Ruben's bike, Ruben asked me, "Where's your bike, fool?"

"My bike chain broke," I replied. I looked over at Eric's bike and saw he was pegless. I could try to stand on the tiny bolts of his back tires, but that would be torture for the whole ride. Also, Eric was too small to carry me the whole way and it felt like an insult to make him the passenger on his own bike. "I could take my sister's bike—*if* this is really worth it?"

"Do it," Ruben said as he started to pedal toward my house.

"Do it . . . do it . . . do it," Jerry repeated in a low voice.

I jogged beside Eric the short distance to my house. "What is this thing you guys want to show me so bad?" I asked. Eric looked over at me with mischief in his eyes. "I know, I know. I gotta see it for myself." He winked in response.

The guys idled in my front yard while I rounded to the back. My dad was gone. Excuses for taking my sister's bike swirled in my head on my way to her Huffy. *She doesn't even use it that much anyway. She's always cruising in her friend Becky's car. It won't matter. As long as I don't get caught.* Her bike was on its side in the backyard, by the porch we used to play hopscotch on. My stride never broke as I bent down, scooped up the bike, and began pedaling.

A loud voice cut through my concentration, causing me to brake with an audible skid. "Chuy! ¿Qué estabas haciendo con tu apa?" Crap. It was my mom on the porch. And she was mad.

"I wasn't doing anything!" I protested, thinking she was talking about jump-starting the lowrider.

"Sí. Siempre haces nada con tu apa. You do nothing with you dad," she said.

"What?" I replied, taken aback. My mom was the enforcer of our family. She was quick to raise her voice and deliver punishment. My mom reinforced all the stereotypes you've heard about the Mexican Mom. She was fiery, gossipy, and sometimes mean. But she was the one in our family who actually dealt with conflict head-on, in a way I find admirable to this day. It never occurred to me then that my dad must have confided in my mom. That he told her about me leaving him in the driveway. I always assumed she watched from inside the house. Besides being quick to deliver punishment, my mom wasn't afraid to lay it all out.

"One day you be old," she said in English. "One day you dad will be dead." I looked at her. My mom had darker skin than my dad. Like caramel. Like me. She had black hair that she kept short. Back then she wore it permed. She had on a baseball cap so that her hair poofed out from underneath. Her hands were veiny and still soapy from cleaning in the kitchen. She looks like me—or rather, I look like her. When people who know me first meet my parents, they say it like it's no contest. I'm my mother's child.

"I didn't do nothing," I repeated.

"Sí. Y you will wish you had—cuando eres un viejito—" My mom stopped, seeing that I wasn't getting it. This wasn't a tangible infraction that she could chastise. This was something more existential she couldn't quite unpack. She said in a quieter voice, "Next time play with you dad."

"Okay," I said as I realized that I had a window of dismissal. I pedaled toward the front yard.

"Took you long enough!" Ruben said. They were circling around my front street, Jerry practicing his wheelie.

"My bad," I replied. "Let's just go." We rode off. Away from my mom who watched us off from the side porch. Away from my dad, who was in the garage by now. Working on another project while the lowrider sat in our driveway.

Ruben and Jerry led the way while Eric and I rode behind them. We doubled back to the football field but then cut across the parking lot toward Kimberly Park. Kimberly Park was three houses down from my house. Back then the major attraction for us was a slide we dubbed "the Tornado." They don't make them like that anymore. We'd climb past the various poles and smaller slides to get to the main show, a spiraling slide where you had to duck into an enclosure and scoot in to start your descent.

Inside this enclosure was the first time I saw the spidery symbols that popped up around town. Even back then they looked sharp and menacing. My cousin Freddy told me they were swastikas. They meant that people didn't want us to be there. I lumped the symbols in with the other curse words and gang graffiti adorning the slide. Ignored them and kept on playing on the Tornado. One time I tried to go down the slide with my legs crossed and almost flew off the side of the first turn. I managed to stay on but got flipped upside down and landed on my head. I can see why they don't make playground equipment like that anymore.

We rode past the Tornado and the tennis court that I swear I never actually saw anyone play tennis on. After that came the Kimberly Park swimming pool. One of our high school teachers, Mr. Diemer, would say that for a town its size, West Liberty had two things that made it stand out. One was that it had a swimming pool and the other was the New Strand movie theater. As we rode past the pool, Jerry called out, "Hey Eric, are your brothers swimming again today? You better tell Oscar to chill or he's gonna be the darkest person in town." Ruben and I laughed. We looked over to see Eric's brother heading to the diving board.

"Shit, he wouldn't listen even if our older brothers threatened him. He loves that pool," Eric said with a smile.

We kept on past the elementary playground. I felt a tinge of excitement as we neared the blacktop. The playground sat on a hill elevated away from the school. During recess all the classes would have to climb a set of stairs to get to the four-square courts and basketball hoops. Rather than going all the way around the school, we bombed down the hill and through an alley as a shortcut.

It takes about twenty minutes to walk from one end of West Liberty to the other. A little less to get across the railroad tracks from my house on the north side to the south side, where Eric and Ruben lived. A few minutes more and you could get to the Mobile Village trailer park where

Eric Maldonado on the playground making
signs he'd never do in front of the church.

Jerry lived. On a bike, with the shortcuts we perfected, you could get
where you needed in less than six minutes.

Ruben started singing "Who Am I (What's My Name)?" by Snoop
Dogg, imitating the vocoder vocals of the intro. *"Eee-ya-ya-ya-ya-yah...
da bomb ... "* We all joined in during "Snoop Doggy Doooogg." He had
memorized Snoop's first verse and continued to rap it out as we biked.
"Went solo on that ass, but it's still the same. Long Beach is the spot
where I serve my 'caine." He was finishing his verse before we came
across St. Joseph's. "You see that it's a must we drop gangsta shit. What's
my motherfu—" Ruben stopped, realizing we were now passing our
church. Without skipping a beat, Ruben and Eric crossed themselves
as we passed by. "En el nombre de la padre, hijo, y espírito santo." They
kissed their fingers. I looked over at the sign on the church wall. It said
"Welcome/Bienvenidos" and had the times for Mass on Sundays. Ruben,
Eric, and I would go with our families to Spanish Mass at 10 a.m. Jerry
wasn't Catholic. I remember being jealous that Jerry only had to go to
temple every few months.

We kept going, toward downtown. We passed City Hall and the True Value hardware store, where we'd go on Fridays to snag some free popcorn. Down the street from True Value we smelled Hobbs Feather Company, a rundown white building that specialized in raw materials for farming. We never knew what was going on there or saw anybody going in or out. All we knew was that it stank when you rode by and you could find random feathers floating around the building.

Turning into downtown we passed by the Eulenspiegel puppet shop. Then the Mexican bar my dad went to every so often. I remember tagging along once while my dad drank with his friends, when I was young enough that it was a weird memory. I remember asking for some quarters only to then lose all my lives in the sole *Double Dragon* arcade game in the back. The old guys at the bar joked that I'd lose money faster at that game than they'd drain from drinking too much.

We made it to what we called "Main Street," although that's not its official name. When someone refers to downtown West Liberty, they're talking about this street. This was the street that had the New Strand Theatre. It also had Hawkeye Pizza and Paul Revere's Pizza, where my older brother worked through high school. Close to the theater was Dreibelbeis, a pharmacy and old-school soda fountain. My wife gets a kick out of the fact that we indeed used to have after-school dates at Dreibelbeis. We would go to the booths in the back of the store and get soda pop and ice cream sundaes. "Oh my God, that's adorable. Just like Archie!" she said when I first told her.

Down the street was La Mexicana, the first, and for a long time the only, Mexican convenience store in West Liberty. It was a small store filled with candies and the ingredients our moms needed for cooking. Stuff the other stores didn't have, like the right kind of lard to make flour tortillas. La Mexicana was a hub for commerce and socialization in town. In high school it added tables and booths in the back and became one of the first Mexican restaurants in town. The Elizondos owned it. Don José and his wife opened the shop and tended to it every day. Until one morning Don José sat on a bench in front of the shop and had a heart attack. He slumped over and passed away in front of his store. His family maintained the business for a few years after, but eventually his children sold it. It was so tied to their dad, and they didn't have the passion for maintaining this little store like he did.

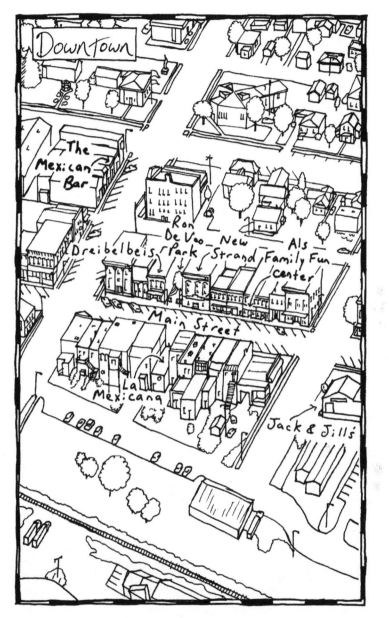

The Main Street of my youth.
Illustration by Zoë Woodworth.

Continuing down Main Street, there was a Jack and Jill and then a Casey's gas station and general store by the town's only traffic light, a single red light that flicked on and off. A glorified yield sign. Jack and Jill was a bigger convenience store than La Mexicana. It had the usual small-town grocery trappings. Families wouldn't do their big weekend grocery runs at Jack and Jill. Instead we would drive on Sundays to Hy-Vee or Econofoods in Iowa City. But Jack and Jill was good for smaller runs, like if you needed an ingredient you forgot.

Our group used the place for snack runs and cash transactions. If we brought empty bottles or cans, the store clerk would scrounge up some cardboard flats for us. We'd have to sort the recycling ourselves and they would have to be clean, the annoyed teenagers would repeat to us. But we could bring trash bags full of cans accumulated from our families and make bank. Sometimes we could walk away with fifteen or twenty bucks. Enough to pay everyone's three-dollar admission fee at New Strand and a little extra toward popcorn to boot.

South of Jack and Jill were the train tracks, intersecting the town east to west. They were significant the way train tracks are always significant to small towns. Jerry, Ruben, and Eric lived south of the tracks. On the west side of town, at the south end of Elm Street, was the former train depot. West Liberty used to be a vibrant hub because of the railroad, gaining hub status by becoming the intersection of major railroad lines in the late 1800s. As of our childhood, though, the only trains that came through town were freight trains, ugly machines full of natural resources whose whistles screamed through the night. We would throw rocks at the passing trains. Put pennies on the track to pancake them for souvenirs.

South of the depot was a holding area where Louis Rich would rotate the turkeys they were going to slaughter. They sat in dozens of cages lined up in rows along a gravel road parallel to the tracks. My cousin Freddy lived down this road. We'd ride our bikes through the gauntlet of turkeys to his house.

Across the street from the holding area was the Louis Rich plant. The new epicenter and reason for West Liberty's existence. The reason why most of our families lived here. Almost all our parents currently worked there or had worked there at some point in their lives. It was a turkey processing plant, which is a nice way of saying they killed turkeys and made them into food.

In high school we went on a field trip to the factory. Everyone wore hard hats, hairnets, white smocks, and work boots, even the man leading our tour. He was a burly white guy with a beard. Since he had the beard, he had to wear a second hairnet over his chin. This looked funny to us and we laughed about it while he led us through the factory floor. He gave us some of the history we'd already vaguely known, like the fact that Louis Rich had been around since 1960. We all knew that because we knew that's why our parents came here. That's why the racial makeup of the town changed so dramatically through the sixties. Why the white families had to deal with all us Mexicans and Asians. He also told us things we didn't know. That before it was Louis Rich, the plant canned tomatoes and had been around since the forties. But turkeys sold more than tomatoes, so here we were. He told us this before we came across a bunch of turkeys on this conveyer type of machine. "This is where they get killed," he said. And we watched while one by one the turkeys went through this contraption. They went in one end alive, got an electric shock, and came out the other end dead. It sounds crazier than it was. Most of the turkeys already looked dead before they went into the shock machine. "It's state of the art, the way we do this," the tour guide said. "It's as quick and painless as we can get."

After the killing floor I saw my dad working in the back. His job was like most of the jobs there, a super-specific action performed over and over in the assembly line. His action was to check the bodies of the turkeys to make sure they were right for the next step. It involved a lot of movement of his right arm, repetitive movement to start and stop machinery. I know this because it messed his shoulder up. Tore it all to hell over the years. He almost lost his job once, when he couldn't move his arm, it hurt so bad. The plant told him if he couldn't work his arm anymore, there was nothing they could do. My family threatened to make a stink. To get lawyers involved. At one point they asked if I could go into an office and translate for my dad. To confront the higher-ups. It never happened and I was beyond relieved. I know English, sure, but I don't know *lawyer* English. The thought of confronting big important white people with my dad's career on the line terrified me. It embarrassed me, too, the fact that he couldn't stick up for himself.

At the end of the tour, our double-netted guide got serious. His eyes squinted and his voice lowered, like he was going off script. "How many people have family that work here?" he asked. All of us raised our hands. Every single one. "Look, I tried to make this tour fun. But I'm not going to lie to you kids. This place is hard and cold and boring. More boring than anything else. That boredom will take everything from you. Your family, the people working here, they do it for *your* livelihood. They do it so you get a better shot then them. Shoot, that's why I'm here." Our guide rubbed his gloved hands as he talked. He wasn't looking at anyone in the eyes. It was like he was talking to himself. "Don't get me wrong, there's nothing wrong with working here. There are a lot worse places you could end up. But go to school. I'm telling you, you're smart kids. Don't end up here. Don't work here." And he ended the tour, raising his voice and pointing out some of the tidbits he'd forgotten as we headed toward the exit.

Walking out of the plant was like walking out of a dream. The sun seemed to shine brighter. The birds' songs were livelier. While filing into our bus, I looked at the plant. Louis Rich was a big white box surrounded by brown fencing. It was the only time I set foot inside the place. Growing up we never had a reason to get too close to the factory. That tour solidified one of the reasons why we stayed away.

Down the street from Jack and Jill, past the train tracks, was a yard full of huge red farm equipment. Machines that farmers would buy and use to work their vast expanses of fields. To me it looked like alien technology. Growing up in town, I hadn't visited a farm until junior high, after I stayed the night at a friend's house in the country. Even then, he lived with his grandma and I didn't actually see any farming done. This is funny because that's one of the first questions I get when people hear I'm from Iowa. Lot of corn? Lot of farming? Yeah, but not for us Mexicans. Our parents moved here to get away from the fields.

After the giant red farm machines we came to the junction of Columbus and Third Street. On the corner was a smaller trailer court called "Kenya Court." We had no clue and I still don't have any idea why it's called this. But once we made it to Kenya Court corner, we usually had three places we could hang out. Left was Eric's house. But it was packed with Maldonado boys and Eric didn't want to get bullied by his older brothers in front of us. Straight was Jerry's place in Mobile Village. And right, past Friendship Park, was Ruben's house. Ruben lived only a few houses down from the racetrack—car races, not track and field like over by my house.

On the day we were pedaling across town, we didn't even make it past Main Street. "Yo, Chuy, is that your sister?" Eric asked as we turned the corner. A panic-shock pulsed through my body. "Yeah, that's her with her chola friends." Oh no, oh no, I thought, hoping she didn't see me with her bike. Nancy was hanging outside the New Strand with some friends. They were at Ron-De-Voo Park, which was a tiny patch of grass beside the movie theater. They were smoking cigarettes and laughing.

"Yo, yo, Ruben, Jerry, let's go this way," I tried to say loud enough that they could hear but not so loud as to attract my sister and her friends. It wasn't loud enough. They rode right by Nancy and her flannel-clad friends. She recognized my friends zooming by and looked over to catch eyes with me. I saw her recognize that I was on her old bike. She flicked away her cigarette and walked onto the sidewalk to block our path. Eric swerved around her but I slowed to a stop. Ignoring her was futile.

She got in close. "What the fuck are you doing? You know I told you that you couldn't take my shit whenever you wanted." I looked over at my friends in front of the movie theater. For all the terror my sister caused me, she always did it in the privacy of our home. My friends looked on with confusion.

"Ay, Flaca, what's going on?" Nancy's friend Becky said from the park. Nancy was hanging out with a group of girls her age. All dressed in blue jeans, black shirts, and various colored flannel shirts. They had hoop earrings and hair-sprayed hair that looked wet against their foreheads. They were all older sisters of kids around my age. I later learned from Becky's younger brother that she terrorized him like my sister did me. They were badass teenage girls who got into trouble. They cruised and hung around West Liberty because there was nothing better to do.

"Nothing's going on. Just gotta deal with something," Nancy called to Becky before leaning in low again. "Here's what you're going to do," she said with a snarl. "You're going to turn around and take *my* bike back home. Fuck whatever Power Ranger shit you and your little friends are playing."

"Chuy, you coming or nah?" somebody said from the theater. I wasn't sure who said it. I wasn't looking over at them. I wasn't looking into my sister's eyes. I knew when we got home, I was going to get it. It was whether I was going to get a regular-ass beating or something extra by defying her in front of her friends. I kept inhaling through my nose. Fighting back tears.

"Nah, he has to go back home," Nancy said to my friends. "Isn't that right, little brother?" she said as she kept her eyes on me. She was gripping the middle of the handlebars so hard her knuckles were white, controlling where the bike would go in case I tried to make a run for it.

"Yeah, I can't go, guys. I'll see you back at school on Monday," I called over. Defeated.

"Smart choice," Nancy said as she let go of her bike.

"Okay, Flaca, are we going to this movie?" Becky asked.

"Nah, fuck this pinche movie. Puro pedo. Let's get out of here," she said as she pulled out another cigarette. "I'll see you at home," she added. They walked out the back of Ron-De-Voo Park toward the alley and got into Becky's car. The bass from the audio system rattled the car windows. Reverberated from the brick walls surrounding the park.

I looked over to see that the guys were still waiting, expecting me to follow them. I turned around before they could see the tears welling in my eyes, about to burst.

"Yo, Chuy, you're for real not coming?" Eric asked. I ignored the question as I started to pedal Nancy's bike back home.

My feet were concrete slabs as I pedaled, running the events through my head over and over. Shame at not being able to stand up to my sister in front of my friends. Fear at the realization that Nancy had granted me leniency. If she'd wanted to, she could have stripped her bike then and there. She could have whaled on me. I thought about my sister's power over me as I pedaled back toward my house.

Nancy was five years older than me, athletic, and had a temper. Whenever we fought, and we did a whole bunch, she would emerge the victor. If things got heated, she had the capacity to beat the ever-loving shit out of me. Some kids had a mean older brother or cousin, or a neighborhood kid who tormented them. West Liberty had bullies in droves. We were bullies, too, mind you. To a lot of people. There was a pecking order. Everyone got bullied and everyone bullied someone else. Of course that's not the whole truth; there were a few tragic kids at the very bottom. Or kids pure enough to not reciprocate and maintain the status quo of violence. But that wasn't us. Everyone I knew growing up had dirt and muck and blood on their hands. My sister had all of the above at my expense. She relished playing the role of the bully.

Reflecting on my sister back then is like reflecting on the West Liberty I knew growing up. West Liberty has a certain reputation as being rough and tumble, even more so in the nineties. The demographics of the town lent itself to conjecture. The surrounding 99.9 percent white towns reveled in the stories of violence coming from ours. Those were exaggerations, sensationalist tales that added to the mythos. But I would be lying if I said there wasn't *any* violence and fighting. Like any other small town, there is a history of pointed aggression popping in and out of domesticated life. For West Liberty, these stories get wrapped up and compounded with unsubstantiated fears. So we witness protocols where visiting teams hold hands when they leave their bus to walk to the locker rooms. Or I talk to people who grew up in surrounding towns and they ask me how many school-wide rumbles I got into.

I can mostly dismiss this gossip. Mostly. What makes it hard is that my sister was my childhood bully. My nemesis. She was the troubled middle child who ran with a group of girls who dressed alike and fought with their families. I still mull the question over. *Was she in a gang?* As I reflect on that, the sirens in my head immediately go off, like they go off when I talk about West Liberty. I'm defensive and embarrassed. Of course she wasn't. Of course West Liberty is safe.

Growing up I heard about two bona fide gangs, the Gangster Disciples (GDs) and the South Side Sureños (Sur 13). I had a cousin who grew up in Muscatine and would brag about all the GDs he knew. Nancy has a huge homemade "X3" tattoo she gave herself on her ankle. Various West Liberty landmarks have had this same symbol, tied to Sur 13, graffitied on them.

But I tightrope across this topic, like I do with most aspects of the town, because gleeful powers that be would like to lump together known affiliates with bona fide gangsters. Would a politician group my dorky, gangly cousin with members of the Mexican Mafia because one time he marked a park bench with the letters *GD*? But Nancy wasn't my cousin, and I remember the glimpse of a razor blade she kept in her bag. She said she would keep it under her tongue if she ever got into a fight and needed it. I never saw her keep it under her tongue, but I remember it glinting among the things in her purse. *You see.* That's how easy these myths about West Liberty get started. I'd be lying if I said I never saw a random razor blade in my sister's belongings, but I doubt she ever used it.

All I know is there were some people in town you didn't want to piss off. My sister was one of those people. And without fail, over and over, I pissed her off. And when I did, don't picture a brother and a sister wrestling each other at arm's length until someone tells Mom; think my sister sitting on top of me to pin my arms down and punching me in my screaming, bloodied face. Now you can see why I rode home that day. I propped Nancy's bike on its kickstand before heading inside to wait out the weekend.

I didn't talk to the guys again until recess Monday morning. I caught a glimpse of Eric and Ruben after church on Sunday. Before they got a chance to talk to me, my mom shooed us away to get back home to tend to her menudo with my tía. I didn't protest.

To my surprise, my encounter with my sister at Ron-De-Voo Park wasn't a focal point of ensuing conversations. They knew it was verging into too-real territory for me, transcending the petty chiding and insults we hurled at each other.

"Yo, Chuy, come play Hail Mary with us!" Jerry called out from the field beyond the asphalt north of our middle school. Hail Mary was a simple enough game. One person was the designated quarterback at the end of the field with the football while everyone else was at the other end. The solitary person would call out a point number and heave the ball to the crowd. If you caught the ball, you acquired the points. Accumulate a predetermined amount of points and you became quarterback. Usually the harder and farther throws corresponded with larger numbers to add dramatic tension. I was terrible at catching any type of ball but agreed to play with my friends to further distance us from the occurrence at Ron-De-Voo Park.

From the depths of our scrum, an arm caught the ball. "Shit, Gin Money on the loose. Racking up a thousand. Chalk it up!" It was our friend Josh Gingerich. Josh had a lot of different names: Josh, Gin Money, White Josh. He was the token white kid in our friend group. Josh rivaled Jerry for the title of funniest guy in our squad. His stepdad was the high school biology teacher, and he relished any opportunity he could get to act a fool in class or at recess. Josh high-stepped with the football to gloat before tossing it back to the quarterback and jogging over to Eric and me. We had both jumped and missed the ball that Josh caught. We tripped and wobbled on the uneven terrain. "Hey Chuy, so you got to see it then, huh? The Sha—" Josh began before Eric cut him off.

"Nah, remember he couldn't go over to Ruben's," Eric said. "He doesn't know about it."

"Oh shit, my bad, my bad. Yeah, you gotta see it for yourself, playboy," Josh said.

"That's what I've heard," I replied. Josh turned his gaze from the current quarterback to me.

"So I never got the full story. Why couldn't you get over there? You guys were on your way, right? Something about some shit went down by the movie theater?" Josh said. My voice faltered in trying to find a response to his question. Eric, sensing the situation, interjected.

"It was something that your parents wanted, right Chuy? Your sister had seen you and said you needed to go and see your dad right away." Eric met my eyes as he talked.

"Yeah, something like that," I said, turning away from Josh's gaze. Eric continued his banter with Josh as they ran for an errant throw in a spot far from us.

I watched Eric as he struggled to keep up with the other boys angling for position. Being as small as he was, he rarely got a chance to catch enough passes to become the quarterback in Hail Mary. For Eric it was a cruel irony that our friend group valued the game so much. He was tiny and unathletic. His older brothers, Sergio and Junior, were bigger than average, way bigger than the average Mexican, so they thrived on the West Liberty Comets team in their day. Eric lived in their shadow. I can't imagine what a terror it must have been to suit up in seventh- and eighth-grade tackle football being a few feet shorter and dozens of pounds lighter than everyone else. One time Eric got injured and hobbled on his leg the whole week after a game. We noticed at one point his hobble was on the wrong leg for a fraction of the day. Feeling bad, we never said anything to him about it.

Eric and I got along particularly well because we both had to deal with so much trauma and bullying—me from my sister, him from being the runt of our grade's litter. Eric's size hinted at how we were in this awkward transitional stage between being little kids and teenagers. If you saw little Eric walking down the street with us, you would never imagine the sailors' mouths on us. Or the fights we could get in on the playground. Or that we were only two or so years away from our first taste of alcohol. At the same time, we still watched cartoons and were a few years removed from playing with Hot Wheels cars in the dirt.

But even though Eric was small, he always had your back. He was quick-thinking and loyal. That's why we tolerated his little-man aggression toward others. We knew if we got into something, he would have our backs, no questions asked. He would stand up for us even if it meant putting himself in the line of fire. Eric proved this in our recess game of Hail Mary when Jerry caught a particularly crowded pass. There was a scuffle after Brent, a red-headed kid with a bad attitude, checked Jerry as he came down from his catch.

"Yo, what the hell!?" Jerry yelled as he shoved Brent in retaliation. Brent's face was ruddy and pockmarked, and he smiled in response to Jerry's shove. Stanley Kubrick couldn't have demanded a better smile.

"I'm just playing the game. What, they don't play football in China?"

A playground audience circled around, like they always did at the hint of a fight. Eric walked over between Jerry and Brent. "You know he's not from China, idiot. Come on, Jerry, he's not worth it." Eric walked Jerry back. Another goon, Darren, appeared amid the crowd. In spite of everything Brent was—hotheaded, a troll, a casual racist—he never took things too far. For Brent, Eric walking Jerry away was most likely met with relief. But Darren was a straight-up racist and bigot. He hated us. He had thin, ratty hair and always looked exhausted.

Darren called out, "Yeah, you know he's not a Chinaman, he's a gook. Aw, the Mexican and the gook, friends forever."

"What'd you say?" Eric said as he let go of Jerry and walked straight to Darren. Darren clenched his fists in anticipation. As Eric closed the distance between them, you could already see the mismatch in size. If they had stood next to each other, like boxers after a weigh-in, Darren would have towered over Eric.

Now it was Jerry's turn to diffuse. He grabbed Eric by the waist and pulled him back. "Nope. Nope. It's not worth it for you either," Jerry said. Darren laughed and pointed.

"Let's get back to the game," Brent said as he scooped up the football and threw it to the quarterback. Jerry, with something to prove, kicked it into overdrive. He sprinted across the field and caught the next five passes in a row, his streaked hair bobbing up and down as he cascaded across the field. He was a force of nature, snatching a few catches from out of Brent's grasp. Brent's face crimsoned at the display.

Jerry honed his skills on the playground at Mobile Village, the trailer court where a lot of the Southeast Asian community resided. Jerry played games with an older group of kids at this playground. We colloquially and simply called them "the Asians" in the way they called us "the Mexicans." The Asians, counter to Brent's mockery, were actually from Southeast Asia, not China. Their parents were refugees from Laos and northwestern Vietnam. In the 1970s Iowa Governor Robert Ray welcomed refugees displaced during the Vietnam War. The Tai Dam people in particular, from Laos, Thailand, and Vietnam, ended up coming to West Liberty. Like my parents from the south, a lot of these refugees found work in factories like Louis Rich.

According to the numbers, the Southeast Asian population was always smaller than the town's Mexican makeup. But to me it always felt like there was a group of Asians with us. Maybe it's because we tagged along with Jerry while he followed the older kids in the trailer court. Because we thought they were cool and people to emulate.

I would bike from my side of town and link up with Jerry, Ruben, and Eric to go over to the Mobile Village. Being on the south side of town, it was next to a cornfield and a few blocks from the town cemetery.

Jerry's house was a mobile home in the main area of the trailer court. We'd have to take off our shoes in the mudroom before we entered the house proper. When a lot of us kids were congregating at Jerry's, there would be a cascade of shoes in the entryway. Once we entered, we were in the kitchen and living room. Jerry always had the nicest and biggest TV among us. When we wanted to watch a movie or show, we'd go over to his place to get the full experience. I don't remember talking much to Jerry's parents. They usually would greet me at the door and point me toward Jerry's room. The middle of three boys, Jerry would avoid his tagalong younger brother, Anthony, and not interact much with his older brother, Phone. Phone would roll his eyes at us and tolerate our loud mouths and shenanigans.

We didn't spend too much time at Jerry's. We'd either go to the Mobile Village playground or to another part of the court away from the main section. There were two ways to get to this smaller section. You could either go out the main entrance and walk around the long way, down the street that led to the cemetery, or you could take a shortcut through a ditch direct to this section. After heavy rains this ditch would get swampy, so some kids added a long plank to act as a bridge. One by one we'd cross the plank. The Laotians in the Mobile Village dubbed this ditch "the Mekong River." One of my friends reminded me of this fact recently. I forget how self-aware and hilarious we could be. Of course it was the Mekong River.

We'd cross the Mekong to get to Da's, Jack's, or Lucky's. Of the older Laotians, Da was the eldest and the de facto leader. They were at least a few years older than Jerry. They'd play card games like spades or pack into a couple cars and head to Iowa City to drive around and get food. On occasion we'd get to tag along on these excursions. I didn't realize Jerry was stuck between groups, this older group of Asians he identified with and younger Asian kids he was too old for. I suspect he hung out with our group of Mexicans by default, that if there'd been other Laotian kids his age he would've been closer to them.

Jerry continued to deal with racism from kids like Brent and Darren. We all had to deal with it in our tackle football careers when we finally suited up to play against the surrounding towns. The towns we played were roughly the same size as West Liberty, both by geography and by population. The huge difference, of course, was that West Liberty was the only town in the area that had any people of color. Point blank, we experienced a whole bunch of racism.

In one instance, we traveled to another town for an away game. Before the game both teams would usually go to opposite ends of the field to warm up. Our coach at the time was Gus Garcia. Gus was mixed race, half Mexican, half white, and he was good at his job, gentle but firm. He stood before us as we filed through our lines doing high knees and butt kicks. From the home team's side we heard a yell. It came from a player standing in front of the rest of his team. Their coach was beside them like Gus was beside us, overseeing. The player bellowed, "Let's beat these fucking Mexicans' asses!" The rest of the team hooted and hollered. Their coach didn't react at all.

Coach Garcia walked over to him. "Really? You're going to let them say that in front of you?"

"I didn't hear anything," the other coach replied, his arms akimbo as he walked away.

I remember Josh talking to us during the pregame huddle. "Okay. Let's not pretend we didn't all hear that. You heard it. I heard it. Let's use how pissed we are and show them what happens when they say shit like that." I remember thinking that we heard stuff like that in West Liberty though. Jerry, Eric, Ruben, and I would get called things like that back home, but playing football against other towns showed people like Josh that sting. He got a small taste of our experience. The opposing player didn't say, "Let's beat this team that has some Mexicans!" No. Josh and the other white kids on our team became honorary Mexicans in their eyes.

In Jerry's case this sometimes happened literally—the other teams thought he was Mexican. One time Jerry responded to how other towns lumped us all together in a memorable way. We were playing a home game against another all-white team. It was after the previous incident, so we had already experienced plenty of Mexican-based slurs and bad blood. Jerry and another player were at each other the whole game. Remember, we were in full pads and helmets by that time. In junior high we didn't have our last names on our jerseys yet, so there wasn't a "Sayabeth" that the kid could read. As Jerry went for catches, the kid would see Jerry's arms, brown as mine, reaching for the ball. As they volleyed for the ball, they would rough each other up. At the end of each play, they would walk back to their teams and talk shit to each other. After Jerry caught a ball in front of the kid, he hissed out, "Nice catch, you fucking spic."

Jerry, incensed, turned around to the kid and yanked off his own helmet. "Wait, what did you say? I'm not a spic. I'm a chink!" And he pushed the kid, who didn't know how to respond. I mean, I can relate. It's more than twenty years later and I still don't quite know how to respond to that. It's tragic and encapsulates a lot of the anger and frustration we felt playing against these racist kids. But there's something there too about how Jerry needed to resort to calling himself a slur for that kid to even know who he was. I imagine it must have been lonely, being an even smaller minority in a town full of minorities. But we all took those words and let them feed our anger and frustration. That's why Jerry was kicking it into overdrive at recess. He was flying in the face of kids who hated him because of his skin and culture. Because he existed where they thought he shouldn't.

Jerry caught another ball and showboated in front of Brent. He sang the lyrics to a Bone Thugs-N-Harmony song as he did a carioca quick step.

"It's the Thuggish Ruggish Bone!" Jerry sang. Before the quarterback threw another pass, the teacher on recess duty blew her whistle for us to line up. We all groaned, dejected that our games were over and we had to go back to our classrooms.

The lining up of classes was chaos. As I began to file in with the other students, I noticed the animosity from the playground had spilled over into the line. Brent and Darren were face to face with Jerry and Josh. Eric signaled me to come over and give them backup.

"Oh, so that's what you're going to do? Get your brownie friends to gang up on us?" Brent asked Jerry, inches from his face.

"Come on, Brent, you're better than this," Josh said.

"Oh, what, like you're better than us 'cause you like these brownies? These *Mexicans*?" Darren responded. They had this way of saying "Mexican" that was a slur unto itself. They didn't need to fall back on the harder names. The way "Mexican" twisted out of their mouths was venom enough.

"We're all better than you, Darren. You scurv," Jerry retaliated.

Darren winced at this slur. It was the closest thing we had to a retaliation to kids calling us chinks, wetbacks, spics, and *Mexicans*. Brent looked uncomfortable in his alliance with Darren. In the grand order of things, there was a class system in play in our altercation. Josh was upper middle class. He lived with his stepdad in a nice house by Wapsi Creek Park. Brent, though not as affluent, came from a respected enough family in town. There are a few family names that have been around West Liberty for a long time and have a certain clout. Darren was the opposite of that. He often wore the same outfit day after day. He was dirty and malnourished. "Scurv" was our slur for any white kid who fit this mold. Not all white kids were scurvs, but all scurvs were white. It was short for "scurvy." Only now looking back do I realize it's the same scurvy that pirates got on long sea voyages.

Brent receded into the line as Darren bumped his chest against Jerry's. "What'd you call me, you chin—" Darren started, but his voice cut off as someone shoved from the side, his head jerking from the momentum. Darren wobbled and caught himself, furious at whoever pushed him.

It was Ruben. He stood languid and ready. "What you gonna do?" The two stood facing each other for a bit.

"Come on boys, time to move it!" the teacher on duty called out from the front of the line.

We gathered behind Ruben. "You all good?" he asked us. Jerry shrugged and nodded for us to forget about it. "Let me know if he starts anything else. So is everybody free after school? It's about time we show Chuy what we have waiting in the cut. That okay with your sister, Chuy?"

"It won't happen again," I replied, my cheeks burning.

"I'm messing with you, fool. It's all good. Let's go. For real Jerry, let me know if those crackas act up." We filed behind him as we walked back to our classes.

As far as I know, Brent never started anything else after that. In fact, we actually got cool with him as the years passed. He sat with us during lunch in high school. He could be a hothead, but he quit being a casual racist. That happened to a lot of the kids surrounding us. They saw that we were kids like them. The proximity forced them to identify with us, like when Josh got called slurs in football. There are otherwise conservative West Liberty alumni who are progressive on immigration. Who are empathetic to that issue. Who are empathetic to us.

Darren was another story. Later that day he got a pen and scrawled marks on his hands and arms. A teacher walked by his desk. "What's that all over you?" she asked.

"Nothing. It's something my dad showed me how to draw," he replied.

"I think it's best you go to the bathroom and wash it off. I don't want you getting any ink on your clothes."

Darren got up and held his hand against his chest as he passed by. He walked in slow motion and made sure we saw. They were the same jagged etchings that were at the top of the Tornado in Kimberly Park. Violent swastikas of varying sizes and intensity adorned Darren's hands and arms. He smirked at our reactions as he walked out of the room. He continued to scribble swastikas on his arms throughout the time I knew him. Sometimes he would press so hard and go over the markings so much he would bleed. His family moved before we got to high school. I suspect they moved to a town that didn't have the racial makeup of West Liberty, which wasn't hard to find in Iowa.

We got through the rest of the day's classes all right. We were bright kids but restless and ornery. Eric got into another argument with a substitute teacher, Mr. Evans. Josh, Jerry, and I acted up, cracking jokes to make the rest of the class laugh. There was a constant war of escalation as the teachers tried to figure out how to separate us in class. They'd move our seats row by row only to find us making faces across the way.

Part of our group posing on the
playground like it was a prison.

One time they turned our desks away from one another, each of us facing a different wall.

The three o'clock bell finally rang. We scurried to our lockers, grabbed our backpacks, and met Ruben by the front entrance of the school. He was standing in a royal-blue Comets jacket that had "Chavez" stitched over the breast pocket. Besides diminutive Eric, and Josh, who was a little chubby, we were all around the same size. Ruben was the strongest, fastest, and most athletic of us. Not only that, but he was the smartest to boot, which proved dangerous in the verbal barbs he could throw out. He had a way of cutting to the core of you when he hurled his insults. We followed his step as we began walking south from the middle school. Ruben had a way of analyzing a situation and responding, whether that meant a well-placed verbal jab to get Eric to calm down or a shove on the playground, knowing the bully wouldn't engage. He was our leader. We never designated him as such. But we knew it all the same. Ruben always kept his hair short. He had an electric hair trimmer he would use on himself. Whenever he would trim, you could see a scar on the back of his head, the result of a childhood accident involving his younger sister and a glass bottle. It mirrored a scar I have on my eyebrow from when my sister made me carry a case of bottles by myself and I tripped onto my face—*onto* the bottles.

We recapped the day as we made our way over to Josh's house. We were on the east side of town. The east side was residential. It was nice houses that led to Wapsi Creek Park. Wapsi had a baseball diamond and a field reserved for flag football.

"I gotta stop by my house and let them know where I'm going," Josh said as we walked parallel to his house. We stood by the door as he hollered to his mom that he'd be back by dinner. Usually we would hang out in Josh's basement. Josh's brother and sister are a lot older. They had moved out and Josh was, in effect, an only child. We'd play video games or watch MTV while his mom and stepdad, Mr. Ottaway, hung out upstairs. If we were persistent, we could convince Josh to let us play with his stepdad's Mac computer, which he had years before any of our families could afford one. That computer mesmerized us.

But there wasn't any time for games today. Josh hollered "Love you too!" from the doorway and we made our way to Ruben's house. As we got closer, the guys got more and more excited. To tell the truth, I was getting annoyed that they wouldn't out and tell me this big secret.

"I'm starting to think this isn't gonna be worth it," I said as we walked into Ruben's backyard. Ruben and Josh looked at each other and smiled. I kept on walking toward the back entrance of the house when I noticed the other guys had stopped.

"Over here," Ruben called out. They had posted up by the rundown garage at the end of Ruben's backyard. I had never given his garage much thought. It was like our family's attic in that it had become this refuge for random knickknacks and junk. Last I'd seen it, Ruben's dad had filled the garage to the brim. As Ruben put his shoulder into the green wooden door, the bottom of the door scraped against the concrete floor and the group filed in one by one. They had me go last. Someone flipped on a dim light. My eyes adjusted from the sunlit backyard to the now open and habitable garage.

"What? What is this?" I asked. They had cleared out all the junk, and in its place were various furnishings. A worn couch, stained and floral patterned, lined the wall. A couple of broken wicker chairs sat in front of an old TV. Eric and Jerry were already starting the hooked-up Sega Genesis. There was a mattress in the corner and a radio on an old workbench. Josh pulled out a poster of Ken Griffey Jr. from his backpack. Ruben grabbed a hammer and nails from the workbench and got to work putting up the poster. Josh plopped onto the granny couch and placed his hands behind his head.

"So, what you think? You're the last one to see it," he said.

It was still very much a work in progress. And no matter how much we gussied it up, it was always going to be a run-down old garage. It had the undeniable must of wet carpet. There were no windows and it was stuffy.

"It's incredible!" I said as I continued to take things in. I meant it. For all its shortcomings, I knew what this space would mean for us. Everybody's house had the potential for interlopers. Parents eavesdropping from beyond our bedrooms. Older siblings barging in. Younger siblings tagging along. This could still happen in the garage, but its distance from the day-to-day activity of Ruben's family was enough to be an annoyance, which meant they left us alone. This was ours. It was our home base.

"We're calling it the Shack," Ruben said as he surveyed the poster on the wall, making sure it was straight.

"The Party Shack?" Josh asked in an epiphany. We all looked at each other. Jerry and Eric turned from their game of *Mutant League Football* on TV.

"Yeah! The Party Shack," Ruben said with a smile, and we all whooped, our hollering muffled by the Shack's walls. If you were outside, you wouldn't have even known we were in there.

I made my way home so as to be back by 6 p.m. for dinner. I was still buzzing at the idea of the Party Shack. Ruben tasked us with getting eggs from our kitchens that week, stockpiling ammunition for the weekend. On Saturdays were the car races at the track by Ruben's house. The racetrack was behind Louis Rich and the West Liberty Community Center. I find it poetic that beside the turkey processing plant were all these social things for the town. The center where they hosted bingo and bailes. The track where white people could watch the car races. The area for the county fair in July.

I arrived home through the side porch that opened right to the kitchen. My mom was setting the plates on the table. She called Nancy to join us to eat. Dinner was a pack of hot dogs cut up and fried in a pan. We called it "chopped weenies." It went excellent with tortillas de harina and frijoles. Only I didn't like beans at the time, something my sister made fun of as we accepted my mom's offerings.

"No frijoles?" my mom asked.

"He thinks if he doesn't eat beans, they won't call us beaners," my sister said.

"Shut up! It's not that. They're gross!" I said. Nancy coiled her fist, ready to strike. I winced. After she returned home on Saturday, she'd found me and delivered two strikes to my arm in the night. The bruises were turning green and purple underneath my shirt.

"¡Ay, cálmate los dos! Chuy, go get you dad. En la garage." I jumped up from my seat, debating whether I should give Nancy a dirty look. I thought the better of it and crossed our living room to get my dad.

In the garage was a surprise. My dad was changing the oil on our family station wagon, but beside it, hauled in from the driveway, was the lowrider. I had never seen it moved from its iconic spot in the driveway. It looked odd waiting beside the station wagon we had used so much. A decoration beside something so utilitarian.

"Apa, ya está la comida," I said in shaky Spanish. I had to speak louder than the norteño music playing from a tape deck. My dad nodded and got up to wipe his hands on blue shop towels. He caught me staring at the lowrider but didn't say anything. The silence forced me to talk. "Why is this inside? You going to fix it?" I asked.

"Maybe," he said as he tossed oil-stained paper towels into the big blue bin between the two cars. The song "La Puerta Negra" by Los Tigres Del Norte swelled while I stood at the door. To me it sounded like polka music. As my dad turned to put away some tools, I took my chance and left, stealing one last glance at the lowrider.

Its new home was significant, or so I thought. If a car or apparatus was in the garage, that usually meant it was next in the queue of never-ending projects. My dad would cycle through cars, lawn mowers, woodworking projects. Anything in the garage was fair game for the next project. Only the lowrider stood untouched by the rotation over the weeks that led into months. It felt like my dad was keeping it hidden away. At first we thought he was sheltering it from the harsh Iowa winter. But when the snow thawed and spring came, the car was still lying in wait. If the clutter of more pertinent projects grew too wild in the garage, my dad would move the lowrider back out to the driveway until there was more room. Back and forth he wheeled the lowrider from the driveway to the garage.

Months passed. Then years. You could tell the passing of time by the corrosion on the trunk of the lowrider where it faced the sun. The cancer spots grew even bigger, bore holes into the metal until you could see into the trunk from the outside. The paint along the sides flaked and peeled. The jagged rust lines along the paint job looked like a desert. The tires deflated and started to crack. If my dad needed to wheel the car the few feet into the garage, he'd have to bring over an air compressor and fill the tires. Within minutes they'd completely deflate onto their rims. In high school we found a beehive forming in the back window. My dad waited until dusk a few days later and sprayed the hive down while covering his face with a rag. He threw the dead hive by the car and left it there to rot.

I never knew and have never asked my dad about his feelings surrounding the car. I have never got the nerve to ask him what he thought about me not working on it with him. My dad is very pragmatic. The last I talked to him about it, he said, "It got too expensive." The maintenance, the upkeep, the legacy. Through the years, on occasion, during the times it was outside in our driveway, we'd get visitors. People would ring our doorbell and ask about the lowrider. "Is your dad the owner? Would he be willing to part with it? I'd pay good money." A lot of times these were other Mexicans. Car enthusiasts from other towns. People who saw that, with a little work and money, you could get that car running, no problem. My dad turned each of them down. One time a college-aged white guy knocked on our door, blonde with sad eyes. He talked fast and exclaimed how much he loved the car. He had driven by it so many times. He pulled out a wad of cash, then and there, thousands of dollars. I craned my neck from the living room sofa to get a better look. As he did with each potential buyer, my dad smiled and shook his head after each sentence, like you do when you don't care how the solicitor feels. No. "But here's the actual money in hand." No. "You won't get a better deal. I'll haul it myself." No. My dad didn't even look at the wad of bills as he told the kid thank you and closed the door. My face burned as I flipped through the TV channels.

As time ravaged the lowrider, my dad and I grew more distant. My interests deviated more and more from his Mexican aesthetics. I found myself in hip-hop and rock music, in American pop culture. My dad listened to Mexican music and radio. During my childhood he had the TV preset to Univision, the only Spanish-speaking channel we got. During high school he got a satellite dish so our house could have more Mexican channels. This also meant I lost a lot of the shows I loved. I lamented that I could no longer watch Conan O'Brien. My parents didn't care as they watched novela after novela. The brief amount of conversation I had with my father diminished even more. I thought we had nothing in common. The more I found my identity, the more the void grew between my dad's sensibilities and my own. We talked about work. Or school. Or let the language barrier be the excuse for not talking at all.

One day I was warming up leftovers in the microwave. I must have been a sophomore at the time. My parents were watching their precious satellite TV in the living room. I was trying to tune out the histrionic acting and corny narration as I waited for the timer to beep when a car pulled up in the gravel beside our side porch. The headlights danced across the living room before the engine cut off.

"¿Quién es?" my mom asked from the living room, looking through the blinds to get a better look at the silhouette in the driveway. She inhaled through her teeth at the sound of a car door shutting. "¡Viejo! Honey. Es Ray."

"Ray?" my dad asked from his seat on the couch, annoyed at the interruption. "¿Cuál Ray? No conozco un Ray."

My mom's voice grew higher pitched, urgent. The silhouette of a man was walking toward our side porch. "¿Como qué no sabes, viejo? Ray! Lowrider Ray!"

I jumped at the beep from the microwave as it finished warming my food. My dad scrambled to his feet as Ray came into the light outside the door. He caught my eyes and stretched out his arms. He had his sunglasses on even though the sun was setting. "It is him, Dad," I said, frozen to the spot.

Ray knocked on the door as my mom shuffled over to the kitchen, chastising me for not letting him in. She opened the door while proclaiming salutations. My dad stood in the entryway between the kitchen and living room, waiting.

Ray and my mom hugged. She asked if Ray remembered me as we shook our "Cómo estás" handshake.

"Saludos. Holy shit. You got big. I remember when you were a little one. To my knee. Time flies, primo. ¿Y tu padre?"

My dad walked from behind my mom. "¿Cómo estás, Olivarez?"

"Señor Renteria. ¡Órale!" Ray responded as they shook each other's hands. My mom started to buzz around the kitchen, scooching out chairs, picking up leftover plates from the table. She asked Ray if he wanted anything to eat, to drink, if he wanted to sit. Ray declined my mom's invitation to settle. "Perdón, Irene, pero I came to see her."

My dad mumbled under his breath. He raised his hands then let them fall onto his thighs. "Okay. En la garage." He motioned Ray to go back the way he came and followed him out the door.

As soon as they left, my mom turned to me. "Chuy. Go with your dad. Now." I followed her instructions and left my cooling food in the microwave. Ray had served his mandatory minimum and was out on parole. First thing he did when he got out was track down every last one of the cars he had sold in the area. It had been ten years since he had been out. Ten years to reconnect and see how far his babies had gone. Memories and stories swirled in my head. Memories of me as a kid in Ray's garage. Stories about how and why he ended up in jail and out of our life.

Before I turned the corner of the house, I heard my dad. "Ray. Tengo que decirte . . ." They were standing in front of the garage door. Ray had his fists clenched. I jogged up to them as my dad finished warning Ray. Doing my best to act casual, I almost bumped into the two as I caught them.

"Primo. Tell your dad to be cool, man, he doesn't have to worry. Lotta time passed. Shit, you don't need to remind me."

I didn't know what to say. I looked over at my dad. He didn't know what to say. My dad turned the handle of the garage door and hoisted it up halfway. I walked over and helped him push the door up the rest of the way. I wanted to preoccupy myself with an action. To look away from this man as he saw what we had let happen to his car. Ray rushed past us, ducking his head under the garage door as it ascended.

"What. What did you guys do?" he said. Shock and anger in his voice. I stood in place as Ray paced back and forth, surveying the damage. He yanked off his sunglasses to get a better look. He came down to his knees before the rotted, see-through trunk. His hand came up to feel the rust and metal. It was a long time before he spoke again. The anger gone, his voice broke when he asked, "What you do to her, man?" He looked up to face my dad. It was the first time I had seen Ray without his sunglasses. His eyes red and tired.

"You right, Ray. A lot of time passed," my dad said in English. It came out like a plea for understanding. I backed away from Ray and my dad, from the garage door. I was an interloper.

I don't know what else my dad said to Ray that night. I don't know what else he could have said. But I felt like it wasn't for me to hear. My head swirled as I walked up the front porch to see my mom.

"¿Y tu apa? ¿Está bien?"

"Yeah. He's okay."

"Ray?" she asked in a softer tone.

I shook my head and walked past her into the living room.

A few weeks after Ray's visit, my dad brought the lowrider out into the driveway. He never returned it to the garage after that. It felt like a penance. Like if it was going to rot away, it would happen in the open for people to gawk at.

Not too long after that, we got a notice from the city. My dad handed me the letter to translate it for him. It was about the car. They said it was an eyesore. A public nuisance. They gave us thirty days to get rid of it. I ran through a mental list of other beat-up cars I saw around town. I thought of the trucks I'd seen in yards, rusted and on cinder blocks. Of white homeowners. I suspected we were getting the notice because of our proximity to the football field. Because of its prominence when coming into town from the highway. In their eyes it must have set a bad impression. I thought to bring this up to my dad after I read the letter out loud. But what would it have mattered? They were well within their rights and we had no plans to fix it up. He took the letter from me and let it drift into the trash. A week later he sold the car to a junkyard for scrap.

Before I started writing this story, my dad had a severe health scare. My mom took him to the same hospital I was born in, Mercy Hospital in Iowa City. He continued working at the turkey plant, now West Liberty Foods. Even got a watch for his fortieth anniversary at the factory. Around the same time doctors diagnosed him with type 2 diabetes. My mom says it was his first time he had to go to the hospital for something we couldn't make sense of. The first time he had to face his own mortality. He's always been healthy. Always been working.

The doctor talked to my brother and sister. Said the diabetes certainly didn't help with his condition, but it wasn't the root cause of the hospitalization. He had an issue with his pancreas. It was excruciating pain and causing him severe nausea and dizziness. As my brother tried to get all the facts straight to relay to our parents, the doctor commented, "You have good English, you know. It's impressive."

My brother, who has lived here all his life, snapped. "Fuck if I have good English or not. We're talking about my dad here." And the doctor found an excuse to leave.

I arrived a few hours after this. My dad was sleeping as my mom sat beside him. She had tuned the TV on the wall to Univision like back home. Mercy Hospital is a Catholic hospital, and next to the TV was Jesus on a crucifix. The hospital nailed the decoration up through the figure's hands. My dad stirred. "Honey. Es Chuy," said my mom.

My dad opened his eyes and sat up in bed. He told me he was afraid. That he thought it was almost his time to meet God in heaven. Not yet, I told him. We sat in the room for a while. That car flashed through my mind. I'd been bringing it up lately. Asking my dad questions about it. That's how I found out he'd finally sold it for scrap rather than selling it to someone he knew. That's how I found out the actual model was a '52 Chevy Fleetline. An idea rushed to me as I sat beside my dad in his hospital bed. We could find another car like that. We could work on it together. I'd been making more money. I could splurge on it. Then I thought of what my mom said to me that day Jerry and I jump-started the lowrider. One day I'd be old and I'd regret not wanting to be with my dad. Not wanting to know him as a person. She was right. Goddammit, she was right. I let the idea of a new car, the possibility of a new project to atone for my past, dissipate in the hospital room. My dad closed his eyes and fell back asleep.

It was never about the car. My dad's health scare lent an immediacy to an act I've been resolving to achieve the last few years. The act of getting to know my dad. I've been hanging out with my parents more. Traveling to West Liberty from my home in Iowa City and getting dinner at the same old house I grew up in on Elm Street. We talk. I force myself to mash together enough Spanglish to reiterate points I would have left by the wayside in the past. I listen to the stories my parents tell. The idea of this book stemmed from some of these stories. From learning about Juan and Irene, the human beings.

Sometimes at night when I can't sleep, I keep myself up with the question of why I didn't connect with my parents growing up. It's a tortuous question for first-generation children. Tortuous because the disconnect from our parents is bigger than our parents. It's a disconnect from an entire culture. Like how I don't know Spanish, like how I still can't force myself to like norteño music. But I've been trying to connect with that culture in my own way. In ways that still feel authentic to myself. I forced my mom to teach me how to cook meals I had growing up. (Gender expectations complicated this.) I asked my dad to tell me something about growing up in Ojinaga. Even if it's awkward, even if it feels decades too late, I'm trying.

My dad is funny. One of my recent visits involved a conversation on how my parents were as babies. How fussy did their parents say they were? How long did it take them to get potty trained in comparison to my siblings and me? My dad, dead serious, declared, "I was potty trained at six months." It took me a moment to register how full of it he was before my mom interjected.

"¡Stás loco! He a liar." And my dad smiled. I laughed a deep laugh, imagining my dad running around Ojinaga as a boy.

There's something else that inspired these memories of the lowrider. In going to visit my parents more often, I ended up home by chance on the day of the county fair parade. This was the parade I had heard stories of the lowrider being in. The lone Mexican island in the sea of white small-town festivities. I pulled up a lawn chair, feeling nostalgic for the parades of my childhood.

I immediately noticed things were different. The whole affair was

Mexican. All these Latino displays intermingled with the rest of the parade. The traditional fair was still there. The convertibles carrying the pageant queens led the pack. But floats sponsored by Mexican restaurants and stores followed. A Mexican luchador walked alongside a float advertising an upcoming lucha libre wrestling match. Floats blasted ranchera music as they passed. One float had a person grilling arrachera meat and passing it down to people like candy.

The high school marching band preceded a float with local musicians playing cumbia tunes. The Shriners were still there, stunting for the crowd. The clowns that brought up the rear, the ones who scared my sister so much, were gone. In their place was a huge cavalry of Mexican guys on horses. Some had their horses promenade and canter. Others waited some distance and then had their horses bust into a gallop for the kids.

The only significant lull in the parade was when a sparsely decorated truck crept by. I noticed some younger kids jeering before one of my tías shushed them. The Trump truck passed by in complete silence on our block. Josh Gingerich walked by with his wife and daughters after it passed. "Did you see the Trump truck?" he asked. "Wasn't that the quietest reception you've ever seen a float get?" I smiled and agreed, hugging my old friend as we laughed about the highlights of the parade. Talked about how much things had changed.

It's not enough to say that West Liberty is Iowa's first majority Latino town. We've read that headline so much it's almost lost its meaning. Sure, one of the biggest hobbies West Liberty people have is to share the latest newspaper article or video about the town. I do it too. There have been a lot of them, from the *Chicago Tribune* to ESPN, the *New York Times* to Telemundo. Each of them has done a fly-by piece amounting to, hey, isn't this kind of neat, this town? There are white kids and Mexicans next to cornfields. This blonde-haired, blue-eyed ten-year-old speaks Spanish better than you. Look at all these Mexican shops. And so on and so forth. These puff pieces are hard to reconcile with the climate and animosity we felt as kids. It's tough. We want to celebrate and our town is more than willing to do so. But there's something else nagging at me about the changes West Liberty has gone through since my childhood.

Liberty Lanes closed down when I was in high school, replaced by Club JTs and rebranded as Flamas. A venue for bailes and quinceañeras.

They filled in the bowling gutters and called it a dance floor. The shops in our downtown, on our Main Street, have changed as well. What was once only La Mexicana is now a series of Mexican shops and restaurants. Hawkeye Pizza became my tía's restaurant, Puebla. Even Jack and Jill, the little grocery store, became Jeff's. If you go in the back you'll find all sorts of carne marinated with homemade recipes. Mexican treats line the aisles. My nephews joke and call Jeff's "Jefe's," which doesn't make sense because *jefe* means "boss" in Spanish, but you see what they're trying to get at.

Despite these changes to the town's makeup, its ownership and embrace of our customs, there was this feeling I couldn't shake. It wasn't the Trump truck—the stories so far prove we've been through more overt bigotry before. I didn't parse it out until I talked to an Iranian singer, who told of the woes of being a touring international artist. She said something that hit me like a gut punch. She laid down this cultural concept that rushed that feeling I had during the parade into focus. We'll call it the three Fs: Food, Festivals, and Fun. When it comes to celebrating diversity or cultural appreciation, the three Fs lie in wait. It makes sense; they're a big part of who we are. Of what West Liberty is. The parade had the three Fs in spades, and the image of the lowrider dancing in the street is definitely part of that.

But there can be this celebration before the battle is won. This patting ourselves on the back before we get to work on the deeper issues. When we are content with the puff pieces. When people think they are advocating for our town but are content with the surface-level Fs. That advocacy ignores our struggles and cultural dissonance. The widening of cultures between my dad and I happened despite the embrace of some aspects of our culture. The festivities ignore the trauma and ugliness of the kids on the playground. The food and fun ignore the internalization of things like swastikas on playground equipment. *Come on, that doesn't fit the narrative, we're trying to have fun here.*

The lowrider grew dilapidated between the parades. The weight of our own lives, the cultural strains placed upon them, all this happened between the parades. There have been less than a handful of people of color in meaningful roles in the town's history, whether that means politically or socially. We still have decades to go—if we ever get there. That can get lost in the celebration. The sacrifices get lost during the cultural shift from generation to generation. Those losses go unaddressed. Think of them with me when you read the headlines. When we are celebrating on the streets together, think of the car rotting in the sun. Think of the work it takes to maintain our humanity, between the pomp and pageantry. Think of a father, a son, and the man who sold them a car.

PART TWO

FISTFIGHTS AND QUINCEAÑERAS

I WAS FIVE YEARS OLD when I got into my first real fight, with another boy from town. We squared up against each other while a gaggle of kids swarmed us in a screaming circle. We were at a Mexican barbecue across the street from my Tío Jose's house. Want to know a funny thing about Mexican barbecues? Our parents cook the ever-loving shit out of our meat. I don't know why. From hamburgers to steak, all of it ends up well-done char. The first time I had a white person's burger was after a football practice in junior high. I looked over at White Josh for guidance on how to navigate the foreign-looking meat from the grill. The burgers were big honking things that looked like mini footballs. They were pink and bloody on the inside and *delicious*. I never looked at our charred hockey pucks the same way.

I could smell the meat burning from the other side of the house while I sized up the kid I was going to fight. Another thing that distinguishes Mexican barbecues from white people's is how unsupervised the kids are. At all Mexican parties in general. The kids go unsupervised for hours while the adults drink and reminisce. I don't remember why I found myself face to face with a kid in my class named Carlos. Carlos was small, even smaller than my friend Eric. But his size was misleading. Because of his stature, his dad enrolled him in martial arts classes so he could defend himself from bullies and riffraff. This had unintended consequences. Carlos had the tools and knowledge to fight against un-trained kids—and a mean streak to exploit that knowledge.

The older kids egging us on were at least fifteen or sixteen years old. They cheered for us to fight one another. Had schemed and set us up to do so. Like a cock fight. "Come on, fucking fight." They swelled and jeered from the circle around us. I could hear the thump of our parents' music in the distance. Smell the coals and lighter fluid from the grill wafting from the other side of the house.

Carlos ended it with a series of calculated strikes. Swift punches to my face. My nose became a faucet. Blood poured from it as the older kids cheered. They grabbed Carlos and hoisted him up on their shoulders.

This story encapsulates a lot of what made the West Liberty of my youth what it was. It's midwestern small-town normalcy. It's lax supervision and the good and bad that exist within that frame. From that first fight when I was five until the very last fight I got into late in my teenage years, the normalized violence of our town had a profound impact on me. By the time I was twelve years old, in 1997, I had already been through and committed more acts of violence than I dare recount. This culture of fighting was a big reason why I stuck with my friends and found refuge in our base at the Party Shack. I'd argue it's also the reason we were getting into so much trouble in the Shack. You can track our age by the severity of trouble we got into—by how bad we lashed out at the town. At first we stuck to egging the race-car processions. We also ventured off and egged houses—of people we didn't like, sure, but there was also an element of randomness. We were agents of chaos. If a house called to us or looked ripe for it, we targeted it. In a stroke of self-awareness, we called it "hoodlumizing," a portmanteau of "vandalizing" and "hoodlums."

After we got tired of egging houses, we looked for more creative and destructive ways to wreak havoc. With the Party Shack as our base of operations, we escalated our pranks and destruction to knocking down and stealing lawn decorations. Messing with cars. Anything we could do quick, hidden in the night. Chances are, if you lived in West Liberty and had something broken, smashed, tagged, or stolen from 1995 to 1998, it was us. I'm remorseful now in my older age. Now that I own a home and think how annoying it would be for some punk kids to come and mess with my mailbox. Josh and I recently joked that we are going to get it so bad in the coming years. There's going to be a cosmic retribution. A payback of youths to torture us like we did West Liberty.

But if I can offer something of a defense, we weren't acting out of pure malice. We didn't know we were internalizing all the things we'd been through in town. Well. Okay. Sometimes there were clear vendettas. You were unlucky to be a disliked teacher with a found-out address. But for the most part, we thought we did our hoodlumizing out of this manic need for *something to do*. To fight the boredom that always came after we exhausted the few possibilities of things to do in town.

One time Ruben smirked at us as he dialed a number. He called the police to report some suspicious kids at the local park. We all gawked at Ruben, who was already out the door, heading the few houses over to Friendship Park.

That was Ruben's modus operandi. The way he pushed us into things. As our leader it was his responsibility to find the escalations. The way to break that persistent boredom. He was the instigator of our group. It was his job to find our limits and goad us into doing something bigger, more dangerous, and more fun. But it was the two of us who started one of our most memorable hoodlumizing endeavors.

———————

We were returning to our Party Shack home base after a good long night of hoodlumizing. The town's coin-operated laundromat was about two blocks from Ruben's house, next to the fire station north of Friendship Park. I noticed this flimsy mailbox across from the laundromat. As we ran by, I punched the mailbox and it flew completely off its stake in an explosion of plastic. The guys exclaimed at my feat, surprised that I took it clean off in one blow. They stomped the beheaded mailbox into a crumpled mess and we sprinted back to the Shack.

Less than a week later, a new and improved mailbox surprised us on our after-school walk to the Shack. That's when we realized that the building across from the laundromat was in fact a woodworking shop. The owner took the destruction as an opportunity to engage in his livelihood. He replaced the defeated mailbox with a proper, sturdy model for the shop. We took it as an affront. A challenge. A defiance to the agents of chaos and the first reprisal in a war of escalation.

We returned that very weekend with a baseball bat. It took Jerry a few forceful swings to finally get the mailbox off the stake. We had to hand it to the shop owner. He reinforced that thing and made it sturdy enough that it took us double the amount of time it should have taken. We waited for a response.

While we waited for this regrouping, the girls at school murmured about a new kid. "Did you hear? There's this new boy in our grade. He has blondish-brown hair and blue eyes. Word is his parents divorced and he moved from Washington. Oh, and you can tell he works out."

Our group's jealousy alarms flared. They flared even more when I saw the new kid in the flesh. He was handsome and comfortable in his movements as he navigated the hallways. It wasn't only that he worked out. It was that he had already hit his growth spurt. He was on the other side of puberty, and his dad had instilled in him a work ethic that paid off in muscular dividends. His looks primed us to hate him. Not only that, but in my first class with the new kid, the girls swooned over his handwriting. His old school taught cursive writing. Hell, even our sixth-grade teacher couldn't stop gushing over how beautiful his handwriting looked compared to our chicken scratches. I exchanged glances with Eric and Josh across the room.

But when the new kid reacted to our schoolroom antics, things changed. When he laughed at Josh's and my tomfoolery after the science teacher pulled up the next in an endless parade of videos, we immediately warmed up to him.

"Hey, you're alright, man. What's your name?" Jerry and I asked after we all got chastised by the teacher and left with a warning.

"You guys are super funny. It's Josh. Josh Magdefrau."

Jerry and I shot each other exaggerated faces, wide-eyed and open-mouthed like Japanese butoh dancers. "Wait, your name is Josh too?" Jerry asked in a high pitch. I immediately thought about our Josh. Josh Gingerich. White Josh.

"I mean, it's a common name," New Josh replied. We knew we were going to have to figure this one out. If this new kid was going to become one of the gang, we'd have to differentiate the two Joshes.

After introducing the new kid to everyone, we did indeed add Magdefrau to the group. We verified that he moved to West Liberty after his parents divorced. His mom started dating someone from West Liberty not too long after they moved here from Washington, another town not quite an hour away. The thing was, this guy his mom moved in with, Josh's not-yet stepdad, was a West Liberty police officer named Hank.

"Your dad's a cop?" we asked Josh.

"He's not my dad. He's the guy my mom moved in with. But yeah . . . he's a cop."

"You're okay with that?" Jerry said.

"With him being a cop or my mom dating him?" Josh asked.

"Shit, I guess both," Jerry replied.

"Well, it's not in my control either way," he said. We agreed that was a good point.

That we added Magdefrau to the group tickled Josh Gingerich. On an objective level, the handsome new kid who looked like a preppy Ken doll, whose "stepdad" was a *cop*, was much whiter than him. Without a word uttered, the official title of "White Josh" transferred to the new kid. Hell, Gingerich partook in calling Magdefrau "White Josh" the most. Only usually it was more severe—most of the time Gingerich would call Magdefrau "White Boy" or "the white kid."

You see, Josh Gingerich had grown up in West Liberty as the token white kid among us Mexican and Laotians. I remember an older kid named Eddy Ortiz going up to Josh at a baile, waving his arms at the crowd of brown faces. "Hey, how does it feel to finally be the fucking minority?"

Josh didn't skip a beat. "Man, I grew up in West Liberty. I've always felt like the minority."

With that Eddy whooped out "¡Es todo Joshy!" and went to relay to his friends what Josh said. So when Josh finally had a chance to transfer the title, however ironic and jovial it was, he relished in doing so. Magdefrau, the new White Josh, laughed with the rest of us as Gingerich laid it on.

Gingerich was doing just that as we walked over to the new White Josh's house for the first time. While Gingerich was joking around, Jerry, Ruben, Eric, and I, the actual nonwhite people, were apprehensive. We weren't sure what to make of the fact that White Josh's mom's boyfriend was a town cop. Our last hoodlumizing adventure flashed in my mind. Would this kid narc us out?

Magdefrau didn't live too far from Gingerich's house. We popped in and he introduced us to his mom. She was nice and seemed excited that her Josh was already making friends, making him blush in response. Josh showed us his Nintendo 64, which was sweet because it had come out the year before and none of us had one. Then the loud sound of boots reverberated off the kitchen floor. Magdefrau continued playing *Super Mario 64* while the rest of us froze, nervous for the interaction. What if Hank somehow recognized us from one of our hoodlumizing escapades? What if he made out the bright streak in Jerry's hair in the moonlight while we were running away one night?

Hank gave away his presence before he entered the side room we were in. "Josh! You got to take out the—" he called, then stopped as he entered. He was in full police uniform, which surprised me for some reason. Maybe I thought he'd change out of his work clothes at the station. "Oh. Well, look at you. I didn't realize you had already made little friends. Little girlfriends. The trash?"

"I'll take out the trash before dinner," Magdefrau said, not looking up from the game.

"And you'll take it out with a smile on your face," Hank said, half joking.

"Yeah, yeah."

Hank gripped his utility belt as if he were about to hoist it up. He smiled at us. "Ladies," he said before making an about-face back to the kitchen.

Under his breath, eyes still on the television, Magdefrau uttered a single word: "Pig."

Gingerich grinned. "Hey Josh, you ever heard of hoodlumizing?"

I also remember this time in my life as quinceañera season. Tradition forced me to be a chambelan in my sister's quince two summers before in '95. Now my Tía Nelle was making me go to the community center on Sunday afternoons to go through the motions for my cousin Cynthia's quinceañera. The whole ordeal with my sister's quince had left a bad taste in my mouth. Being with my friends and going out in the night was the embodiment of freedom. We made our own rules away from our parents and authority figures. Going through the traditions, rules, and dance steps dictated by my mom and tías was the complete opposite.

Sunday's looming procession rehearsal weighed on a day already heavy with Mass in the morning. At least we got to meet up at the Party

Shack since I would already be in the area to walk the few blocks to the community center. I was feeling the ennui of the day as we gathered in the Shack and introduced Magdefrau to our base of operations.

"Whoa. This is sweet!" said Josh, as Ruben and Eric revealed the Shack like they had to me a few years earlier. Jerry and Josh Gingerich were watching VHS tapes on the TV. Ruben had a big chunky video camera and it was a hobby of ours to record ourselves doing skits and goofing off. They were watching a scene we recorded a few weeks prior of us recreating hood movies like *Boyz n the Hood* and *Juice*. Back then, with irony, we called ourselves the "Pu-Tang Clan," and the movie they were watching was one we dubbed *Pu-Tang: The Lost Empire*.

I couldn't stay long though. "Dang, alright. I got to go to this stupid quince rehearsal," I said as I got up from the dirty couch.

"What's a quince?" Josh Magdefrau asked.

From their chairs watching TV, Josh Gingerich and Jerry pounced. Jerry started. "What? You don't know what a quince is? A quinceañera. Yo, Gin Money, this guy doesn't know what a quinceañera is."

Gingerich picked it right up. "That makes sense. White Boy probably hasn't been to un baile either."

Magdefrau bristled at this latest usage of "White Boy." The other Josh had been laying it on thick lately, relishing any opportunity to shine light on Magdefrau's Otherness. You could tell it was starting to get on New Josh's nerves and he would push back at times. But after deliberating and choosing not to engage, Magdefrau let out, "What's a baile?"

"Oh my God! Dude, you guys didn't have shit in *Warshington*, huh?" Eric said, his pronunciation of Washington a jab at how Magdefrau had said it when he introduced himself on his first day of school, the way Goofy says "gawrsh."

"We had lots of things but not a lot of Mexicans," Josh replied. "But to bailar is to dance, right? So you guys go and dance? So is a quince a souped-up dance?" His phrasing of bailar and quince was funny to Jerry, who laughed at how floaty and white it sounded.

"Hell no, we don't go dance. Only our parents go and dance," replied Ruben.

"I'm confused," said Josh.

"If you have to dance at a quinceañera, then it means you're one of the unlucky ones," I said, only adding to Josh's confusion.

Ruben, realizing it would be easier to show Josh, made the call. "Let's all go to the rehearsal with Chuy so we can show this fool what this is all about."

My immediate reaction was to balk at this proposal. I hated going to those rehearsals. I was terrible at picking up the steps of the choreographed dances my tías attempted to teach us. The girl they paired me with by height, a nice enough girl named Blanca Bueno, could barely hide her disdain when I missed a cue or stepped on her feet. It was torture and I didn't want to give the guys ammunition to razz me on this front. But Ruben had called it and the guys were already clamoring to get their things. They were inundating Josh with what he should know about our community center. I followed them out of the Shack.

By the time we got past the racetrack, Ruben and Eric were finishing up the general outline of what the bailes were. It went something like this. A baile was a multifaceted social gathering. At the top level, it was the place where our Mexican parents and grandparents went to dance. A baile could happen anywhere, but in our town it happened in the West Liberty Community Center by the turkey plant. It was a big box, brown and utilitarian on the outside. Besides our Mexican functions, bingo and 4-H competitions happened there during the summer fair.

While our parents were dancing away until midnight or later, the kids were there, too. I have early memories of running through the crowds of adults. While the mass of elders pulsed to the music, we counter-rhythmed, snaking in and out of the crowd. The kids would play games like tag. Or look after and play with their younger siblings. Or go get beers for our parents between songs, when it was quiet enough for them to tell us what to get. I remember babies bouncing in their mother's arms to the tune of the band. Having a fussy child wasn't an excuse to leave. Our parents kept dancing until the exhausted kids fell asleep in their arms. By the end of the night, passed-out children were strewn about chairs with coats as blankets. There was always someone to watch over the fallen kids while someone else danced.

Save getting cracked around in "La Vibora de la Mar," where the dancers interlocked hands and snaked through the venue with ever-increasing speed, the fun was to be had outside. Beside the community center was a big open field. To some that might read, "beside the community center there was nothing." But to us it meant there was an opportunity. It was a big, unsupervised recess in the nighttime, a kid's dream. That's where I first got to know and hang out with Ruben and Eric.

One game we played was hide-and-seek. We'd huddle up in a mass, putting one foot in the middle. Eric knelt down and started figuring who would be "it" for the game. We used variations of "Eeny, Meeny, Miny, Moe" for this. Eric usually started with our favorite variation, "Mississippi Tiene Pelo en Su Pipi," which translates to "Mississippi has hairs on their penis." Eric tapped a foot, shooing it away. Then he switched up to our second-favorite rhyme, "Chino, Chino, Japonés, Come Caca, No Me Des," which meant "Chinese, Chinese, Japanese, eat shit, and don't give me any." Even though we knew that technically this wasn't a diss to Jerry Sayabeth since he wasn't Japanese or Chinese, it still felt like an affront to him. Our parents called all our Asian friends "Chinos," no matter how many times we told them they weren't. It was sort of like how they called all our video game systems "Nintendos." We would never chant "Chino, Chino, Japoñes" in front of Jerry, but it was too fun to say it when he wasn't around.

If we weren't playing games like tag and hide-and-seek, we were playing variations of football games. The most popular and simplest game had the name I am most ashamed to admit we used. Ask any small-town Iowan about this game and they'll know it. We called it "Smear the Queer." The game was simple enough. Throw a football in the air, and whoever catches it or scoops it up is the target. That person doesn't stop running until someone tackles them, wherein they relinquish the ball and the next brave or foolish soul grabs it for their turn. There are lots of stories and acts we did as kids that give me pause now. Things that were racist, homophobic, and violent. In a lot of ways, it was the normalcy and casualness of these things that make them so hard to look back on. It's hard to admit I had some of the most fun times of my life playing a game with such a violent and homophobic title.

But to hide details like the name of this game would be to let us off the hook. It is what it is, and that game gets wrapped up in the other games we played by the community center. I'm sure of it—the highest, most visceral moments of joy happened at this stage of my life. Playing and messing around until our parents stumbled out of the center in the early morning. They would yell out our names, that it was time to go, and we'd crawl into the car for the ride home. The thump and bustle of the night would fade as exhaustion kicked in.

This was generally what bailes were for me as a kid. Until I had to be in Nancy's quince, explaining all this to Josh Magdefrau on the way to Cynthia's quinceañera rehearsal.

"That's all it is, man. Being put on display and hoping you don't mess up the dances," I said as I kicked at the gravel of the parking lot. We were nearing the door and into the community center's shadow. My palms were getting sweaty at the thought of the guys watching me as I flubbed the steps.

Before we reached the door, my Tía Nelle burst through it. "There you are, Chuy, we were waiting for you! You were supposed to show up at one-thirty today. Come on, get inside. You're the one who needs the most help anyway." She let me through but blocked the rest of the guys from coming in. "Uh-uh-uh. You boys can watch the girls another time. Ándale pues. Turn around and bye-bye," she said as she shooed them away. It was another situation where the group realized that the adults were the ones calling the shots.

My Tía Nelle's family were our neighbors. Their house was across from our backyard. Their mailbox was on our front porch so the mailman didn't have to cut in the gravel alley. My mom was the oldest of the De La Paz family. It's a huge clan. She has something like thirteen or fourteen siblings. (I always have to ask my mom what the exact number is.) The majority of these siblings are sisters. When my mom found her way to Iowa, a handful of the sisters came with her. The others stayed in Del Rio, Texas. It always felt like my tías were the ones who influenced and raised me. At social functions our dads would huddle and close themselves off from us kids. But our tías would engage and play with us. We were matriarchal.

The De La Paz sisters who landed in West Liberty with my mom, Irene, were my tías Berta, Irma, Pauly, and Nelle. Nelle was short for Enedelia and we pronounced the double Ls mexicano style like "Nay-eh." Nelle wasn't the youngest but she felt like it to me. She was vibrant and funny. She usually had a sly one-liner or zinger at the ready. In games of lotería she was our go-to card caller because she was good at it and because her overemphasis and metacommentary on the game elevated it. She wouldn't just call "El Venado" when the card showed up. She changed her voice and sang out "¡El Venado! ¡El Venado!" like the song played at the bailes. Our entire extended family, my cousins and tías, would laugh and holler at Nelle's commentary. Holidays were a cacophony of joy. Boisterous and shrill gritos punctuated the games we played.

Only my Tía Nelle wasn't loud or joyful in the silent community center as I got into my line opposite Blanca. Tía motioned to her sisters to start the music. We began rehearsing our choreographed waltz. My steps were unsure as I tried to remember the last time I went through the dance. Blanca pressed my hand and led me left when I thought to go right. We finally got halfway through the dance and created flanks for Cynthia and her brother Javy.

For all our explanation and overview of quinceañeras to Josh Magdefrau, we didn't actually convey to him the point of the festival. Quinces are traditional and symbolic celebrations to note the transition from girlhood into womanhood. We didn't hammer home this point because we didn't know what it actually meant. I watched Javy look over to his mom for a cue, then stumble forward with his sister as they walked between our lines. It was weird to see Cynthia and her brother in this manner. I knew them as my neighbors who I played games with. Javy was about three years younger than me and like a little brother. He shared at least three of his mom's qualities—her penchant for jokes, her smile that revealed deep dimples, and her ability to be a smart aleck. We had a fraught relationship, the type where we would play and he would say something that got under my skin and I'd make him pay for it. Like my sister did to me.

Cynthia was a tomboy like Nancy but built stockier. She held her own in the rough games we played in the dirt. She would even defend her little brother against me if things got too rough. But she gave off a different vibe during these rehearsals. Even without the lavish and ornate dress she would eventually wear, she presented herself regally, with the seriousness my tía wanted me to have for her daughter's big day.

Here's something that was at least true for our two Mexican families: the difference between the freedom offered to boys and girls. It was vast and immeasurable. Think of all the factors in play that let us boys have opportunities to go hoodlumizing. All we had to do was tell our parents we were spending the night at someone else's house and that was that. Our sisters had the opposite expectations. Our parents watched their every step. They weren't allowed out of the house past six at night. There were countless arguments over whether Nancy could spend the night at a friend's house. Many times my sister lost that fight and had to stay home. I would usually rub it in like the little brother I was, only for her to beat me up, completing the violent circle of our relationship.

I looked over at my sister in our chambelan and dama rehearsal lines. She had long ago perfected the steps and looked as serious as Cynthia as they navigated the waltz. There was something about these quinces that spurred on our fighting. Looking back at it now, it was our expectation that things would change. Here was this big symbolic gesture that things would be different. That our parents should treat my sister like an adult. But ever since her quince the previous year, our childish fighting had only grown more severe. We fought and fought. She was close to seventeen, I was going on twelve and had hit puberty. A photo from my sister's quinceañera is forever immortalized on our living room wall. It adorns that wall to this day. My sister and her extravagant white dress take up most of the space. She looks happy and hopeful. At the time I was eating a lot and hadn't quite figured out how to navigate my growth spurt. I was a little chubby in the face, which was something Nancy loved to torment me about. In the photo I'm in a suit that doesn't fit right. I'm all cheeks and smugness. There is an ever-so-slight disdain for the camera in my face. I hated that photo growing up. Its place on the wall meant I had to look at it every day in our living room.

As my eyes followed Nancy, they caught a familiar face at the front door of the community center. My feet tripped up as I recognized Jerry Sayabeth's toothy grin. *Oh crap.* The guys hadn't left. Jerry's head made way for Josh Magdefrau to get a better look at the procession. Jerry caught that I had spotted them and gave me an exaggerated thumbs-up. I was about to nod at them to scatter when I realized I hadn't been paying any attention. The second half of our choreographed waltz had started. I realized this because Blanca pulled my hand to follow the procession, *hard*. She must have tugged a few times and resorted to yanking me along to catch up with the couple drifting away in front of us. The pull surprised me and I looked away from the guys at the window, only to trip over my feet as I turned back and cascaded to the ground. Blanca stumbled but righted herself, taking a few steps into another pair who caught her. I watched them equalize themselves from my spot on the

The quinceañera photo in all its glory.
It still hangs on the living room wall.

concrete while my Tía Nelle cut off the music. I could already hear her shoes clacking on the floor as they made their way over to me.

What I did next was a mistake. To this day I don't know why I did it. To try to salvage something with my friends at the window? Because I didn't care about the rehearsal and wanted to show my disdain? It felt like autopilot. Like a way to take hold of the situation before my tía could get at me and embarrass me further. I sprang up from the floor with both arms outstretched, like a gymnast after completing a big move. I smiled big for the other kids in their line. Some laughed. Most looked at me with shock. My Tía Nelle interrupted my victory routine. I steeled myself for her wrath. From a distance I could see my own mom coming in for the follow up. Nelle got in close to me. She didn't yell at me. She was mad, sure. But her reaction threw me off guard.

"Look, Chuy. I know you don't care about this. But I do. Cynthia does too. Please. Por favor. For her. Get it together." Her voice was shaky. She stood up and put her hands on her face before moving them back through her hair.

I didn't know how to react. I let my arms drift down to my sides as my cheeks flushed with embarrassment. I didn't have a chance to respond because my mom had reached us. A torrent of Spanish scolding flew from her mouth as she pushed me back to the line. I looked over at the window to see that the guys had left, then over at Nancy, who had fire in her eyes.

We hadn't made it to the car after rehearsal before Nancy started getting at me. She made fun of me the whole way home. "Oh my God, you little chunker, I can't believe you fucking fell like that! And why'd you have to get up all stupid? Like an idiot. I saw your stupid-ass friends watching you. You did that shit on purpose, huh?"

"No, I didn't!" I said as my mom tried to shush us from the front seat.

"Yeah right, you wanted all the attention."

I tried to ignore my sister's taunts as we pulled into the driveway. She changed her tactics as we walked into the kitchen. "Or did you really mess up that bad? You don't know how to do these easy-ass steps? Oh yeah, you're the kid who still doesn't know how to wipe his own ass."

Like I said before, our fighting had gotten worse. It was increasing in frequency but also in severity. This was because, despite all my sister's ribbing that I was getting chunkier, I was also getting stronger. I was fighting back. My sister could still beat me up, but I was getting a few shots in. Sometimes I could hold my ground enough that my mom would have to intervene. Reactionary. Like how I sprang up from the ground at rehearsal. I spit out, "You know what? You're mad 'cause I know that these things are stupid and a waste of money. Nothing changed after your stupid quince."

"Shut. Up," she said.

I continued, "I don't care that you and Cynthia get these stupid parties for yourselves. You'll always be a bitch."

Nancy lunged for me and tackled me to the ground. In one swift motion, she grabbed the side of my head. I managed to get out a yelp before she slammed my face against the hardwood floor. Unlike when we were younger, I was able to use my weight to roll her and got one punch in myself before my mom ran between us screaming. I dashed through the kitchen into the bathroom, slamming the door as my mom continued to yell at Nancy to stop her pursuit.

The boy in the mirror fought back tears. Maintained emotions. I messed up. Before I could think about what to do next, the doorknob

Nancy at her quince. For some reason, I feel
like she was thinking of me in this photo.

of the bathroom rattled and twisted. Oh no. The door popped open
to reveal my mother before me. She had used a knife to pick open the
flimsy bathroom lock and stood before me wild-eyed, knife in hand.
She chucked the knife into the bathroom sink and grabbed me, yelling
at me the whole time.

"Ama, what are you doing? You can't bust open the door like that."

"¿Por qué no?" she replied as she wrestled me back toward my sister.
Like I've said, my mom was never one to avoid confrontation. I stopped
fighting back when I saw my sister. She was still in the same spot as
before, avoiding my eyes. My mom forced us to apologize to each other.
We got out half apologies, knowing this was only the latest in a string of
fights we'd been having for as long as I could remember.

Everything I did made Nancy furious. Me existing got under her skin.
It took me a long time to realize that it wasn't calling her a bitch that
caused her to get so mad that day. It was that I had got at an ugly truth.
That she expected something to change after her quinceañera. But it
was all pageantry. She wanted to go out and be with her friends like I
got to. She wanted to get out from under our mother's watchful eye. She
wanted to date boys and live her life. But all she got was an uppity little
brother who didn't know how deep his insults cut.

After the fallout I dawdled around the house. My wandering left me
in our backyard. The backyard between our house and Tía Nelle's.

Flanking the yard were big gnarled trees full of cicadas and birds. I was sitting under one of these trees in a spot that used to be my mom's garden. She hadn't planted anything there for a long time. Now it was dirt. The tree I was under drooped over and had lots of branches that created this natural enclave, a secret spot my sister and I would use with Cynthia and Javy. We begged my dad to make it into some type of Swiss Family Robinson tree house, but he never had the time or money. We stole some pieces of wood and nailed them to the tree to make steps up to a clubhouse that would never exist.

I confirmed that the pieces of wood were still nailed to the trunk and stood there for what felt like a long time. My vision blurred and my face got hot as the pieces of wood on the tree went out of focus. It was almost a relief when my cousin Javy came out of his house. He had this goofy smile on his face as he walked toward me, oblivious to me wiping the tears from my face.

"Hey, did you have a nice trip?" he asked in a singsong voice.

"W-what?" I asked.

"A trip. When you fell on your ass," Javy replied, making a tumbling gesture with his hands. He laughed then, big and shrill.

There's a thing I do when I get mad, real mad. I still do it to this day. I bite my tongue. I don't know why. My sister pointed it out to me after a fight one time. "Why do you do that? Bite your tongue. You're gonna bite your own tongue off one day and I'm going to laugh."

What a weird detail for someone else to notice, right? But that was how frequent and intimate our fighting was. Javy didn't notice it then. That I was feeling the pressure in my throat. The guilt and hatred and powerlessness. That I was biting my tongue so bad it hurt. I lunged at him, tackling him to the ground. Recreating the move Nancy had performed on me earlier that day, I grabbed Javy's head. Slammed it against the ground. He wailed for his mom.

There's a sliding scale for the way little brothers cry. I say that because that's what Javy was to me. Our shared yard and play space meant our two families interacted like one close unit. We'd all walk over unannounced to play games and have meals. The sliding scale for crying is in relation to how severe the act was, which directly correlates to how much trouble the older sibling will get into. Javy's muffled screams in the dirt brought me back to reality. How would it look if I messed up Tía Nelle's rehearsal and beat up her son on the same day? I had to act fast.

"Oh crap, oh crap. Hey, hey. Dude, it's okay. Hey, don't tell your mom. You're fine, man." Somehow this only made Javy's screams louder. "Please. I'm sorry. What can I do?" I pleaded. Snot was running down his face as I realized I was still straddling him from our tackle. I bolted upright at the realization, still pleading. "I'll let you come in and play my brother's old 3DO."

It was a miracle. Javy cut off his crying mid-yell.

"For real?" he asked between breaths.

"Yeah, come on, let's go play. We still got *Super Street Fighter*. I won't pick any cheap characters or nothing," I said as I helped him to his feet. Despite hamming it up for maximum parental attention, Javy's crying was real. I'd slammed his head down hard. He was doing that thing kids do after a bad one, when they try to breathe in and shudder, gasping for air. We went inside and straight to my older brother Johnny's room. Or rather, his old room. Johnny was ten years older, which meant he was twenty-two and out of the house. He kind of didn't feel like an older brother, our age difference was so big.

Johnny had moved out of the house and left some of his old things in boxes in the garage. My friends and I would rummage through this stuff. It was the younger-brother jackpot of multimedia. We looked through old cassette tapes and CDs, movies, and video games. I should give credit to these discarded items as formative artifacts. Relics that jump-started my tastes. We would take old Snoop Dogg CDs from one box and memorize the lyrics, or we'd recreate scenes from the movies in another box. Like I said before, our older siblings were the zeitgeist. These leftover items were a blueprint. When I look back at this cycle of fighting and bullying in our families, my brother doesn't come up. Not for me. He was old enough that I don't remember him ever hitting me or picking on me much. I do remember he trapped me in my cobija once, until I screamed for air. But it was only that one time and he never did it again.

The leftover things I was most into were Johnny's video games. I scoured each box for games and brought them to his old room to play. He had left behind an old 3DO system that Javy was now booting up. The last time we played, I got into a fight with Javy because he hadn't washed his hands after eating candy. He gunked up the controller and I made him pay for it. I bit my tongue as I noticed his dirt-caked hands from our scrap outside.

We started up *Street Fighter* and soon forgot about the real fighting that had occurred. After a bit, Javy broached the subject.

"Hey, so I was going to say though. My mom told me to tell you that we're going to have extra rehearsals now. On Saturdays." He kept his eyes on Blanka, his character on the screen.

"What? Why!?" I said, letting my controller fall into my lap. We were sitting on Johnny's old couch. Technically my couch since this was my room now. It didn't feel like a bedroom though. My parents couldn't afford to buy a new bed, so sleep was a choice between the couch here or the couch in the living room.

Javy kept his eyes on the screen as he won the round against my immobile Ryu. He chose his words. "She just said we need extra practice."

It clicked then. That it was because *I* needed the practice. Now I had to give up my Saturday afternoons too? We still had about a month before the quinceañera. Rehearsals taking up both days of the weekend was the last thing I wanted. Before I could respond, our house phone rang. Johnny's old cordless phone trilled beside the couch. The caller ID displayed Ruben's dad's full name and number. Javy kept on playing, beating out the match while I picked up the phone.

"Hey, what's up, man?" I asked.

"You have to check this shit out."

Not this again. I knew it was coming. I knew I shouldn't even ask. "Check what out, Ruben?"

"Nah-nah. I got to show you."

I looked over at Javy's grubby hands on his controller. Oblivious.

"Just *tell* me, man," I snapped, then caught myself. For all the anger and fighting I did with my family, the anger that exploded from my sister toward me and my temper that I distributed further toward Javy, we kept it to ourselves. Within our family. It was almost like a secret. You can see why I'd keep Nancy's bullying secret, but even my bullying of my younger cousins I kept under wraps. I wasn't proud of this side of me, of the anger that arose when my cousins got under my skin. I took a breath, remorseful that my anger had flared at my best friend.

Ruben gave in. "Okay, okay. Suit yourself. It's the goddamn mailbox."

Waves of endorphins kicked in. I forgot about Javy mucking up the controller. Nancy's assault was a distant memory. "Across from the laundromat?" I asked.

"Yeah, that one. But like I said, you have to see this thing. You won't believe it."

"After school?" I asked. Wishing I could go right now.

"Hell yeah, man, I gotta see your face when you see this."

––––––––––

Murmurs of "the Mailbox" spread throughout our friend group during school on Monday. That the woodshop had replaced the old one, but yo, you had to see it to believe it. It was all I could think about after school while we all walked to the two Joshes' houses. They both had to check in with their parents after school; none of the rest of us had to.

Josh Magdefrau's house was closer so we went there first. We were all half listening to Eric as he talked about pressure points, how you could use them against someone else to incapacitate them. "It makes it so you can take out someone twice your size. Here, I'll show you," Eric said to Jerry while making his fingers into pincers, laughing. Magdefrau hushed everyone as we stopped in front of his house.

Officer Hank was home by now and Josh had to check in with him and do his chores real quick. Josh had us wait in his driveway while he went inside. We talked and goofed off while we waited. Jerry let Eric attempt a pressure-point hold on his clavicle. He made it a point to deadpan that he didn't feel anything before squirming away.

The screen door slamming shut stopped our shenanigans. It was Hank with Josh behind him. "I told you we were leaving," Josh said.

"No, no. I can't allow my guests to leave before I address them properly. Ladies," he said as he bowed.

"Oh snap, it's the five-o!" Josh Gingerich said. Magdefrau shot him a look. Hank chuckled. This interaction had been evolving. Hank would greet us at his house with various insults and jabs. Most of these were variations on how effeminate we were. When he was feeling particularly caustic, he called us pussies. It was always done in this singsongy voice. Lately Gingerich had been fighting back, throwing in some references to how Hank was a cop. He'd call him the popo, five-o, la jura, or if he was far enough away, pig. Magdefrau hated these interactions and tried to get us out of the house whenever Hank was home.

"Come on, guys. I finished my chores, Hank," Magdefrau said as he motioned for us to leave.

"Aw, but we were just getting started," said Hank. Gingerich agreed. He liked to trade jabs with Hank. The rest of us were tense in those situations. We always felt like it was taunting the enemy. We raced to catch up with Magdefrau as he reached the driveway.

"Go have fun at your princess parties," Hank said from the doorway.

"Oink oink," shot back Gingerich before catching up with us.

Josh Magdefrau got into it right when Gingerich reached us. "For real, man, you got to ignore him."

Gingerich smiled and shrugged. "He's the one that keeps on talking shit. What's he going to do?" The rest of our group walked in silence.

"You don't know him like I do," Magdefrau said, quieter.

Gingerich looked over to Ruben to talk about the other Josh like he wasn't there. "Look man, it's not my fault that the White Boy lives with the Pig. That we're forced to put up with insults 'cause his white ass needs to check in."

Magdefrau took off his backpack and slammed it to the ground. *Here we go.* This had been building for a while. Gingerich never stopped calling Magdefrau "White Boy." At first Magdefrau found it funny. Then he stayed quiet when Gingerich said it. Then he started getting mad and pushing back. Now it pissed him off. Over the edge.

"Quit calling me that. For real." Magdefrau walked face to face to Gingerich. His voice grew louder as he got in the pocket of his anger. "You need to check in with your parents too! That's where we're going right now, right? To check in with *Mr. Ottaway.* The biology teacher. How much whiter could you get? You're white too, Josh! Like me. And that has nothing to do with Hank. I have nothing to do with him. I want us to have less to do with him and leave him alone but you talk shit back . . ." At the end of his torrent Magdefrau stammered, but then he found his words and crescendoed with a simple and definitive " . . . White Boy!"

Gingerich struggled for a retort. We all looked at each other for a moment as Magdefrau's words seemed to ricochet off the trees and hang in the air. Magdefrau was beyond angry and had stood up for himself. But it was also the first time he had called Gingerich "White Boy" and we found that hilarious. We all erupted at once. "Damn, dude, he called you white!" Eric said to Gingerich. Jerry and Ruben exclaimed and ran around the two Joshes as if they were doing touchdown celebrations. Gingerich stood shell-shocked. After the hooting and hollering died down, I realized that the two were still staring each other down. That our eruption didn't dissipate the tension. With them side by side, their difference in stature was clear. Magdefrau stood a couple inches taller.

"Okay, okay. Guys, we're losing time. Remember the mailbox?" I picked up Josh Magdefrau's backpack and handed it to him. Him putting it on gave Gingerich an opportunity to disengage and start toward his house. Gingerich was quiet the rest of the way to the house, deflated.

It was Ruben who brought it up. "So if neither of you is going to be White Josh, then we got to figure out what to call both of you. We can't keep calling you by your last names."

Magdefrau spoke up when Gingerich didn't answer. "Well, you guys can call me what my dad used to call me." He whipped his head back to us. It was like a movie, the way this punctuated this interaction. Cue the Sergio Leone music sting and title as the wind blew his hair and he said, "Zane."

"Zane?" Jerry asked. Gingerich perked up at this, looking over at us with a hint of a smile. Jerry pantomimed mulling it over, bringing his furled fingers to his chin. "I like it!"

From then on, like a switch, we called him Zane. We had that power. To change who we were. We confused our teachers and parents when we insisted that everyone, including them, now call him Zane. But they weren't there when he stood up for himself like he was in a Western.

After Josh (no longer White Josh or Josh Gingerich, simply Josh) checked in with his stepdad, Mr. Ottaway, he began to warm up. That's the way our group operated. Someone would get under someone else's skin and take it too far. It would take a moment but eventually we'd maintain social equilibrium. We didn't apologize to one another. Enough time would pass for us to pretend things never happened. Maybe we were able to move on because we figured out a way to retire the White Josh moniker. Regardless, our excitement was growing as we made our way to the woodworking shop. That's what mattered. What we'd hyped up all throughout school.

Nothing prepared me for what we saw that day.

"Holy . . . " Eric said, trailing off, his mouth agape at what lay before us. We were speechless at the giant mailbox before us. It was Frankenstein's monster, a reinforced custom-made behemoth of a mailbox.

"Be cool, be cool," Ruben said to us under his breath. We had planned to walk by the mailbox. To play it cool. To not draw attention and look like a bunch of kids doing recon. But it was too crazy. We stopped to admire the audacity. The actual mailbox was heavy steel. Industrial bolts capped the screws connecting it to its stake.

Zane uttered in amazement, "I don't even think Hank has tools big enough to take those out."

Ruben urged us to keep walking. "Guys. Come on," he whispered before smiling and adding, "I told you, you had to see it."

"Talk about taking it to the next level," whispered Eric. The post towered at least a foot over him.

"Yo. Fools. Come on. We'll have plenty of time to plan," Ruben said, finally getting our attention. We gathered ourselves and walked the rest of the way to the Shack. There we admired the tenacity and sheer lunacy of that mailbox. We scrapped the thought of taking it out like the previous two times. I would've broken my hand trying to punch out that mailbox. And it seemed like the shop owner designed it to be impervious to baseball-bat strikes. It reminded me of song lyrics, "So high you can't get over it, so wide you can't get around it." This was the challenge to end all challenges. We decided: Saturday night. During the races and the bailes. Come hell or high water, we were going to somehow take that thing out.

The rest of the week was a slog in anticipation of the weekend. We got through class with tapping feet and shorter-than-usual attention spans. Hallway conversations covered different methods and approaches we could take that coming Saturday.

There was one interesting school development that managed to steal away my attention, however. Another new kid. The opposite of Zane. He was a Honduran kid named Javier. Like a lot of other immigrant kids we got from Mexico, Honduras, and Guatemala, Javier didn't know a lick of English. These kids had a rough time. They spent most of their time sequestered in ESL classes. They struggled whenever they were in class with the rest of us, getting ignored or made fun of. I usually felt bad for these kids. But Javier was a little different. You could tell he was one of the cool kids before he moved. He had full slicked-back hair and wore these gaudy gold necklaces. He carried himself with the intent of someone who should have ruled the school. The only problem was the language barrier prevented him from communicating that with the rest of us.

My memories have only the slightest sketch of Javier, which is telling of how little I cared about him and the other kids like him. In a lot of ways the Mexicans who'd lived in West Liberty all their lives separated themselves from these new immigrants. In a lot of ways they were at the bottom of our schoolyard social strata. Growing up in West Liberty, there were always discussions and arguments among ourselves about how Mexican you were. How assimilated you were. How white you were. If it meant that much to the two Joshes, you know it meant something to the rest of us. Another way to look at it is how proud you were of your parents' culture. It became complicated and messy because that conversation rolled into all sorts of other cliques and groups.

There were the vatos Nancy hung out with. Kids who thought they were, or were actually, gangbangers. There were the paisa kids like my cousin Tito who loved the norteño music and culture of our parents and dressed up in cowboy boots and hats. Then there were the friend groups like ours. Mexicans who mixed with the white and Asian kids in town. Who leaned into the small-town traditions, football and homecoming. West Liberty didn't get an official soccer team until I was in high school, but that was a good way to see the different factions. There were the Mexicans who played football and those who played soccer.

The vato and paisa kids would say we were coconuts: brown on the outside, white on the inside. That our culture brought us shame. But I'd argue that, despite my indifference toward Javier, we weren't quite there on the spectrum. There were a couple of Mexican kids in town who *only* hung out with non-Mexicans. Who weren't connected with the culture at all. I remember talking to one of those kids who straight up admitted to me that they wished they were white. For all the complexity of the relationship I had with my parents' culture growing up, despite all the times the "more Mexican" kids would call me a coconut for not knowing Spanish, I never once wished that.

You also have to factor in some outliers. A handful of interracial families with half-white and half-Mexican kids. (A girl I know said her Mexican West Lib friends called her an "unfinished taco.") And a few families that came to West Liberty way before everyone else. Rather than coming for the turkey plant, they came to help bring the railroad into town more than a century ago. I imagine for some of those kids, Mexico was a concept. Like how it is for my wife, who's of Irish and Scottish descent but has no real family or connection to those places.

Astute readers will catch that Javier didn't fit into any of these groups I've detailed so far. First is the obvious but still significant: he wasn't Mexican. Javier was a recent immigrant from Honduras. A country that, I'm embarrassed to admit, took me a long time to realize wasn't a state in Mexico. Here's the thing—Mexicans in America have this reputation and status. They think they're the only Latino or Hispanic group that matters. Some of that is in jest, and some of it is other people in the country putting it on us. It's like how both the racist kids on the playground and our parents assumed Jerry was Chinese and we had to explain to everyone what Laos even was. A similar thing happens to, say, Salvadorans, Guatemalans, Hondurans, and Puerto Ricans. Talk to anyone from one of those places and they'll regale you with stories in which they had to tell someone, "No, I'm not Mexican. Yes, it's different . . . " West Liberty's Latino population has grown more diverse in recent years, with an influx of Hondurans and Puerto Ricans in particular. But they were a very small percentage in my childhood. Which, of course, led to complicated discrimination based on country of origin. I would even overhear adults at Mexican parties talking smack about these "new immigrants" coming into town.

But even if Javier weren't Honduran, even if he were Mexican, there would be a huge divide between him and the other kids in town. You see, he was the Latino equivalent of fresh off the boat. All the other groups I've detailed navigated a duality of cultural existence. From the vatos to the assimilated Mexicans, we picked and chose where the slider would go on the Americanized gradient. We got to pick based on what we thought was cool. The paisa kids who dressed like our parents were still bilingual. Even if they didn't engage in small-town traditions like homecoming, they still understood what those traditions were. Javier and other kids like him didn't have the privilege. They struggled to understand the new language. Messed up the intricate customs and social structures in place on the playground. This is why they were at the bottom rung of the popularity ladder.

One time Javier came up to me at recess, talking to me in Spanish. My Spanglish disappointed and annoyed him. I'm sure his heart sank when he found out I couldn't communicate with him. I should have been a refuge, an oasis from the other kids who shunned him on the playground. Embarrassed, I found my friends playing on the barren field and excused myself. Javier walked over to a bench with another immigrant kid from Mexico. We left them alone while we played American football.

The other development unfolding during the week was at home. Bit by bit, first in my brother's old room, then in the garage where there was more space, I was rehearsing the steps to Cynthia's quinceañera procession. It could have been my Tía Nelle's pleas, or the threat of punishment from Nancy. But I put work in to remember the order and steps I had to do with Blanca. No lie, I gained a small amount of pride by the end of the week, when I realized I had the dance down pat.

I greeted the dance floor with confidence on our extra Saturday rehearsal. My brain pushed away the anticipation of our mailbox mission that night as I took Blanca's hand and led her through the flanks of older boys and girls. When we reached our spots, we pivoted away from each other in perfect unison. My tía couldn't contain herself as she let out a hoot from over by the stereo system. Nancy reacted, too, with an ever-so-slight nod at her little brother. A sign of affection from my sister was so foreign to me that I didn't know how to react. I missed my chance to nod back before we reset our lines.

It felt good. And dare I say, a little fun. It felt good not to hold the rehearsal process up. We even got to work on the next piece early. Both Nancy's and Cynthia's quinceañeras had two choreographed songs. There was the more formal introductory procession, then a looser song. For Nancy's we did a country line dance to Brooks and Dunn's "Boot Scootin' Boogie." If you played that song for me today, I could still do a semblance of that line dance. We did an up-tempo cumbia song for Cynthia's.

For a moment or two, while my Tía Nelle hammed it up and taught us the steps, while we laughed and learned, I forgot about our plans for the night. But as soon as tía called for the end of the rehearsal, looking at me when she told everyone they were doing a good job, the plans came back into sharp focus. Whatever bit of fun I'd had in the community center, that night was sure to trump it. I grabbed my things and walked out into the sunlight, past the racetrack and the few houses to the Party Shack, where I found the guys in deep conversation, planning out the heist.

We had settled on it being a heist in clandestine planning in the school hallways. It wasn't enough to desecrate or vandalize the mailbox.

We had to take it. When I walked into the Shack, Zane was relaying a key bit of intel that he'd revealed to me earlier. Gingerich was prodding, trying to find holes in the info.

"Are you sure? That seems like something you made up," Josh said.

"I'm serious. I checked the clock each time Hank comes in from the evening shift. He comes straight from the police station and arrives right around 10:40. Which means that the shift changes over at 10:30. That's when we go."

They huddled over a coffee table with a wobbly leg. Somebody had made a crude schematic of the mailbox with various notes on its weak points and potential methods to dismantle it. Ruben reiterated Josh's earlier question. "You for sure for sure? That's pretty early in the night." We usually didn't go out and hoodlumize until past midnight. The town would still be active at 10:30.

"I'm positive. If we want the most amount of time where we are *guaranteed* that the coppers will be on the other side of town, we strike at 10:30. On the dot."

We looked at each other. We had decided. I knew it by the smirk across Ruben's face. "Well, shit. Then that's when it will happen."

————————

The rest of the day was spent in anticipation. More sweaty palms and tapping feet. Finally the sun set and the roar of the races filled the night. We scraped open the Party Shack's door and cascaded into Ruben's backyard. Ruben and I had developed rudimentary hand signals for the group, things like "follow me" or "scatter." Basic communication we needed to convey in silence. We felt like operatives in the field.

It didn't take us long to get to the woodworking shop. Ruben, Zane, and I led the way. Jerry and Eric followed, watching our backs. Josh brought up the rear.

"It's 10:28," Eric said, looking at his watch. He was the designated timekeeper. We huddled together, darting glances in all directions for potential headlights.

"Okay everyone, bust out your shit," Ruben said. We unsheathed various tools and weapons. Jerry and Josh had screwdrivers and wrenches in different sizes. Ruben and I had the baseball bats. Eric had a crowbar. "Jerry. Josh. You know what to do," Ruben said as he made way for the two to get at the mailbox.

We hadn't had a chance to look at the type and size of screws on the mailbox during the day. The plan was to see if we could assess that and take them off at once. Jerry and Josh worked in tandem, cycling through tools. They whispered expletives as they worked. "Dude, none of these will work!" Josh said in desperation.

"We have to try them all before we make too much noise," I replied.

"10:35," Eric said from the side, one hand on his watch. This was a repeat of the last time we tried to take out the mailbox, before we were able to knock it off with Ruben's metal bat. That ended up with loud clangs that reverberated in the night. Clangs that made your hand vibrate and sting. That was the last mailbox though. This new and improved model would take a Herculean amount of effort and noise to bash. The weapons were the last resort. We waited as Josh and Jerry continued to fumble with their tools.

"Come on, come on," someone said, not realizing they were saying it out loud.

A loud clang shot out from where the guys were working. "Oh, shit!" Jerry whisper-yelled. They had dropped one of the wrenches in their haste and it had fallen onto some other tools, metal on metal. A dog began to bark a few houses down. "Damn, damn," Jerry continued.

"10:40. Yo, we gotta go to the next phase," Eric pleaded. Ruben looked over at me for confirmation. This was taking too long. We had to resort to bashing this thing and hoping we could get it off like last time.

"Damn, okay. Eric, hand me the crowbar. Chuy, fuck the wooden bat, go straight for the heavy-duty one." I nodded and exchanged my wooden bat for Ruben's newer and more expensive metal one. We patted Jerry and Josh on their shoulders, indicating that they should gather their tools and be on the lookout.

I swung first, a big marvelous swing with all my might. A metallic crack echoed, a call-and-response from the laundromat across the street. We looked on in desperation. There wasn't even the slightest ding on that cursed mailbox. Ruben tried next with a walking lead-in. Ruben was always stronger than me. Besides his wrestling training in the winter, he played baseball in the summer. The mechanics of his swing were perfect as his crowbar clanged against metal. Ruben shook the sting off his hands as we again marveled at the pristine mailbox taunting us.

"10:45," Eric said, desperation squeaking through his voice. "It's now or never, guys!" My ears were ringing from our strikes against the mailbox. Another dog joined in with the first, barking and howling at the racket we were making. For all our talk and planning, our mission was looking to be a failure. In the distance, across from the railroad tracks, I saw a pair of growing yellow dots. Headlights coming our way. Now or never. We jumped into hyperdrive, trying to beat the snot out of that mailbox. We took turns over each other, like what I imagine two railroad workers hammering down a spike would look like. All semblance of a plan, of an attempt to be quiet, were gone. We crashed down on that mailbox with a fury. Out of breath and panicking, I almost cried when that mailbox stood before us, intact and immaculate.

"Yo! We got to call it. That car's heading this way," Eric said. He was already starting to shimmy away from us and the mailbox. Sure enough, the once-small headlights merged together and were getting closer. They were almost to the post office, which was only fifty feet or so from the railroad tracks. If it was a cop and they crossed those tracks, we would have to abort. I watched Ruben for the "scatter" hand sign, moments from giving it myself. "What should we do?" Jerry and Josh said to us, tools spilling out of their arms.

Then, over all the commotion, came another noise. A dinging. A red light flashed on the horizon. Eric squealed and took a couple more steps away from us. A flash of panic struck the group. We all thought the light came from a cop car. But there wasn't any blue mixed with the red. It was the lights from the railroad crossing. The dings accompanied the barriers that came down. That halted the headlights before the track. The wail of an incoming train followed.

"It's a train!" I yelled over to Eric, motioning for him to come back. The trains running through West Liberty could last a few seconds or a few minutes. But it could have been a whole hour and it wouldn't have mattered. We had made zero progress on taking out the mailbox. The train roared in our ears. We couldn't hear each other. I let my bat go limp as I watched Ruben renew his attack on the mailbox. The train was so loud I couldn't hear the blows of his crowbar or his screaming curses. That was it. The mailbox had bested us. In the fury I contorted my hands into a scatter sign and went to turn to the group. Then I felt a hand on my shoulder. I watched in awe as Zane signaled to Ruben to back up.

I'll never forget the image of what happened next. Zane stooped under the mailbox, like he was going to give the post a bear hug. The mailbox was so tall that it came up right above his shoulder. With the train thundering past as a backdrop, Zane heaved and shuddered. He did that thing that happens to weightlifters when they're trying to break a world record. His muscles shook and convulsed as he attempted to rip the mailbox post from the very ground. Our entire group watched, slack-jawed. We could see, but not hear, that Zane was yelling through gritted teeth. Our mouths opened wider as the post began to jerk loose from the soil.

By the time the train passed, Zane had finished yelling. It was as if the two noises were one. He had done it. He'd pulled the post right out of the ground like he was a giant. The dinging of the railroad crossing subsided as Zane stood before us with the mailbox and post in his arms, smiling like he had done the impossible. "Scatter!" I yelled as Ruben and I helped Zane carry the post. It took the three of us to carry. We whooped and laughed in the night. When we got to the Party Shack, we took turns lifting that behemoth of a mailbox and post over our heads. Every few minutes we'd break out into chants of "Zane! Zane! Zane!" Some of us more enthusiastic than others. Josh Gingerich joined in on the chants, but I could see that he did so with less enthusiasm.

And the woodworking shop? They never did construct a new mailbox. They probably got a PO Box after that.

We buzzed in the Party Shack, thinking we would stay in the rest of the night. At this point we were actually sleeping over in that garage, on couches and mattresses with sleeping bags. We nestled the mailbox in the corner of the room, each of us giving recounts of Zane's feat of strength. After some time our energy died down and we went through the ritual of calling who got to sleep in what spot. Then Ruben bolted upright.

"What, are you guys done or something?" he asked while walking behind the workbench on the side of the Shack.

"What do you mean? We did everything we wanted," Eric said, pointing to our spoils.

"It's still early," Ruben said. This was true. Since we went out per Zane's time frame, it was not quite midnight. The races had been over for a bit and the town had died down with them. "And I wanted to try this bad boy out."

"What the hell? Where'd you get that?" Jerry asked.

Ruben held a gun with both hands. It was a long, slender rifle. Wood-paneled and gunmetal black. It had a lever on the bottom like in old Western movies.

"Don't worry about it," Ruben said as he aimed the gun in different directions, one eye closed as he looked down the barrel.

"What do you mean, don't worry about it? It's a gun," Eric replied, making sure to stay out of the line of Ruben's sight.

"Relax, guey, it's a BB gun," Ruben said. He said it like it annoyed him that he had to break it to us. "But we got to go try it out. Come on, guys. Get up, let's go."

Gingerich was the first to dissent. "Don't you think we did enough already, Ruben? That wasn't exactly the most elegant hoodlumizing mission we pulled back there." Ruben ignored him as he made his way out, leaving the door ajar.

"What are we even going to do with that?" Eric asked me. I shrugged. There was a mood of apprehension as one by one we got up to follow Ruben. I couldn't quite put my finger on it. Was it as Josh said and we felt it was too risky to go back out into the night? Or was this an extension of the qualms I'd been having about Ruben lately? He always wanted to push us to the next level. Either way, the open door was a challenge. We filed out of the Shack, a thick haze of fog greeting us in Ruben's backyard.

"You see, fools. It's meant to be," Ruben said, the BB gun slung around his back.

We walked without talking. Down the alley behind the Shack and to the corner by the racetrack. The place was a ghost town. The fog and quietness gave it an almost eerie quality. The fact that none of us were talking added to this quality. We trailed Ruben in silence, off the sidewalk and into the middle of the road.

About fifty feet away was a minivan parked on the side of the road before the entrance to the fairgrounds. If it weren't for the fog, I could have seen the community center in the background, past the fairground entrance. But with the fog as thick as it was, we could only make out the van.

Ruben took the gun off his back and held it to his side. "So who's going to take a shot?" he asked. This was it. The challenge. We all looked at Ruben, confused. A couple of the guys averted their eyes.

"Chuy?" Ruben asked.

I didn't answer. I wanted nothing to do with this. It's strange to say now, the reason for my apprehension. There was something more to this interaction that was putting me off. For all the bad shit we did in our hoodlumizing days, it always felt we were on a level playing field with the town. Like with the war of escalation with the woodworking shop. Sure, we had used tools and bats. But it was always manual. By our own hands. This gun, even if it was only a BB gun, felt like cheating. I know, it's a strange concept: honor among hoodlums.

Ruben must have felt this tension. "Come the fuck on, guys. It won't even do anything. It's a BB gun." Still silence. "Zane? You want to keep the streak going?" Zane shook his head in refusal. "Alright. Fine. Got to do this myself."

Ruben lay on the ground on his belly, the rifle in both arms in the prone position. We all knelt down, waiting for the shot. We waited for a while; Ruben was milking the moment. That's what it was for. The moment. That's why we did these things, and why Ruben pushed us into them. That's why at reunions we still talk about Zane pulling that mailbox from the ground. Without us making these moments, this place would have been a ghost town, the fog the only thing occupying it at night. These adventures were born out of our idle minds and hands. They were about pushing back and making moments that mattered.

Ruben pulled the trigger and the entire rear windshield exploded on impact. A thousand shards of glass rained down on the asphalt at once.

"Oh shit, scatter!" I yelled for the second time that night. We ran in different directions, making sure not to all go down the alley. Ruben and I had formulated this concept together and drilled it with the rest of the group so it wouldn't be obvious we were all going to our home base. In the fog, I could see someone flick on the lights of the house by the van. As I turned to sprint through backyards, the shards of glass glinted in the street.

———————

The shards of glass were still on the road the following Sunday, though the van was gone. I ignored the pangs of guilt and walked the rest of the way to the community center. My head was a fog during rehearsal. I struggled to concentrate on the steps. It was a slog. But for how unfocused and distracted I was, I got through unscathed, no falls or chidings from my aunt. We ended the rehearsal and got to go home for the night.

Sunday nights were usually low-key. We would have leftovers for dinner and I'd watch *The Simpsons*. I was getting ready to watch that week's episode upstairs in my parents' bedroom, where I'd watch shows on their TV while they watched novelas downstairs in the living room. This meant I was next door to Nancy's room when I heard the muffled argument break out between my mom and sister.

I turned down the volume of the TV and walked over to the door. My sister was making her case. She kept saying she had made plans to go out with her friends and couldn't break them. My mom was raising her voice. Forbidding Nancy from leaving so late on a Sunday night.

My sister's voice matched my mom's in ferociousness. "You know what? I'm going to go. What can you do to stop me? There ain't shit you can do when it comes down to it. I know that."

My mom erupted into a torrent of screaming Spanish. She called my sister all sorts of insults, her and her no-good friends who she got into so much trouble with. My mom dared Nancy to take one step down those stairs and see what would happen.

For all the anger and verbal escalation my mom rained down on my sister and I, I don't remember her ever hitting me. The only adult who ever hit me as a child was my grandmother. My mom's mom. The severe figure in the photos. In our brief time together on this earth, she was the only grown-up who gave it to me. To this day, my cousin Freddy talks about the worst time my grandma got at me, after I got jalapeño juice in our cousin Daniel's eye. My grandma smacked me so hard I floated up toward the ceiling. But I don't remember my mom hitting us like that. Until that night when Nancy finally said, "You can't stop me. Try it."

At this point I had tiptoed into the hallway between my parents' room and my sister's. I remember the theme song to *The Simpsons* was starting. I noted how strange that felt, the juxtaposition of the cheery theme song with my mom screaming at my sister. I watched my sister attempt to push my mom out of the way.

Something activated in my mom. The next gear. She smacked my sister like my grandma did to me many years ago. A sharp crack against the music of the TV. My mom pushed and wrestled Nancy back into her room.

She said to her in Spanish, "You don't think I can stop you? Eh? Eh?" She continued to yell out "Eh?" as my sister cried and struggled against the overpowering weight of my mom.

"Get the fuck off!" my sister said between cries. She finally got a good angle and pushed my mom away. I remember them there, in a standoff, looking like they were about to fight. Both breathing hard. Not noticing me. I walked back to my parents' room before my mom gave her one last chastising. Nancy slammed the door and my mom's heavy footsteps thudded down the stairs.

I hastened back to my spot on the bed in front of the TV to pretend I was still watching. It didn't take long for the door to spring open. My sister's eyes were bloodshot. She walked straight over and blocked my view of the television. "Get out."

"I'm watching thi—" I began.

"I don't give a shit. Get out. Now."

For everything that happened with my sister, I didn't feel sorry for her. I was still a little brother, and as a little brother it was my duty to not know the weight of the situation. All I knew was that I was there first and was already watching my show. I froze, attempting to plan an appropriate response as to why I deserved to continue watching. Nancy didn't have time for that. She attempted to snatch the remote beside me. My reflexes kicked in and I grabbed the other end before she could take it. We each tried to pry the remote from the other's grasp for a few seconds before it flew in the air and crashed to the ground. We pushed each other away, both of us scrambling to get to the remote first. I surprised my sister and pushed her away hard. Harder than I had meant to, harder than she realized I could push. I gave a triumphant "Ha!" when I scooped up the remote a few feet away. But my triumph was short lived. The double-A batteries had fallen out on the remote's crash to the floor. I stood up to find my sister in the same spot in front of the TV holding both batteries in her hand.

I remember it in flashes. The few moments before she chucked that battery. Before I realized what she was planning to do. The moments directly preceding that are a blur. I must have said something to deserve it. Some snot-nosed thing about what had happened with my mom. Some clueless little-brother thing like Javy would say to get under my skin. Only I don't remember. I only remember the few seconds of recognition, when I saw the look in my sister's eyes. Her fist was clenched over one of the batteries, with the intent to throw it at me with all her might. In those few seconds I turned away. Attempted to shield my body and face. But I was too slow. Nancy put all of herself into that throw. She sent the battery flying like a missile. Like a shot in the night. The double-A flew through the air and hit my right eyeball with a thud.

It was instantaneous. The pain and visual explosion. Like lightning, like the battery was a hot coal shot into my brain. The visual aura was like lightning too. Like electric capillaries searing against my closed eye.

My scream tore through the house. This wasn't a yell to get someone in trouble. This wasn't mere pain. This was the worst pain I had ever felt, coursing through my body like a current. It traveled through my body and out of my lungs as I collapsed to the ground. The pain caused me to float outside of myself. I remember my sister getting close to me. Saying things as she held me. Pleading with me. But she sounded far away. I remember a warm feeling in my jeans. Not realizing I had wet myself from letting my body go, the warm feeling was a few microseconds of respite. The pain came in waves.

I came back into my body and brought my hands over my eyes. The first words that came out mixed with my screams. Cries of panic. "I can't see! I can't see!" I convulsed on the ground, trying to find some way to configure my body so the pain would stop. My mom's voice mixed with my sister's. But the moments after this are a fog. The memories are hazy. Locked away and hidden. I don't recall how long it took for the pain to subside. I know we didn't seek any medical attention and stayed at home. But my memory stops with my cries, the helplessness and panic, the thought that my sister had blinded my eye.

The fallout from what I now refer to as "the battery hit" lasted a long time. Longer than I realized. As an adult I went to a new optometrist for a routine eye exam. He shone a light on my eye and asked me to look up. "Huh. You have some significant scarring on the bottom of your eye here. Any idea what that could be from?" I told him I had an idea. From an incident long ago. He dropped the subject and continued the exam.

I wasn't able to see out of that eye for the rest of the night and into the morning. If I tried to open it, painful pink auras replaced what should have been sight. Before school my mom stopped me, after my sister left the house. We hadn't talked to each other the rest of the night and I avoided her for weeks after. My mom talked to me in broken

English with tears welling in her eyes. "Chuy. Please don't tell you teachers what happened. Nancy. She already in trouble. Ay, por favor Dios, este chamaca. If you tell she could get in big trouble. They'll take her away."

The anger swelled inside me. I knew my sister was getting into trouble out on the town with her friends but never knew the extent. My mom spared me the details. She pleaded with me to wait a couple days, and if I still couldn't see out my eye then we'd go to the doctor. But Nancy couldn't afford to get into any more trouble. The anger grew when I thought of another reason why my mom asked me to be quiet—so that my parents wouldn't get in trouble, either.

My mom wiped her eyes. "Okay. You going to be late." I walked away from my mom and out of the house without saying a word.

I don't remember if I bandaged my eye; I don't think I did. To not attract any attention at school, I kept my mom's secret. Kept all the pain and embarrassment bottled in. From teachers and administrators but also from my friends. I never told any of them why I was covering my eye with my hand and wincing at the light.

It wasn't too hard to keep my secret. Tall tales distracted my class. The legend of how Zane pulled out a mailbox from the ground with his bare hands was passing from person to person in the hallways, the details growing and morphing like all our stories did. It was interesting that we chose to divulge and cultivate this tall tale while keeping the account of shooting out the van window secret.

I detached myself from my friends for the next few days. To not talk about my eye, yes, but also for another reason. They were so boisterous and engaged in recalling Zane's story. Eric and Jerry took turns regaling the girls in class with their points of view, piggybacking details on top of one another. But I didn't feel like celebrating. I regained my eyesight by Tuesday morning and after a few more days my aversion to light dissipated, but my mood was still sour.

It hit me in class at the end of the week during free time. The paper on my desk blurred. Wet dots blotted my math problems. *It didn't matter.* All the crazy moments our friend group made in the night. The story the guys kept recalling to our classmates. None of it mattered. That power and freedom we felt were meaningless. Why would it matter when I would come home and be so spectacularly taken down by my sister? With one battery she showed me how small and vulnerable I was. No one noticed that I was crying into my desk. That I shook in silence, tears cascading down my face. I regained my composure when I noticed the bell was about to ring, using my sleeve to hide any evidence of my emotions.

It wasn't until I walked through the hallway and into a bathroom that I found someone *had* noticed my silent crying. Javier, the new kid from Honduras, had followed me from class. I ignored him while I went to the bathroom, but he stopped me after I washed my hands.

"¿Por qué estabas llorando?" Javier asked, blocking my way to the door.

"What? What are you talking about?" I mumbled, surprised and embarrassed that he had caught me. I tried to disengage and walk away. Javier was bigger than me and stretched out his arms so I couldn't get through.

"Estabas llorando. En la clase," he said. I ignored him, making my way to the paper towels to dry my hands.

Here's the thing. I took Javier's tone as a mocking one, but there could have also been genuine concern and curiosity. I imagine my crying at my desk really did confuse him. But in the bathroom he thought I couldn't understand him and grew annoyed that I couldn't understand his Spanish. "En la clase," he repeated before bringing his hands up to his face to pantomime crying. My face grew red as he imitated my cries from class. Embarrassment turned to anger that came from deep inside. My fists clenched. My tongue stung from biting it so hard. I thought Javier was testing me. But he was too big to fight. The cyclical nature of violence and bullying I've detailed so far was trickle-down. The bigger and stronger tortured the smaller and weaker. Those smaller and weaker found someone even smaller to pass along their anger. I couldn't lash out at Javier like I did my little cousin Javy. Javier knew this as we stared each other down in the bathroom.

My anger turned to horror when the bathroom door opened behind Javier. Ruben barged in and stopped, surprised to see Javier and I sizing each other up.

"What's going on?" he asked me. I needed to stop this interaction. To preserve my integrity before my friend. I froze at the question.

Javier spoke up. "Este gringo estaba llorando en clase," he said, not knowing that I could understand him. "Pinche bebé," he said while bringing up his hands to fake cry again. Javier was happy he had an audience. Thinking he had an ally in Ruben.

Ruben nodded to Javier. "Oh yeah?" For a second it seemed like Ruben was going to walk past. Part of me hoped he would so I could push my way through and get out of there. But Ruben caught Javier unawares and shoved him against the tile wall. Javier made a noise as the impact knocked the wind out of him.

"¡Es mi amigo, guey!" Ruben shouted. Javier's eyes grew wide. His face contorted as it dawned on him that he was now in a two-on-one situation. Ruben and Javier started to argue with each other in Spanish, fast and barbarous. Javier attempted to shove him and squirm away, but Ruben's wrestling technique prevailed. He had him pinned good. "Chuy, man, what's this about?"

I wanted to bolt. To tell Ruben I had no clue what this guy's problem was. Part of me wanted me to hit Javier. Ruben gave me a look. A moment. To ask me what I wanted to do next. To give me the opportunity to escalate it.

Javier began to make his case in frantic Spanish. Telling Ruben how it wasn't his fault he saw me in class. He was about to get to the part of the story where he found me crying like a baby when I snapped. It was the fact that he was spilling my secret, yes, but it was also the *Spanish*. The fact that he was making his case to Ruben thinking I couldn't understand him. Out of desperation and anger I ran up and cut Javier off.

"I can understand you. I can understand you!" I pushed Ruben aside and grabbed Javier by his shirt. My anger was all encompassing. In choosing fight or flight, I had chosen to fight. But that fight response manifested itself in a different way.

Physically fighting him wasn't enough. I wanted to make him hurt. I knew the way. I twisted the knife. "But can you understand me? Huh? I see you in those ESL classes. Stuttering. Messing up. I see that you don't understand half the things our teachers say to you but you pretend you do."

Both Ruben and Javier didn't know how to take this. But it was too late. The floodgates were open. My rage swelled. "Don't you get it? When you can't speak English." Javier twitched at these last few words: *speak English*. He knew what that meant. I had struck a nerve. "When you can't say basic shit. They make fun of you. Don't you get it? It's embarrassing. You're embarrassing us."

At this point I was on autopilot. Javier looked at me in bewilderment. I remember the whites of his eyes, he had them opened so wide. He didn't say a word. I continued in my fury. "Yeah, I can understand you, but can you understand me? Can you understand that you make us all look bad? Fucking answer me. Don't you get it? Can you even fucking answer in English or are you too goddamned stupid?"

Javier reeled. Shell-shocked that I took things there. Ruben too. Ruben looked at me differently then. He had never seen me blow up before. My secret was out. The rage from my interactions with my family had spilled out. "Yo, yo, chill, Chuy," Ruben said, getting between us.

I let Ruben push me away before walking out the door on my own accord. There was a metallic taste in my mouth. Blood from biting my tongue. The adrenaline was draining from my body, replaced by an immediate and deep shame. I messed up. It happened so fast.

It's hard to convey how mad I got back then. The best way to describe it is to divulge the reputation I got among my friends. It wasn't the last time Ruben would see me so mad. Between seventh and eighth grade, I got a reputation for having a horrible temper. For snapping and hitting those around me. The violence and anger contained in my family spilled out among my friends and kids in school. "Have you seen Chuy mad? Like really mad? It's scary."

The reputation for being the "mad one" transferred from Eric to me. Eric had a short fuse, but you could see it coming. Our group contained and diverted his anger. But the guys told me it was different with me. It takes a lot to throw me over the edge, but when it happens, it's bad. Ruben, who is one of the toughest guys I know, to this day says that I'm one of the scariest people he's seen angry. That it's like he can tell when the anger takes over. That it's all I can see and feel.

I don't know if Ruben told the guys after the incident with Javier. All I know is that I was trying to put it all behind me by the time we were doing our daily walk after school. I let the guys continue to expand and contort their Zane story. Jerry and Eric were in front asking Zane for details. Ruben patted my shoulder as he walked in step by me. He gave a slight nod before picking up his pace and joining the conversation. I hung behind the guys, joined by Josh.

"Tired of that story too?" Josh asked while matching my step.

"Something like that," I said, relieved he wasn't asking me about the bathroom incident. We let the distance grow between us and the guys in front.

Josh perked up. "Hey man, I didn't get a chance to tell you yet. I got my own copy of *On the Road* the other day."

"Is that Sal and Dean?" I asked.

"In the flesh," Josh replied, handing over the book. Our obsession with *On the Road* was the latest development in our scavenging of my brother's things in the garage, where we'd found a biography of Jim Morrison (Johnny also owned The Doors' full discography). According to the biography, Jim was obsessed with Jack Kerouac, so of course we had to read him too. Josh liked rummaging through my brother's media more than my other friends. We bonded over how it influenced our tastes. Josh had a way of making things all right. We had that way with each other, talking about the next movie or band we should get into and making each other laugh.

Even more raucous laughter from the guys in front interrupted us. Eric and Jerry were taking turns imitating Zane pulling out the mailbox from the ground. They looked like WWF wrestlers. Like "Macho Man" Randy Savage and The Ultimate Warrior shaking the ropes, convulsing. Ruben and Zane laughed while the wrestlers tore an invisible stake above their heads. "Fucking stupid," Ruben said between laughs.

Josh stopped talking then, annoyed. We walked behind the guys the rest of the way to Zane's.

We went inside Zane's house because he had promised to show us his collection of Godzilla figures. We were too old to play with the figures, but Zane piqued our curiosity when told us he had amassed a collection in his youth. As we congregated in Zane's kitchen, Hank pulled into the driveway. Off early.

By this point we understood that Zane would want to leave at Hank's presence. The screen door slammed before Hank's heavy footfalls came up the steps into the kitchen. Zane ran down from his room empty-handed.

"Alright, I'm good, guys. Let's go. Hank, I'll get the trash on the way out," Zane said while keeping his forward momentum, motioning for us to follow.

"Whoa, whoa, whoa. Leaving so soon? I didn't even have a chance to bow and have you ladies curtsy back," Hank said while bowing to us in his full police uniform. The gear on his belt swayed while he moved.

I was sitting on the kitchen counter. The rest of the guys were standing in various spots of the kitchen, leaning against walls. Eric and Jerry started to follow Zane, blowing off Hank. In the corner of my eye I saw Josh. He had this look on his face. Like he had planned for this moment.

"Yeah, yeah, whatever, *fucking pig*," Josh snapped.

It wasn't what he said, though I don't think Josh had ever flat-out called Hank a pig before this. Not to his face. No, there was something about the proximity of all our bodies in that small kitchen space. And the way Josh had said it. With venom. Like he had taken a glove off and slapped Hank across the face. Zane grew wide-eyed at Josh's barb.

Something changed in Hank. His features morphed before our very eyes. His face crimsoned with rage. His joviality dissipated. He was no longer Zane's mom's boyfriend, the guy who messed with us and laughed as we messed with him back. He was a police officer laying down the law.

Hank slammed his heavy lunch thermos on the kitchen counter, making me jump. "Alright, listen, you little pissants. I don't work my ass off dealing with all sorts of shit that this town throws at me. You wouldn't believe the shit we deal with out there. Only to set foot in *my* home and have a bunch of ingrates disrespecting me." Hank wheeled around to each one of us while he talked. Jutting his finger in our faces for emphasis. The color drained from Gingerich's face at the realization of what he had unleashed. Zane looked at the floor, his hands limp at his sides. "Now, before you get the hell out of my house, I need each and every one of you to know something. That I am your superior and I don't deserve your disrespect in *my* own house. You got that? No. That's not good enough. I need you to say it. Yes, sir. Say. It."

It seemed like forever. How quiet it was in that kitchen while each of us waited for the other to squeak out "Yes, sir." Zane said it last. Hank then let us know it was time to leave. Without Zane. We tried to become as small and quiet as possible as we filtered out of the house, scrambling away and erupting in talk when we got far enough down the road.

"Dude, what the hell, Josh, why'd you say that?" Eric said.

"I didn't know he would get like that. Not after we've said stuff like that before," Josh said in defense. "My bad, guys. I don't get why he was getting at you guys though. You didn't say anything."

The guys continued to chastise Josh as we made our way to his house. But their anger at how boneheaded he was gave way to a sort of low-key admiration. The crazy white boy called a cop a pig to his face.

In remembering this encounter, something sticks out to me: when Hank snapped at us and talked about the shit that the town was throwing at him. It very well could be that the reason Hank was so stressed out, the things he couldn't believe the town was throwing at him, was *us*. Our hoodlumizing escapades. If only he had known he had the culprits in *his own house*. I'm sure there was a lesson in there somewhere, but as kids we never learned it.

The cyclical power dynamics I've detailed continued all throughout junior high. Power and violence, freedom and authority, tradition and assimilation. I committed terrible acts of violence against my friends and extended family. Things I have apologized for. Things I haven't apologized enough for, from poking Josh Gingerich's eye while we wrestled to recreating vicious wrestling moves on innocent boys and girls on the playground. There are folks I grew up with who can describe me as an antagonist in their childhoods. To them I was the evil kid who dropkicked the girl at recess when she was minding her own business. Or the older kid who almost popped someone's arm out of its socket when I got mad at him in a game of tag. I could say that we all did it to each other. That it was normal like all the other messed-up things we did as kids. But I don't want to excuse anything. I had a rage inside of me that I couldn't contain.

For all that I remember about the lead-up to Cynthia's quinceañera, I don't remember the party itself. That is a good thing. It means that it was boring, that it was uneventful enough that it must have gone off without a hitch.

It took a few months after the battery hit for my fighting with Nancy to continue. Only these were becoming more and more like true fights rather than the hits my sister would administer in our youth. It felt like each fight was becoming the worst one. We would whale on each other. Scrambling and screaming until our mom broke us up. It was always our mom who disciplined and stopped us. I felt like this was too emotional a task for my dad, who always managed to sneak away into the garage while we walloped one another.

There was something else that increased our animosity toward one another. Something that happened before our last fight, the last physical fight I ever got into. It was a summer day after eighth grade. It had been a few weeks since Nancy and I last fought each other, which meant tensions were building.

I was watching TV in the living room and Nancy was in her bedroom when my mom ripped open the front door, terrified and in hysterics. She fumbled with the phone and dialed the police. She got it out in circular spurts, that someone, or some group, had done something to our garage. On the side of it. She didn't know who. Only that *they* had done it. "Ay, la pinche chamaca," my mom kept repeating after hanging up the phone.

"Ama. You're scaring me. What's going on?" I repeated. "What'd she do?"

My mom told me to go and look for myself. A terrible feeling permeated my every step as I walked out the front porch. I circled around my dad's aging lowrider to check out the north side of our garage, the side facing the football field and empty parking lot.

My knees buckled at the sight of it. It was completely bombed with graffiti. Nasty black paint scrawled across the entire side of the garage. There were gang names and numbers. Names and words I had vague understandings of. I knew they were bad. Dangerous. Threats and warnings.

Our mom refused to answer as the police officer knocked on the door. It was Hank. His presence contributed to the off-kilter vibe of the situation at hand. It was weird to see him on duty. The last time I had seen him in uniform, he was chewing us out in his kitchen. Now he was here because my mom had called the police for help. I opened the door in a daze. Hank gave me a silent nod of acknowledgment.

"What's going on here?"

By this time, my sister had slunk from her room and was solemn as my mom motioned for me to tell Hank. To show him the wall. I had Hank follow us outside. Nancy walked in silence as my mom choked back sobs. I watched my sister as we circled to the writings on the wall.

She kept a poker face as Hank talked on his radio. My mom could no longer hold back as she began to cry.

A few other police cruisers pulled into the gravel parking lot. The cops surveyed the graffiti as they walked over to us. They took photos. There were gawkers and passersby. My Tía Nelle and her family came through to console my mom through her hysterics. She got so worked up she began to dry-heave by the lowrider.

I stood by while Hank and a younger officer talked to Nancy, asking her questions while pointing to different parts of the wall. She talked in a quiet voice, answering in short bursts and only when necessary. After a while they dismissed her and pulled me over. Hank put his hand on my shoulder as he talked. I needed him then, to tell me what to do and how to feel.

"You know what this is?" he asked me. I shook my head. "It's nothing. Typical stupid kids. Random bragging and tagging. Done in the middle of the night. Some kids that think they're gangsters had an open wall and too much time on their hands." He squeezed my shoulder a little harder. "You tell your mom that. Okay?" I looked up at Hank in confusion. "Look. Chuy. She's scared, okay? We talked to your sister and we'll get to the bottom of things. But you should tell your mom this was just some random punk kids. Okay?" he asked again.

A knot formed in my throat. I had thrown around the word "hate" before. Had yelled it at my sister after fights. But this was different. I *resented* my sister then. Held it against her for the violence on the wall. For how it felt like the walls were closing around our family. This wasn't random kids. *We* were random kids with our stupid hoodlumizing. This was different. This was something my sister had brought upon us. Her enemies had found our house and scrawled personal warnings and attacks on our family. This wasn't random at all.

"Okay," I told Hank. And I said what he told me to say to my mom, consoling her as she ran through the events later that night. My sister holed up in her room, refusing to talk to anyone.

After this my parents switched everyone's bedrooms around. The graffiti added to the suspicion that Nancy would sneak downstairs and out of the house at night. My parents moved from the upstairs bedroom down into Johnny's old room. My sister took my parents' old bedroom where the battery incident occurred. I was in the bedroom next to Nancy's.

My resentment toward Nancy grew. In a way she got a reward by getting the biggest bedroom. And I thought it was unfair that she wasn't changing her ways. That the warnings on our garage wall didn't scare her like they did the rest of the family. Like they did me. It was this resentment, mixed with years of bullying and pent-up emotions, that led to our last fight. The fight to end all fights.

It happened in Nancy's new bedroom. Nobody else was home. Nobody to pull us apart. I don't remember quite how it started, that fight. I know it was the worst fight either one of us had gotten into. I bet it started with something innocuous. Nancy calling me fat or us arguing over someone's music being too loud. However it started, we ended up at each other's throats.

It's hard to remember the details of this fight because I've blocked out most of them. All I remember is the end of it. After both of us were bloody and bruised. Our strength, skill, and fury matched each other. Punching Nancy's face had ripped and reddened my knuckles. Hers were the same. That's a weird detail that people who haven't gotten into a fight wouldn't know. That it rips your knuckles to shreds. We could tell which kids got into lots of fights by how often scabs formed on their knuckles.

That fight lasted a long time. Longer than any of our previous ones. There was no one there to stop it. Not a parent or adult. Not ourselves. At the end of the fight Nancy was on top of me, pummeling. It was like she was punching my face to dust. Knuckles slamming against ground beef. This should have been the end. I should have cried and said I give up. We had done that before when Nancy demonstrated her dominance. But I was too strong now. Too angry and resentful. Too stupid.

I managed to roll my sister off and get at her face like she did mine. It was all lefts and rights. Sloppy and ferocious strikes. She screamed a raspy scream. Blood oozed and spritzed from her teeth, like she had bitten into one of those vampire capsules we got at the fair when we were kids. But I kept on going. Kept on punching. It was all I could see and feel. It was all the years of feeling too weak. Of not knowing how to deal with my emotions. It was what my friends had warned me about—it's scary when I get mad. It's like jumping into an abyss. Nothing could stop me. Not even Nancy screaming "Get the fuck off!" I kept on punching.

The end of the fight was this. In desperation Nancy grabbed my hair and yanked me off her. In the ensuing scramble, one of my punches landed straight on her stomach. She made a sound like I had knocked the breath out of her, then she inhaled. This wasn't a result of her reacting to the blow but something else. That inhale wasn't physiological but born of fear. Fear of something bigger than either of us.

I should have known then. Right then and there. I was too young and stupid to put it together from that inhale. It wasn't until Nancy pleaded with me that it clicked. "Wait, wait, Chuy, stop. Stop. Punch me in the face all you want but don't punch my stomach."

I knew enough to know that our fight was over. We stood apart, breathing heavy and broken. Sprays of blood dotted the carpet around us. "Don't punch my stomach, okay?"

My voice came out of my throat like someone else was doing the talking. "What do you mean? What's going on?"

Nancy wiped the blood from her mouth onto her arm. She had a fat lip. I could feel my cheeks swelling. The cuts around my eyes stung. "So we're done? That's it," Nancy said.

"Nancy, what's going on?" I asked again. The adrenaline seeped out of my body, replaced with an unknown fear creeping up. Nancy ignored me. Walked out of her room, down the stairs, and outside, where the setting sun was turning everything red and purple.

The sound of the front door slamming shut confirmed it. I was alone in Nancy's room. In the house. In silence, not knowing what else to do, I cleaned the carpet and sheets. Got soap and water and hid all traces of our fight. I took a shower and winced when the hot water hit my puffy face.

It was well into the night when my sister returned. She calculated it so she could stay out as long as possible before getting back right before my parents returned from whatever random errand they were running.

"Chuy," she said from the door, soft-spoken. I dropped my guard as I realized there was no fire in her words. "That had to have been it, right? The last one?"

A strange feeling came over me. Warmth via embarrassment and relief. "Yeah, I think so."

"Good, 'cause I can't afford to get into it anymore like that. *Shit*. Where'd you learn to fight like that, little brother? You can throw a punch," she said, her hand wafting up to her face.

"I learned it from you," I said. Nancy laughed at this, which caused her to wince and inhale through her teeth. "Where did you go? I cleaned your room."

"Nowhere. Around. To go be pissed. I saw Becky and Maria. You know what I told them? I told them I got jumped by some of those bitches we've been getting into it with." Nancy smiled, which looked crooked from her fat lip. "That was ignorant of me because of course they got all mad. We ended up looking around for them for like an hour. They kept on asking me where I thought they were." Nancy said this with a hint of pride. Like I should be proud we had beaten each other up so bad that her friends thought a gang of her enemies jumped her.

———————

The next few months everything else dissipated. I didn't hang with my friends as much. Couldn't focus at school. I regard those months as the time when Nancy and I got to know each other. As equals. As, dare I say, friends. Would you believe me if I told you Nancy and I are the closest in our family now? How messy and complicated human nature is. For the longest time Nancy was my archnemesis, the one who caused me the most harm in the world. But all it took was one fight to change our relationship.

That's what I thought at the time at least. That I had gained my sister's respect. There was another thing that I bet led to our new relationship, though. In a sudden and jarring way, through horrific violence, I found out Nancy's secret. She was a senior in high school, pregnant, and running out of time. It was only a couple months before she would have to tell our parents. Looking back at it now, I can see that my sister needed someone in our house who at least *knew*.

In those few months of getting to know each other, Nancy schooled me on various subjects. She was my unofficial mentor. I imagine that knowing Nancy and I were now in cahoots must have terrified my mom. Nancy taught me how to sneak out of our second-story windows onto the roof of the front porch and down the porch columns to freedom. The shuffling of bedrooms had the opposite effect that my parents desired. My parents thought they would be able to hear people coming down the stairs and sneaking out. In actuality it made it easier for Nancy and me to sneak out. Nancy is the one who showed me it was possible.

In this time of getting to know each other, little things popped up that helped me see the way things were for my sister. All the little affronts to her based on the fact that she was a woman in our culture. Things that I had internalized but never thought about came into focus. Like our mother's expectations of how we should act. The fact that Nancy got into trouble for wanting and doing the same things I did with my friends. I started to notice how my mom would serve my brother and I food, like we were little princes. My mom would never serve Nancy and even told her she should work on getting everyone else food. You can imagine how my sister took that.

Nancy got me hip to her music and divulged her self-inflicted tattoos. Chief among them was a big X3 on her calf. The first time she showed me, she pulled out a lighter to sanitize the sewing needle, then dipped the needle in ink and, slowly and painfully, pricked her tattoo. Nancy showed me the ritual but left out the part about needing to use India ink for it to be permanent. I would blow out ink from pens around the house, which meant the ink would evaporate from my skin after a few months. Nancy did this to protect me from my own stupid impulses, because sure enough I tried to give myself some scratchers.

The worst two were direct results of my fascination with my older brother, Johnny. A direct result of the rummaging through my brother's things I did with Josh. The first was a rudimentary skull flipping someone the middle finger on my ankle. The backdrop was a pot leaf. Only I didn't know exactly how to draw a pot leaf and had never smoked anything in my life. Among the things Josh and I found in my brother's stuff was a huge broken bong. My brother had tucked it away behind a speaker in the corner of the garage. I aborted the tattoo on my ankle as I had run out of room on my "canvas" and the skull and leaf were converging into one ugly blob. Thank God Nancy left out that crucial India-ink ingredient from her demonstrations.

Other kids in West Liberty were doing what I was doing, emulating our older siblings and giving ourselves scratcher tattoos. Our junior high looked at it as an epidemic. There were all sorts of atrocious tattoos on kids who thought they were the baddest things in the world. It got so out of control that the school ushered us into the cafeteria for an emergency guest talk from a dermatologist who specialized in tattoo removal. She was there to tell us our tattoos were bad. Real bad. And we should wait until we were old enough to get them done by professionals.

I remember proudly showing Nancy the other most egregious tattoo. This one I had dotted on my forearm. It came from my brother's Jim Morrison biography that begat our obsession with *On the Road*. One of the lyrics old Jimmy says at the end of a song is "Stoned . . . Immaculate." He says it with such force and mysteriousness. I still don't know what it means, but by God it sounded cool, so I tatted it on my arm.

Nancy made no effort to hide her feelings. "Dude, what the fuck is that?" she asked. "You got to think about what you're putting on yourself, pendejo. Little brothers, I swear. What does that even mean?"

"It's from one of Johnny's CDs," I said while unrolling my sleeve.

"*More* white-boy shit? Why you trying so hard to be Johnny, anyway?" Nancy asked. Her question threw me off guard. I had never thought about it. She didn't let me answer. "I wouldn't want to get anything associated with that fool anyway. You think you got it bad from me, little brother? Johnny used to *fuck me up* when we were little."

Nancy continued talking. She switched gears to talk about music some more. I half listened. What was a throwaway factoid to my sister was a revelation to me.

I had always assumed that Johnny never hit Nancy. That he didn't torture her like she did me. It was because he was always so chill with me. I never thought about the fact that he was old enough that I wasn't a threat. It was a different story with his little sister. Johnny getting at Nancy completed the cycle. It was the missing link that made the trickling down of hits and fights make sense.

It reminds me of a recent conversation I had with a friend from West Liberty. This friend was younger than my friend group by a couple of grades. Back in the day this seemed like a huge age difference. But as you get older, you realize that four years is a drop in the bucket.

The conversation dealt with our older siblings hitting us. It's not true for every Mexican family but goddamn true for my family and my friend's family. The concept is this. When our immigrant parents came to America, they brought with them antiquated forms of punishment. It was the seventies and early eighties. A different time for parental punishment. So our parents would unleash on our older siblings. No doubt my parents and grandparents got at Johnny and Nancy. The memory of my grandma's slap was further proof.

But something happened in the transition to the eighties. Our parents began acclimating to this new world. And they also got older and frailer. They didn't have the fire they used to have when doling out punishment. So when I was growing up, my parents never once hit me. And I had watched enough TV to know that form of punishment was outdated. Danny Tanner never hit any of those girls on *Full House*, so I would have called out my parents if they did any worse.

But here's the rub. We weren't free from it. Because our older siblings had good memories and vendettas. They remembered how it was in the old days, and they made sure to give it to us if our parents didn't. Many times worse than what they got. Kids don't have the same impulse control.

My friend laid it out for me. "In a lot of ways our older siblings *abused* us. We abused each other. And our parents let it happen. Our culture and town and households let it happen."

I bristled when my friend told me this, the same way I bristle at the question of whether West Liberty is safe or not. There are words that have a charge to them. *Abuse. Trauma.* My friend was seeing a therapist to make sense of these words. I started making excuses for my family, town, and upbringing. I did that thing people do: compared the things we did to each other to more severe acts. I didn't have the stereotypical case of a father constantly beating his son with a belt. I didn't *feel* like what we did to each other was abuse. It was normal. It was childhood. "Just because it was normal doesn't mean it was right. Doesn't mean it didn't *fuck us up*."

After some time talking with my friend, after knee-jerk reactions and excuses, it clicked. I thought about when Nancy told me about our older brother. When I figured out how the loop closed on this phenomena of sibling cultural punishment. This loop of conflict permeates through many Mexican American families in the Midwest. In West Liberty. In a lot of ways we are still dealing with the emotional fallout.

But there's another thing mucking up the water. The other factor is the guilt we have in knowing our parents were trying the best with what they had. We suspect and hear rumblings of the struggles our parents withstood to get here. We hear stories about how West Liberty was so much rougher and more racist for our older siblings. So we internalize that guilt. Let it fester. We don't talk about the trauma. Because we don't feel it was as bad as what this new land forced the older generations through. We ignore it. Or let it disappear into our untold family histories.

That's what made my relationship with Nancy so different. The fact that we actually started to talk about that trauma. Our truce forced us to look at each other and cut off that cycle. Of course I didn't think about any of this stuff when Nancy was talking to me in those few months. I just knew that it felt good to talk to my sister. That she was interesting and badass and it was cool to hear her insights on how to be cool.

One day I answered the phone and was greeted by a voice I didn't recognize. "Hey. Hey, is this Chuy? Yo, is your sister there?"

"No, she's out. Who is this?" I answered.

"Tell her I called," the voice said.

"I don't even know who to tell her you are."

"Fine. Fine. Tell her it's Ruben and that I've been trying to get ahold of her."

And he clicked off. There was a brief moment of confusion. Ruben? Like my friend? But the voice on the other end was deep and husky. A man's voice. I told Nancy later that night.

"Oh my God, that idiot got my number, huh?" she said. It was a guy. *The* guy. We called him Big Ruben, to differentiate from my friend Ruben but also because they were planning on naming their child after him. Big Ruben's calls began increasing in frequency. He would only call when he was sure my mom wouldn't intercept.

My mom and sister's relationship was becoming even more strained. I started to cover for my sister as she snuck out her window. I would turn up the volume of my video games when she climbed down the bannister. I would tell my parents that the private number that called was a wrong number or one of my friends.

We didn't talk about the pregnancy. I didn't ask her any questions about it. I felt like it wasn't my place. And it seemed like too big of a subject for me to tackle. Nancy wore baggy enough clothes that it would take a while for anything to show. But we knew that sooner or later my mom would figure it out. That everything would hit the fan. I chose to ignore it with my sister. To talk about music and movies. To cruise the block as the reality of life weighed down on our family.

Everything changed one night when I heard the all-too-familiar sound of my sister on the roof. By this time Nancy would tell me when she was planning on sneaking out though. The fact that she hadn't said anything to me was out of the ordinary. I opened my window to the crisp spring air.

"Hey, what's up, what's going on?" I whispered, catching Nancy off guard. As soon as she turned around, I knew something was different. There was an intent in her eyes. She had made a decision.

"Chuy, I got to get the hell out of here, don't tell Mom," Nancy said in one breath. She never stopped making her way to the side of the roof.

"What's going on? Where you going?" I asked.

"Out. Look. Don't tell Mom. For real." It was a statement, but the look in her eyes was asking. Begging me to promise. One last act to solidify our friendship on the roof of our house.

"Okay. Okay, I won't."

As she scurried down the roof like we had both done so many times before, I knew this time was different. I convinced myself she would be back by five in the morning like all the other times. Back before my dad got up to get ready for work at West Liberty Foods. But when she wasn't back by the next afternoon, I wasn't surprised. When my parents figured out she was gone all night and wasn't returning the next evening, I wasn't surprised then either. She was gone. My sister had run away.

I started to worry after the third day. After my parents filed a police report. Guilt began to creep in about not telling my parents the truth. About not letting them know everything I knew. After a week the guilt turned to fear. Each night was an exercise in imagining what horrible things had happened to my sister out there. Nancy was tough, but she would have come back by now, right?

The aura of our house, brought on by my mother's sisters and friends, didn't help my emotional state. Every night would bring a different tía or woman from the town to console my mom. My Tía Nelle was around a lot, to talk my mom through her pain but also to get to the bottom of the things. After a few nights there developed this ragtag group of women hell-bent on finding intel on my sister. They would take turns calling leads they had acquired and putting boots to the ground when new info revealed itself. By the end of the second week, with no new information on my sister, things were dire. The guilt and fear racked my every action. If only I had told my parents about my sister leaving first thing that next morning. Would they have found her by now?

But the group of women in my house was steadfast. My mom and Tía Nelle worked methodically. They talked into the late hours of the night, trying to figure out what town my sister could be in. Watched hours of news channels for any pertinent info. It was my tía who broke the news that last Saturday night. She had gathered some key info from her daughter, my cousin Cynthia. She talked with the group in energetic Spanish. It was the same unbounded energy she displayed during our games of lotería, only there was nothing jovial or happy about it. She was on a mission to find her niece.

The group of women followed my mom and aunt as they filtered out of our kitchen on a new mission based on Cynthia's information about *some guy* in Columbus Junction. CJ was a nearby town like West Liberty, with a meat processing plant and an influx of Mexicans in the last few decades. My mom left my dad and me alone in our house. We were to wait in case we got any calls or, however unlikely, if Nancy were to return.

During this whole saga, any time Nancy's rebellion came up, my dad would let my mom deal with it. There was something about how emotional things could get. How charged and confrontational they were. My dad couldn't handle it. He would escape to the garage after half-heartedly trying to stop our fighting. It made sense that my mom, always the one who dealt with Nancy head-on, was the one to assemble the task force and look for her. Dad and I ate frozen meals from the microwave and waited until we passed out on a futon in the living room.

The next morning my mom returned with a sheepish Nancy. Cynthia's intel was sound. They found her in Columbus Junction. She told them everything. About her pregnancy. About how she was living with this guy. The guy. The baby daddy. My mom, faced with the real possibility she would lose her daughter, bent and negotiated a deal. It was a gambit. She told Nancy it would be better for her to be at home and have the support of her parents. She gritted her teeth—*and the guy could come too.* It's a common parental epiphany, the need to relinquish control and work with what you have.

Big Ruben moved in with us while Nancy's due date loomed, and for a while it kind of worked. My parents had a tenuous grasp of normalcy with their daughter. We all felt it, that we needed to stick together. Little Ruben was born in the spring of 1999. In the grand scheme of things,

Big Ruben was in our lives for a flash. Part of me suspects that my mom knew it would happen. That her gambit was a long con. I imagine part of the allure for Big Ruben was Nancy's rebellion. How she was working against her parental figures. That there was an authority figure to beat. I'm reminded of our hoodlumizing escapades. We all wanted to push back. But once his kid was born and he faced the life of familial status quo, Big Ruben balked. He was gone in an instant. But our family stood together, closer than before. And Nancy raised her child as a teenage mother.

———

I was getting prepared for high school the summer Little Ruben was born. My sister's birthday is three days before mine in July. I turned fourteen and she turned seventeen. I was starting my high school journey as a freshman while she was on track to completing it as a senior. My mom would take care of Little Ruben as we both went to school during the day. The fact that Nancy had a kid before she graduated high school was something of a trend in West Liberty, like the homemade tattoos that school officials noticed cropping up in junior high. They noted that there was a big upward swing in teenage pregnancies in my sister's grade. Almost all of them Mexican girls. In many people's eyes, she was a statistic. At no other time did this narrative creep up more than when I was in Mr. Carter's World Cultures class that fall.

Mr. Carter had dirty-blonde hair and old wire-rimmed glasses that conveyed a bookish appearance. But he also lifted weights and was an assistant football coach with tree trunks for arms. World Cultures was a politics class, but really it was a Mr. Carter class, meaning he brought up tough discussions he thought we should tackle head-on. He liked to play devil's advocate and moderate spirited discussions on topics that were bigger than us. On things like police brutality, abortion, and racism. We watched *Schindler's List* and discussed parallels to today's society.

One of the legends swirling around the school was that it was Mr. Carter who came upon a student who crashed at Bothell's Corner on Highway 6. He held the student in his arms while she passed away. I never knew if this was true or myth mixed with fact. It doesn't matter for the purposes of this story. What matters is *that* was the story we shared in hallways. We thought Mr. Carter was a good man. Tough and strong but fair.

Which made things all the more complicated when I walked into World Cultures class that day to find my sister and four other girls in desks at the front of class. The school bell chimed, signaling for us to take our seats. Mr. Carter walked up in front of my sister and the other girls. He commanded our attention without a word. I was smart enough to figure it out before he opened his mouth. My face grew hot with embarrassment. My stomach queasy.

He began. "Everyone, as you can no doubt gather, we have something a little different planned for you today. We are joined by these young ladies. Your fellow classmates. All of them seniors. All of them young mothers. Now, before we go on, we have to acknowledge something in this room." Mr. Carter looked over at me. The feeling in my stomach grew. I hated this attention. This embarrassment. "We have to acknowledge that it's a little strange that we have one of these ladies' younger brothers in attendance. Chuy, I imagine this might be a little awkward. Is this alright with you guys?" I nodded that it was okay. It felt like things were being done for me. Like I wasn't in control of my own actions. I was a spectator of the scene before me.

Mr. Carter looked at Nancy. That's the first time I noticed, really noticed, how shy and small my sister looked up there. She squeaked out a response. "It's okay with me. It's good he's here," she said. Seeing my sister in front of the class was further proof of something I've said earlier. Ask a thousand different people their story of West Liberty and you'll get a thousand different responses. This is true of how people recollect other people as well. We were vastly different things to different people. Would you believe that if you asked Nancy's high school teachers, they'd say she was the shyest person they knew? One of the nicknames her friends kicked around before they landed on Flaca was Shy Girl. I always scoffed at this name. She never was shy around me, I can tell you that much.

It threw me off guard. Everything about how she behaved toward me was out of sync with that shyness. Her abuse toward me as a child. Her larger-than-life nature while mentoring me. Her stubbornness in pushing against my family. My sister, for all the good and bad we put each other through, is a character deserving of a place in great literature.

She is complex and fierce and the kind of person I aspire to be. When I'm at my lowest, when I'm afraid, I turn to her attitude toward life for guidance.

That was all gone in that classroom. When the girls were in a fishbowl for us to gawk at. She looked small and unsure then, like she was waiting for someone to tell her what to do.

The feeling in my stomach turned into a knot as Mr. Carter began leading the girls through questions. The gist of the discussion was something like a cautionary tale. It wasn't completely that. It'd be a disservice to Mr. Carter to describe it that way. But he was playing devil's advocate, and part of that advocacy was putting these girls front and center so we *would learn something from them*. From their stories. The why and the how. The ways we could prevent this from happening to us as freshmen. "So. You didn't use protection?" Mr. Carter reiterated after another girl brought it up. I could feel myself sweating in my armpits. I was feeling queasy, like when I drink hot tea on an empty stomach. What kind of question was that? The girls answered solemnly one by one.

"No, I did. I did. I don't know if the condom broke or . . ." It was Nancy. She trailed off, lost in a thought. This was weird. Really fucking weird, to be hearing about things this way. I felt like I shouldn't be there. That none of us should be there. This wasn't fair. It wasn't our story to hear. Not in this way. My sister's broken and stilted answers fueled this feeling.

There was something this discussion was getting at that was eating at my insides. Something I couldn't articulate until well into my adulthood. I remember that feeling of helplessness. Of feeling something for my sister. I recognize it now. For that brief moment in class, I felt something for my sister that I never felt before or since. *I felt sorry for her.* That was it. The rub. She was a pawn in this cautionary tale. She was a statistic. Give me pissed-off Nancy. Give me Nancy fighting tooth and nail to get what's hers. Give me my sister who doesn't wince when inking herself with tattoos and who calls me out for how stupid mine are. Don't give me a statistic cowering in a hard plastic school chair.

Nancy struggled to articulate herself against another one of Mr. Carter's questions. One of her friends prodded her, trying to lighten the mood and open her up. "Come on, Shy Girl. Es todo Flaca."

Nancy wasn't able to find her footing and answer. The silence hung in the room before Mr. Carter switched gears. I thanked the Lord when

I saw that time was running out for our class. I could feel I had sweated through my shirt. The fabric stuck to my back as I adjusted.

"So. We're almost out of time. I wanted to give you ladies one last thing to say before we're out of here. Because we have lots of kids here who are going to be in similar situations. They'll face things that you all have faced. And I want to know what you have to say to them."

Some of my peers scooched their chairs, which sounded like thunder in the silence of the room. The girls didn't know exactly how to tackle Mr. Carter's open-ended question. "What I'm asking is, do you have any regrets? Nancy?" He started with her because he thought it'd be the easiest answer. I'm projecting. But how could he not have thought so? Everything about my sister's demeanor screamed regret. The way she held herself and couldn't find her footing. I wanted this to be over. To get up and out of that classroom.

"No," my sister said. Mr. Carter's classes glinted in the fluorescent light as he cocked his head to the side.

"None at all? After everything you've been through. From everything we've gathered so far it seems like things are tough for all of you."

"Yeah. It's tough. So?" Nancy said. I looked at the girls around her, who were shuffling in their seats like I had been before. One of the girls, Nancy's friend, the one who told her "Come on, Shy Girl," was smiling.

Nancy continued, and as she talked, something in her changed. She was doing that thing where your own words fuel your confidence. The words cascaded as she went.

"I don't regret nothing. I never will. Yeah, it's tough, so what? So am I. I'm tough. Look. Everyone here can judge me. Can think all sorts of things about me and what happened to me. But I don't regret shit," Nancy continued as Mr. Carter tried to take the floor. "You want to know something about me. I'm one of the most stubborn people you'll ever meet. And I won't regret nothing 'cause I know that will make you people happy. I know bitches want me to fail. So no, I won't regret anything. Not my son. Not my choices. Not ever. Ain't that right, little brother?"

Nancy's friends laughed when she finished her mini speech. It felt like the whole class turned to look at me. If this had been the beginning of the class, their stares would have mortified me. But the feeling in my stomach was gone, the checking of the ticking clock subsided. Before I could say anything, Mr. Carter diverted the conversation. He wanted to wrap things up on a different point. He asked another question to the girl next to Nancy.

I didn't see anyone else then. Only my sister. She looked at me and I at her. And there it was: an ever-so-slight nod at her little brother. The bell rang and everyone got up at once to return to their lives. To talk loudly and tell stories. To already forget about this lesson in a string of lessons thrown at us in high school. But before the buzz signaled to the class to get up, I saw my sister. And I nodded back.

PART THREE

LESSONS IN
B-BOYING

Chuy's Mix CD of Breaking Jams* and Other Misc. Stuff**

1. Alice DJ, "Better Off Alone"
2. Zombie Nation, "Kernkraft 400"
3. West Street Mob, "Break Dance—Electric Boogie"
4. Babe Ruth, "The Mexican"
5. Rufus Thomas, "Itch and Scratch"
6. Dennis Coffey, "Theme from *Black Belt Jones*"
7. The Jackson Sisters, "I Believe in Miracles"
8. The Mohawks, "The Champ"
9. A Tribe Called Quest, "Scenario"
10. DJ Shadow, "Organ Donor (Extended Overhaul)"
11. Bomfunk MC's, "Freestyler"
12. Jimmy Castor Bunch, "It's Just Begun"
13. Incredible Bongo Band, "Apache"
14. Parliament-Funkadelic, "Flashlight"
15. M.O.P., "Ante Up"

*Raving songs we started breaking to plus legit breaks + hip-hop and
 everything in between
**Party Shack jams, etc.

I KNEW WHAT I HAD DO before she even hung up the phone. My first real girlfriend was breaking up with me. *She* wasn't even breaking up with me. She had gotten a friend to call me and break up with me *for her*. How pathetic was that? When I clicked off my house's cordless phone, I clicked it right back on and called Jerry Sayabeth. It was time. I was ready.

"Jerry? It's me. Yo, you still got that *Battle of the Year '97* tape you guys were watching? Could I borrow it? Like come over right now and grab it from you? Yeah like *right now* right now. Okay, I'll be over."

That was it. That's when I started breaking. That's when I flipped the switch and began a twenty-year career in dance. That's when I made the first step of the journey away from the wall where I would watch the Laotians dancing at the mobile court toward that self-guided path to identifying as a b-boy.

It was 1999 and a lonely summer was ending. I had turned fourteen years old at the end of July. Going to Jerry's that day was a last-ditch desperate attempt to figure out what the heck I was doing with my young life. Things had been getting worse and worse since Ruben and I had a fight to end all fights at the beginning of summer. Since I had started running with a new group of friends, friends who were causing more destruction than the gang at the Shack ever did. Since I started shunning them and got a girlfriend. I tried to pour everything into her until she had her friend call me on the phone to say, "She just thinks it would be better if you guys were friends." I later learned that my now-ex was listening on the other line for my reaction.

My world was crumbling around me. I needed to act, and that *Battle of the Year* VHS tape was my lighthouse in the fog. It bellowed for me in the mist, emanating from Jerry's VCR player. I booked it from my house to make the trek across town to the mobile court.

Walking in a small town in the encroaching dusk is a spiritual experience. It fills your mind with wonder. Floods it with thoughts and insight in the solitude. More than anywhere else or any other time, I am most like myself walking in the twilight of my hometown.

Before I knew it, as if I had stepped outside my house and directly onto the front porch of Jerry's mobile home, I was there. I knocked on the door while slipping off my shoes, adding them to the ever-present pile of shoes at the entrance to their home. Jerry's mom popped open the door before I could count the pairs.

"Aw, good. You eat too. Come, come," Jerry's mom said while ushering me inside. Jerry's parents never said hello but always welcomed me into their home. His mom pulled me into the kitchen and thrust a plate into my hands. Before I knew it, my plate accumulated fried fish, a baggie of sticky rice, and sauce to go with the sticky rice. I thought it strange that the sauce smelled fishier than the actual fish. I thanked Jerry's mom and nodded at the dad of the household.

I found Jerry tucked away in the corner of his room at his new computer. That was a thing. That was *the* thing back then. This was around the time when computers were finally accessible to poorer folks like us. It felt like how you imagine families felt in the fifties, when they would crowd around the unveiling of a television. Our families could afford these big boxy Compaq or Dell computers. These off-white heavy machines were our access to a world outside West Liberty.

"Long time, no see!" Jerry said, craning his neck from his computer screen and back.

He was right. I hadn't seen Jerry much since my fallout with Ruben. Out of all my old friends, he was the only one I kept in touch with, but it was only sporadically, and mostly over our shared interest in dance. Over his shoulder the fuzzy monitor shone back at me, displaying a rudimentary logo my friend was working on. He was nudging an *M* so it fit above a *W* in MS Paint. "I think that's it. That's the one. The official Midwest Breakaz logo," Jerry said while he admired his work.

I let out a low whistle as I unwrapped the baggie of sticky rice on my plate. "That looks sweet," I said after my first bite of rice. Jerry nodded. The Midwest Breakaz was the name the Laotians had given their breaking crew.

"Bro!" Jerry said with exaggerated gusto as he noticed me eating. "How many times I gotta tell you. You can't be just eating the sticky rice by itself. It's weird. At least eat it with the jeow! That's what it's there for." He was talking about the sauce nestled between the rice and fish, but it was too late.

I gulped down a mouthful of rice before smiling back. "I can't help it. It's too good on its own."

Jerry rolled his eyes and got back to the Midwest Breakaz logo. It happened in a flash, how all the Laotians in West Liberty got into break-dancing, as they called it. All of a sudden they knew how to do these incredible spins and flips. They learned the moves the way other trends and fads and cultures managed to find their way to our small town—through cousins on the coast. Jack and Randy Lovan were the best of the group, and they learned from their cousins out in California. They would go on summer vacations and soak up as much knowledge as they could, then come back to town and teach all the other Asians. They would practice their moves in their yards at the trailer court or in the carpeted basements of their uncles' houses.

"Anyways, this is what you wanted, right? *Battle of the Year '97*, boy! Be sure you make it all the way to the end for the battles. That's when things get real crazy."

I exchanged the plate of uneaten food for the tape, cradling it in my palms like it was a vessel of pure energy.

"So that's it? You're gonna start breaking?" Jerry asked.

"Yeah. I'm going to run home, watch this for inspiration, and start right after."

"Okay, okay, that sounds like a plan," Jerry said, ripping off a piece of fish on the plate with his fingers. "Why all of a sudden now though?"

I told him all the gory details of how Cheryl had her friend April break up with me over the phone. April lived in the mobile home next to Jerry. At this bombshell he got up and peeked through his blinds as if to check that they weren't currently plotting against us.

Jerry got it after I finished telling him the story. He had a first-row seat to all the drama with our old friend group, knew how much I was

Jerry Sayabeth acting a fool at the mobile courts.

twisting in the wind without them. "This will be good for you, man. Breakdancing is the shit. You get a move and you feel like you're the king of the world. You should get going so you can get some good practice in."

I thanked Jerry for the tape and got up to leave. There was something bubbling out of me though, something I couldn't help but ask. "What are your plans for tonight?"

It was a cool Saturday night in the middle of summer. The races would soon be roaring. A perfect night for hanging out at the Shack. Jerry took a second to gather a response. "You know. The same ole, same ole."

"Gotcha," I said before giving the Midwest Breakaz logo one last glance.

The words came out of Jerry in soft, rapid succession, like they were too real and precious for him to speak in a regular cadence: "You know, Ruben's been asking about you. We all have, man. We miss you. He's sorry. You should come hang with us sometime when you're not breaking."

It was the last thing I wanted to hear. I had already made one life-altering decision in getting this tape. Forgiveness and reconciliation were too much to pile on top of that.

"Yeah. I should sometime," I said before giving Jerry dap and peacing out. Jerry's mom smiled at me while the men held their poses at the table.

After putting my shoes on, I started to run home. It was like I was sprinting in a race with the VHS tape as my baton. I was trying to outrun the last things Jerry said, about Ruben being sorry. I didn't care if he was sorry. I wasn't ready to forgive him. Or to say sorry myself. I ran so fast it felt like my lungs would burst. It was getting to be nighttime and my feet were a blur in the fading light. I gasped for breath, doubled over on my front porch. No time to rest too much. I fought through the sting in my throat and went inside to my room.

Soon the old *Battle of the Year '97* tape was playing on my television. All its past owners had played and replayed the tape many times and the footage was fuzzy as a result. It didn't matter. The garbled footage had my full attention. Battle of the Year is a breaking event held in Germany every year. The event invites breaking crews from all over the world to perform showcases. A panel of judges picks the top four crews to compete against each other for first and second place. The tape was a two-hour document of the best showcases and those top battles. I sat and watched the entire tape, showcase after showcase, battle after battle. I noted the different styles of the groups from Europe compared with those from Africa or Japan. I rewound particularly impressive moves and freezes, which most of them were to me.

In a simplistic way, you can break down breaking into two camps: the power heads and the style heads. Power is what most people think of when they think of breaking. It's the spinning moves—headspins and windmills. The moves flashed in music videos. The stuff most impressive to people who don't know anything about the dance. The Laotians in the trailer park dedicated their training almost exclusively to power moves. A lot of times they would take off their shoes and practice their power moves in socks to make it easier.

In contrast is style. Practitioners of style concern themselves with footwork and musicality. The best way to describe footwork is staccato movement low to the ground. It's when you're stepping around on the floor on your hands and feet. Good footworkers take traditional steps like the six-step and Russian taps and piece them together in creative ways. Of course, categorizing breaking into these two camps is an oversimplification. A good all-around breaker takes elements of everything, transitioning from power moves to freezes to footwork as a complete package. That's not even to get into the discussion of power heads who are able to do their power moves in creative and stylistic ways.

The majority of crews on the *Battle of the Year* tape concerned themselves with power. In the early to mid-nineties there was a wane in the breaking scene stateside. I'm careful not to say that it died in America. There were still very active scenes on the coasts and in bigger midwestern cities like Chicago. But that huge explosion of dancers in the eighties, the one that infiltrated the suburbs and small towns, had dissipated. Before the Asians started trying swipes and headspins in town, I had never seen anyone move like that in person. But while the dance faded in the American consciousness, it picked up steam around the world. The mid-nineties saw a surge of dancers everywhere from France, Russia, and the Netherlands to Japan, South Korea, and China. The worldwide representation was immediately clear in the diversity of crews on the tape. But for the most part they danced alike, with that power focus. At the time I, of course, had no clue about the intricacies of power versus style. All I knew was that everything changed when the sole U.S. crew started to dance: Style Elements.

Style Elements. They deserve their own paragraph in this book. For their impact on the worldwide dance scene. For their impact on me. It was immediately clear that they were different. True to their name, they had *style*. They were unique and creative. All the other crews danced to the same type of funk or electro beats. Style Elements started their showcase to the sounds of machine-gun fire and warfare. They pantomimed being soldiers, crawling on their bellies to get to their marks on the floor. This was weird and different. It was theatrical. From there they took turns dancing to the soft guitar opening of Metallica's "Enter Sandman." I watched the rest of their showcase in silence. They were light-years ahead of anyone else sharing that stage. Their movement was more complicated and bombastic. Style Elements got best showcase and won their battle for first place. It was no contest. While watching I felt a weird sense of pride that these American dancers went to Germany and stood out against the rest of the world. I felt this connection and representation. Style Elements hailed from Southern California, and even though I was so removed from them, I felt connected. It was the first time I felt something like patriotism. I smiled at this thought while I grabbed a sweater.

There was nothing left to do. I *had* to try something. There was too much inspiration and energy pulsing through my body. By then it was well into the night. I walked outside into the now cool summer air. A flat spot in the backyard by our old swing set made an adequate spot to try my moves.

My "moves." Despite all my watching of the Midwest Breakaz across town, I hadn't done any dancing of my own. I had no moves to try. I did what I could think of. I flopped around in the silence of the backyard. No handstand or cartwheel was safe. I revisited all manner of basic somersaults and elementary school tumbling maneuvers. I could smell the grass stains accumulating on my sweater. Every once in a while I would need to wipe the dew off my hands.

I imagine it must have looked a sight, this boy trying to walk on his hands and spin on his back in the grass in the dead of the night. I didn't care. This exciting feeling filled my lungs. Filled my every breath. I fell out of a particularly daring maneuver, landing on my back in the soft yard. The night sky loomed overhead as I sprawled on my back, my arms outstretched toward the heavens. Our town was small and insignificant enough that there wasn't enough light pollution to dilute the radiance of the stars. My breath labored as my chest rose and fell in time with my exhalations. The air was cool but humid, a combination that made clouds of breath materialize every time I exhaled. Each inhalation stung as I got back onto my feet. It didn't matter. Nothing else mattered. I got up and kept trying every move I could think of. I haven't stopped since.

I know, I know. We've got to talk about it. The deal with Ruben. I've been delaying it, trying to shut it out and preoccupy myself with other things. But if we're going to talk about why I started breaking, we've got to talk about the state of my friend group at the time. It also means diving into the topic of development in teenage boys. I've already talked about how we started drinking by this age. The other factor was hormones. Ah, yes. I'm talking about how we started to catch up with Eric and his many girlfriends, trysts, and dalliances.

One day at the Kimberly Park pool, our friend Veronica noted an unfamiliar white girl checking us out. Veronica had long black hair that she wore in double Dutch braids. She was Mexican like Ruben, Eric, and me, but went to a different church than us. She went to a blue shed by Wapsi Creek Park called the Independent Pentecostal Christian Church. Sometimes Eric would make fun of her church, saying, "What you guys do in that blue shed, talk to snakes and speak in tongues?" Thing is, Vero could give it as bad as we could. If Eric would get at her too much, she'd make fun of his height or talk about the latest gossip to cut him down. In many ways she was the communications person between the girls and guys in our grade, which she could weaponize whenever she wanted. Veronica felt like the leader of the group of girls we hung out with, like how Ruben was the leader of ours.

Something else about Veronica both connected her to our friend group and put her off-limits from it. She was the youngest sister of the legendary Galvan boys. The Galvans who ruled the school with our older brothers. Arnie Galvan was Ruben's wrestling and life mentor. The veiled threat of a pounding by Arnie scared us away from pursuing anything with his little sister.

Arnie and the other older guys who mentored Ruben were around a lot back then. As he grew into a teenager, they saw more and more that he could be an elite athlete. The little brother they never had. I felt like sometimes they were judging us, Ruben's dorky, less athletic friends. I could imagine that was why Ruben kept pushing and pressuring us to be better. To do crazier stuff. He was passing on those expectations from them to us.

I didn't talk to the girl at the pool that Vero pointed out. I wanted to keep going off the diving board and goofing off with my friends. But Ruben jumped at the chance. He found out her name was Samantha and she was from West Branch, our official town rival. Samantha liked to swim and would get dropped off at West Liberty to go to the pool in the summer. (Remember, ours was the only small town in the area that had both a pool and movie theater, which meant lots of cross-town visitors in the summer.) Ruben jumped at the chance to holler at a girl from outside our friend circles.

Even though none of us were old enough to have a learner's permit, we would "borrow" our parents' cars and drive them around town. We started driving to Samantha's country house on the outskirts of West Branch, hanging out with her and her friends. As you can imagine, this did not sit well with the West Branch guys who got wind of our excursions.

One fateful night Eric, Zane, and I were at my house, bored, waiting on word from Ruben on what we'd be doing, when the house phone rang. It was Ruben, panicked. He rushed into a call to arms after I got out a "Hello?"

"Yo, Chuy. You need to get over here. These guys are fucking pissed. They're saying they can't take it no more. They're after me. Come quick!"

"Whoa, whoa. Hold up. Who's after you? Where you at?" I asked, snapping my fingers at Eric and Zane to get their attention.

"I'm at West Branch. Get over here!"

Eric, Zane, and I took the cordless phone and piled into my dad's Nissan Pathfinder. A strange feeling came over me. As I tried to get the exact location, Ruben wouldn't give it to me.

Ruben's voice rose on the phone. "Just get over to West Branch! They're after me. Can I count on you?"

That was it. The question. Can I count on you? Something felt weird about this. Then Ruben hung up. I looked over at Eric and Zane.

Eric pleaded in the silence, "We gotta go help him, right?"

"But where do we go? He wouldn't tell us," Zane answered. With thoughts of a mob of angry West Branch boys jumping my best friend, I shut off the car.

"If we don't know where he is, we can't help him. We got to wait to see if he'll call back." Eric and Zane didn't protest as we got out of the car. Not knowing what else to do and without Ruben telling us what to do, we were at a loss. We ended up walking across town to Ruben's in the night. The entire walk I tried to fight that feeling creeping up. That strong suspicion that Ruben had made it all up. That this was another one of his tests to see how down and loyal we were. I tried to suppress this line of thinking; my internal monologue was in a shouting match with itself. I didn't tell Eric and Zane my suspicion as we made our way to the Shack and waited for any sign of our friend.

The roar of Ruben's parents' station wagon signaled his return. Before Ruben said anything to us, I could tell he was beyond pissed. Eric tried to ask him if he was okay, but he wasn't having any of that. He yelled and the sound of his voice echoed across the gravel alley behind the garage.

"Nah! Nope. Don't even try to come up to me and say anything. Your true fucking colors show. I can't count on you for anything. Some friends you guys are! It's pathetic. Won't even come when I'm telling you I'm in danger . . ."

As he talked, something in me snapped. Something that had been building for a long time, a resentment and an anger. I was sick of being pushed and tested, over and over, to fit what it meant to be a man in the eyes of the older kids in town. I unloaded. Screamed and got in Ruben's face. I shouted my grievances laced with profanities. This was it. The end of us.

It wasn't enough for Ruben and I to meet outside the Shack, to admit we hurt each other and show vulnerability. We thought we had to do it through a meltdown. "That's it. I'm done. Done with you and your constant need to see if we're down or not. We were there, fool! We were in the car and out the stupid fucking door. We'd follow you to the ends of the earth. *If* you would have told us where you were at. But you wouldn't! 'Cause it wasn't about that, was it, Ruben? I'm tired of all this shit. I'm done. We're done."

I drifted away from the rest of the gang. Aimless and lonely going into my freshman year, I sought another outlet or group of people to connect with. Enter Aaron and Justin, two white kids in my class who befriended me. The worst influences a kid could ask for.

———————

Aaron and Justin were both blond-haired, blue-eyed kids who lived in the country outside of West Liberty. After school I'd join them as they went to hang in a house of miscreants by the high school. We'd mill around as Aaron's and Justin's older brothers and their friends smoked weed and talked shit about their teachers. They were all either seniors in high school or recently graduated with nothing better to do. They were a group of rough, poor white guys with time to kill and younger brothers to make impressions on.

If we weren't hanging out at the riffraff house by the school, we were spending time at Aaron's house in the country. Aaron's family were victims of one of West Liberty's great tragedies. A couple of years before I started to hang out with him, his dad killed his mom and committed suicide afterward. This isn't the only horrific murder in the town's history. In fact, it's not even the West Liberty murder that warranted a two-hour episode of NBC's *Dateline*. That episode was about a cold case in '92 where somebody bludgeoned a guy in his house.

No, Aaron's parents' case was open and shut, a tragic footnote in our town's history. Aaron never talked about it and I never asked him about it. One time a girl messed up and called him a son of a bitch and he shut down. We all understood she didn't mean it like that, but we got why Aaron would react the way he did, too.

When I say we spent time at Aaron's house, I should say we spent time at Aaron's grandma's house. After the incident with his parents, his grandma took care of Aaron and his older brother. Their grandpa had passed when they were young, so it was their grandma with all the weight of their tragic backstory on her shoulders.

She was the sweetest lady. Warm and unsuspecting of the shit her grandsons got into. Aaron, Justin, and I were angry and looking for something to do. One question best sets up the destruction we wrought. Aaron and Justin had heard legends of our hoodlumizing escapades at the Shack. Our mailbox feud with the woodshop. Our clandestine drinking sessions with our parents' alcohol. One night after I talked about some of the things we did, Aaron asked, "Well, what's the worst thing you guys ever did?"

I didn't have to think long. "I guess it'd be the time that we shot out the window of this van. I mean, Ruben shot it out while we watched him do it."

Aaron's smile revealed deep dimples in his rosy cheeks. "Oh, we can do way worse than that!"

And we did. Aaron and Justin would spend the night at my place and we'd terrorize West Liberty. Or we'd stay at Justin's place in the nearby tiny town of Atalissa and go to work there. We took Ruben's shooting out the van window as the initial bet. Our subsequent actions were us raising the stakes.

We took bats and smashed *all* the windows of targeted cars at night. Slashed tires. Pissed on the door handles of the cars we didn't destroy. It was all a different feel from the hoodlumizing days with the old gang. I can look back at most of those excursions at the Shack with a hint of whimsy. With a bit of romanticism. Yeah, we messed with that woodshop guy proper, but we weren't trying to hurt anybody. With Aaron and Justin, it was senseless. It wasn't about a sense of adventure but rather this dull, angry cynicism. We'd have Aaron's sweet old grandma take us to Walmart or Target. While she shopped, we'd go to the watch and jewelry section. I'd go up and browse one section, and while eyes were on

In all our baggy pant, Starter jacket glory.

the brown kid, the two all-American white kids would be snatching as many watches as they could fit in their Starter jackets. We accumulated thousands of dollars in stolen goods.

This racial bait and switch gets at an interesting side of my relationship with Aaron and Justin. Hanging with them and their brothers in the house by the school was a unique experience because it was the first time I was the minority in West Liberty. They were all white. I had never felt that before in town. Not at the bailes at the community center or even hanging with the Laotians in the trailer park. We were all variations of brown. It was weird being the token Mexican among these rough white kids. Aaron and Justin fed into that. They exoticized me and my stories about the Shack. This relationship fueled our vandalizing and one-upping of my past deeds. The irony is not lost on me, that

I separated myself from Ruben because of his need to push us closer to the edge only to have these guys and their tokenism shove me off into the abyss.

One day we scoured Aaron's older brother's bedroom. He had old car magazines and gore-filled comic books that we would take turns gawking at. A Trapper Keeper filled with printed-out pictures caught me off guard. Aaron's brother had printed them on those old graph papers with the margins you'd have to tear off. There were White Zombie and Marilyn Manson logos. But I hid my emotion when I came across a small run of Nazi imagery. There were cherub-proportioned Klansmen drawn in this rounded cutesy style, heiling Hitler in front of swastika-adorned banners.

Aaron spoke before I could say anything. "He's fucking dumb. I keep on telling him that white power shit is stupid." I stuffed the pile of papers back into the Trapper Keeper. I didn't know how to take the images. Or what they meant about how my new friends' older brothers felt toward me. Tokenism aside, Aaron and Justin genuinely liked me. But I knew deep down that there was something toxic about my relationship with them. That together we were worse than the sum of our parts. I wish I could say that after I saw those pictures I made a fuss. That I did something like gave Aaron an ultimatum to renounce his brother and those fucked-up drawings. But I didn't. I was a lonely, confused kid who needed something to hang onto. If I had to put those drawings back in the Trapper Keeper and pretend I never saw them, that's what I had to do. It would take something bigger to get me to distance myself from this path.

I suspect that breaking saved my life, that it saved me from my own worst impulses, from the path of destruction and loneliness I was going down. It provided an identity and an alternative to all the other endeavors in town that didn't quite speak to me anymore: drinking, football, vandalism. They all drifted away when I started to break.

At first I practiced in secret. No one knew I was practicing rudimentary tumbling in my backyard. Only my Tía Nelle saw what I was doing. I imagine she thought I was crazy, trying front handsprings and somersaults in our backyard for hours at a time. It didn't look any crazier than

A lost kid right before I started to break.

all the times I'd fight imaginary Putty Patrollers from *Power Rangers*, though, so she left me to it.

Around this time, my dad surprised the family with a big box from Walmart. In a fit of keeping up with the Joneses, he'd impulse-bought the family a computer. The first thing I did was look up dance moves I could try. I had exhausted the list of tumbling moves your average kid can do on the playground. It was time to actually try some bona fide breaking moves. Ask Jeeves and MSN Search were my access points to knowledge I was too afraid to ask of the Asians. My search queries revealed an avalanche of resources. Websites with GIFs of faceless avatars going through the positions of the six-step. Message boards and chat rooms of kids like me asking what the secret to flares was. If I had the time and patience, I could try to download QuickTime movies of particularly impressive dancers.

In my initial deep dives on the web, I came up with two bits of information to whet my newbie appetite. The first was a tutorial on how to do moves called Nikes and L-kicks. They were variations on the same move, a freeze you did in a one-handed handstand. The difference was in the position of your legs. An L-kick is self-explanatory: go up on one hand and make a ninety-degree angle with your legs. A Nike is an L-kick except while upside down you curl one of your legs to emulate the iconic Nike Swoosh. As far as freezes go, both of these are basic. But they're rite-of-passage beginner moves. Daring enough to separate kids who are afraid to be upside down on one hand. I psyched myself up a few times before attempting my first proper L-kick, only to chicken out and bail the first dozen (or two) times. But after a few days of practice, I could nail L-kicks and Nikes on either hand. I hadn't seen any of the guys in the trailer park pull that off.

The other bit of information I found was an article written by an OG dancer about how it was in poor taste to refer to yourself as a "break-dancer." The way he worded it, the original dancers in the seventies used to call themselves "b-boys" and "b-girls." It wasn't until the breaking explosion in the eighties when the media labeled it as "breakdancing." This term became associated with the exploitation and shunning of the dance by the mainstream media. As a fourteen-year-old newbie, this blew my mind. It was like a litmus test to see if you were actually down for the cause. From then on out I'd correct anyone who misspoke and said the cursed term. "No, no, no. *Actually*, you should call me a 'b-boy,'" I would tell them with a certain air of smugness. "Instead of saying they're breakdancing, you can say they're b-boying and b-girling," I'd add. Which is counterintuitive and unnecessarily gendered, but I didn't care. I was part of this inside club. Connected to other breakers across the world who gave a shit about what word you used to call yourself. It meant something.

I took this new sense of pride and my L-kick variations across town to Jerry's house. Jerry bought a slab of linoleum and rolled it out in the yard between his and April's mobile homes. As I walked up on the yard, Randy and Jack were taking turns seeing who could do the most flares in a row. Randy and Jack were cousins but had different body types. Randy was squat like a wrestler while Jack was tall and sinewy. The rest of the group—Tim, Jerry, Da, and Larry—circled around the linoleum slab and chanted out the number of flares each person hit.

The flare was born out of the pommel horse in gymnastics. Your legs swing in wide circles in front of and behind your body, the entire trajectory of the move done with only your hands touching the ground. Both Randy and Jack would peter out and drag their feet on the ground at around three or four flares. I joined the sidelines as Randy rubbed his hands together for one final try at his personal best. He wound up and busted out six clean flares. We all screamed out "Four! Five! Six!" as he let the momentum of his body go and spun on his back to a stop. We jumped up and down and congratulated Randy.

After that the circle opened up. Da, being the leader of the group, would call out the next person to go out into the circle and try out a move. In the past he would shoot me a smile and say, "Chuy, you gonna bust it out or watch the whole time?" I'd put my hands up like I was apologizing and mutter that I couldn't do anything. This time I steeled myself for the inevitable callout. "Chuy, can you follow up those flares?" Da said while patting Randy on the back.

The music from Jerry's boom box in the grass came out tinny and distorted. The bloops and bleeps of Alice DJ's "Better Off Alone" spun on a burned CD. It provided the perfect backdrop for the moment. The Asians loved dancing to "Better Off Alone." It was like their soundtrack. It was either that or nondescript techno music. I would beg Jerry to burn these songs onto mix CDs because I didn't know the names to download them from Napster. The ratio of nameless techno songs to "Better Off Alone" was like two to one—all roads led back to Alice DJ.

I took a deep breath and shuffled out into the middle of the floor. I tried my best to emulate the toprock of the other guys. Toprock is the upright dance that's all shuffles and steps. Back then we believed it was an afterthought. The thing you rushed through before you got down to the *real* breaking, the stuff low to the ground and acrobatic. I rode the beat for a couple of seconds while Da said, "Oh shit, Chuy's actually getting down!"

The other guys noticed and started clapping along to the beat, chanting out a "Hey!" on every snare of the music. I said a little prayer that my L-kicks would find themselves sturdy. *Please Lord, let me not crash like the hundreds of times I did in my backyard.* I did a little spin to add some style to the approach and went up on my right hand. After my first L-kick, I got up and immediately switched to the other hand for a Nike. Then it happened. Time stopped. My hips stacked up over my shoulders and I froze in place. A bird's wings flapped in ultra slow motion.

It felt like an eternity, the time I spent suspended upside down on one hand. In reality it was something like two and a half Mississippis. But it didn't matter. The group *exploded* at my sticking of the freeze, yelling and running around. It almost felt like they were going to hoist me on their shoulders.

Afterward, when the rest of guys left and it was only Jerry and me, we talked while stretching on his linoleum. "Hey, that was a pretty dope freeze, Chuy. You've been practicing! You should hit up Danny. He's pretty close to your house and he's been dancing by himself too."

Danny Hoang was another Laotian in town, but he lived about three blocks from my house. Danny was an interesting case study. He was lighter skinned with dark black hair in a fierce bowl cut. Kind of like the way I didn't quite feel at home in my friend group, he didn't belong to the rest of the Laotians. Part of it was that he didn't live in the trailer court. Another part was that he was quieter and more introspective than the other guys.

I approached Danny in the hallways of our high school. We were all freshmen and the lockers seemed made for kids twice our size, towering over us as we navigated the halls. "Hey Danny, I heard you started breaking? I did too, we should practice together," I said while we shuffled off, trying to find our next classes.

Danny mumbled, especially when something took him off guard. He managed out, "Oh? Oh yeah, I heard you started up too. Yeah, I'm down. Where've you been practicing?"

My backyard setup wasn't adequate for real dance sessions. "I've been messing around in my yard, but my dad doesn't have any extra cars in the garage right now. We could practice there."

Danny agreed to my proposition and we walked to my house after school. In talking to Danny I found out we had a lot more in common than I realized. We both had older sisters who were cooler in social status than us. We both liked the same video games and cartoons. He was geeky like how I was geeky. And that disconnect we felt from our friend groups extended to our families and cultures. He couldn't speak Lao with his parents like I couldn't speak Spanish. We were both stuck in the middle of all these different cultures: our families, our friends, our town. Everything was pulling for our attention and embrace. But it was the dance that most connected us. We formed an alliance and began to practice together after school every chance we got. My previous friend groups faded away. Aaron, Justin, and I became acquaintances, merely greeting each other in the school hallways. There wasn't enough time and attention to give my old friend groups. Breaking was all that mattered. Well, that wasn't totally true. I was happy to move on from the shenanigans that I got into with Aaron and Justin, but I still very much missed Ruben and the guys. But breaking helped fill that void, so I practiced as much as I could.

We spent hours practicing in my garage on cardboard we hobbled together. We practiced moves with names like coffee grinders, apple jacks, broncos, and electric crabs. We helped each other with the dynamics and mechanics of foundational moves we read about online. Danny, being closer to the mobile-court Asians, was better tapped into the music they listened to. He brought over mix CDs with songs like "Kernkraft 400" by Zombie Nation. I managed to get my hand on a bargain-bin CD of "breakdance jams." These were old electro songs from the eighties with a few funk tunes peppered throughout. One of the intros burned into my head, from the song "Break Dance—Electric Boogie" by West Street Mob. It goes, "Y'say a one for the trouble, two for the time, a c'mon, y'all, let's breakdance!" The word "breakdance" was in this robotic synthesized voice we loved to emulate.

In our practice sessions it became clear that Danny was the better b-boy. We had similar builds and heights, with roughly the same amount of athleticism. But it was how quick Danny got movements that set him apart. He had this ability to watch a move and recreate it with ease. His movement vocabulary expanded with each practice. In contrast, I was a slow learner. It would take me three or four days to learn the same moves Danny learned in an hour—if I ever got those moves at all. While Danny hit his freezes with authority, mine were sloppy and subpar in technique. But that was the beautiful thing about breaking. It didn't matter. While Danny was a good-at-everything generalist, I was *really* good at the actual dancing aspect of it all. My toprock, that part of the dance we thought was a preamble to the "good stuff," became intricate and stylistically complex. I had *style*. I attribute this to my obsession with the American crew in that *Battle of the Year '97* tape I still watched. I found clips of Style Elements online and took their movements as gospel. If I couldn't be as clean and consistent as Danny and the other Laotians in town, I could be a creative counterpoint.

Practicing my moves on the cardboard in my garage.

Danny and I were a good duo and we made it official. If we couldn't be in the Midwest Breakaz, we could make our own crew, as partners. One day Danny was perfecting his windmill. We thought of the name after Danny got up dizzy from the move: Dizzy D. Okay, okay. But if Danny got a *D* name, what could work for me? I thought about my newfound obsession with musicality and style and came up with the idea of being "jazzy." That was it! I could be Jazzy J. *J* for my actual first name of Jesus. No one ever calls me Jesus, not even my parents. To this day I insist everyone call me Chuy. But the allure of the alliteration to match Danny's name was too strong. We trained with a new intent, proud of our fresh new identifying monikers. Jazzy J and Dizzy D were the new kids on the scene.

Our individual styles solidified as we got more comfortable in our dance practice. While that happened, our bodies accumulated bumps and bruises. Besides the obvious injuries, there was inevitable wear and tear. By-products of moving in this new way. Occupational hazards that came with the dance. We both developed gnarly callouses from dancing along our palms doing footwork. I had to call practice early one time because my callouses had ripped and bled from dancing so much. We'd get bruises and floor burns in the strangest of places on our bodies. Along our elbows when we were practicing forearm freezes. Peppered across our shoulders when we practiced windmills and coin drops into backspins. Later in life, I would watch a documentary with b-boy Crazy Legs that describes these very injuries. He said, "We call them b-boy burns!" I always felt pride that we developed these very same burns in our garage sessions. These markings on our bodies were signifiers of our trade. The way you can tell a bicyclist by the size of their calves or a powerlifter by the scabs on their shins from the barbell scraping flesh. You can tell a breaker if you look hard enough at their shoulders and palms after practice.

One signifier is what we call "the breaker bald spot." I have one, as do countless other breakers across the world. It's what happens to a dancer's head when they do enough headspins, head glides, or any other number of moves performed on one's noggin. You develop a callous and bald spot on your head. I've seen dudes in their twenties with otherwise full heads of hair and a racing stripe of baldness down the middle. The bald spot isn't even the worst part. The worst part is the flaking and shedding of your scalp as you develop the bald spot. It's like super dandruff, big pieces of skin that look like mini Frosted Flakes.

One practice I relayed the horror of finding these flakes during school while talking to a cute girl. Danny laughed hard at this. His face crimsoned. "That's too funny," he said while shaking out his wrists. "You have to collect somebody's real dandruff to show her that yours is different." We both smiled at the absurdity of this.

It was nice to chat with Danny. He had a reputation for being serious and stoic at school. Truth is, I did too—I could be downright shy in class. So it was a relief when we let our guards down and warmed up to each other in my garage. Those were good times with a friend. It wasn't all jokes and stories, though; we were there to train alongside each other. To push each other to get better. There were practices where hours would go by and we'd be so focused we wouldn't say a word to one another. There was an understanding that we didn't need to talk. That our dance and progression could do the communicating for us. We'd make gestures when someone was close to getting a move or whoop out encouragement when we finally got said moves. Those times were good too.

The Iowa winter snuck up on us like it often does. One day the cold was bitter and never went back. It got so cold that we activated a long-dormant old-timey fireplace in the corner of the garage. That winter was a montage. Day after day of lighting up the garage fireplace and heaters, then warming up as we took turns dancing and working on our moves. When we first lit the fireplace, we noticed the smoke and soot would accumulate in our noses. "That can't be good," Danny said after he wiped his nose and noticed black mucus. We cracked open a window from then on but prided ourselves on the fact that we still danced in such conditions.

By late December we had made marked improvements in our dancing. I no longer felt like an outsider dancing with the kids at the trailer park. Danny encouraged me to embrace my style influences. To keep focusing on creative footwork transitions and musicality. This resulted in me standing out from everyone else. In return I was Danny's ultimate cheerleader. Every time he got a new difficult move, I'd jump up and down and congratulate him. We made a good duo.

While we trained in my garage, we heard rumblings of other dancers coming up in town. That's how crazy the late-nineties breaking boom was. In a town of about three thousand people, you could have different groups of kids learning the dance, not counting the curious who learned a worm or basic baby freeze solitary in their houses. There were about four dedicated factions of "real" breakers in the area. There was Danny and me, or rather, Dizzy D and Jazzy J, training in my garage, and of course the Midwest Breakaz in the mobile courts. Then there were two other groups we caught wind of.

The first was two younger cousins, Tony and Marc Frausto, who were practicing in Tony's bedroom. They called themselves Da Bomb Squad. Tony was this stylish kid with a hint of aloofness about him, while Marc was a goofball loudmouth who balanced Tony's energy. I was cousins with Tony and Marc in a roundabout third- or fourth-cousin way, but I didn't know them well. I heard their parents would drive them to the larger city of Muscatine to dance with a whole bunch of kids that were real good. I sniffed out something about how they danced at this all-ages nightclub called The Edge. It all sounded mysterious and intriguing. Tony and Marc were in the class two grades below me. Back then that seemed like such a huge difference in age. We didn't interact much, but I resolved to approach them the next time I saw them and ask about this Edge place.

The other group we heard about was even younger, in the grade below Tony and Mark. They were babies, so young I didn't pay them much mind. The group consisted of two Asian kids, Keven Xayasene and Nicky Quangvan, and their Mexican friend, Clemente Cota. They practiced at Nicky's house, which was ten minutes from West Liberty in a tiny town called Nichols. Nicky and Clemente both lived in Nichols, and Keven got dropped off at their houses. Nichols is one street with a couple of neighborhoods flanking it. It's so small that people in West Liberty can call it "podunk." Nichols was part of the West Liberty school district, so Nicky and Clemente were honorary West Libertians. They called themselves Triangulum Tribe and were training hard in the confines of their town.

I sought out other materials to supplement tutorials on the internet. Rewatching Jerry's *Battle of the Year* tape had ground it to dust. In my sleuthing I came across a site that would change my life, the way it changed lots of other dancers' lives across the world: Freestyle Session. A b-boy promoter named Cros One out of San Diego hosted the site. It was the mecca of online breaking resources. It had forums where people connected from individual scenes across the country. My heart skipped a beat when I found out that if you sent in a check or money order, you could order breaking VHS tapes.

Right before Christmas, *Freestyle Session 5* came in the mail. It had taken so long, I was starting to get the feeling it was all a scam and some con man on the coast had played me. But no, here it was in my hands. The level of moves was mind-blowing. It made the dancers from '97 look like amateurs. On display were the best dancers in the country. They were Style Elements's peers. The first battle featured my favorite crew. They actually got beat by the up-and-comers. This new tape inspired me the same way I connected to Jerry's tape months ago. *Freestyle Session 5* was on a constant loop in my bedroom. I studied every battle dozens of times before I shared it with Danny.

The first time I watched the tape with Danny, I primed him for one section in particular, not because of the dancers but because of the music the DJ played during their dancing. There was something about this mix of songs that struck a chord with me. I would later find out that he was spinning some classic breaking tunes. The same songs that DJ Kool Herc would play for dancers in the block parties in the seventies. There was "The Mexican" by Babe Ruth and "Itch and Scratch" by Rufus Thomas. The dancers got hype to the theme of Blaxploitation kung fu flick *Black Belt Jones*, which then transitioned to The Jackson Sisters's song "I Believe in Miracles."

"Check out this music, Danny, it's awesome. You can tell it's what these breakers dig," I said as the battle first started up. Danny didn't react to the music and instead continued to comment on the moves. I tried to bring up the music again and told him I found some of the songs on Napster. We could train to these songs in my garage. Again no comment. It felt like when you show someone a funny video and wait in horror as they don't laugh at the funny parts.

I got up and played one of the songs from a different battle, a song called "Champ" by The Mohawks featuring a funky organ melody. Danny revealed how he felt. "I don't know. I like the music we already dance to. This sounds weird to me. Like it's all old and slow. It's definitely not the stuff we would rave to."

I did a bad job of hiding my disappointment. He didn't care about these dancers he had never met in real life. And the music *was* weird. Although I recognized some of the songs as samples Dr. Dre and hip-hop producers used, most of it was like nothing I had heard before. But this was what all these *real* breakers were getting down to. Later when we went to practice we played the same songs as before. My new musical discoveries were left unburned on my computer.

It wasn't the last time Danny and I wouldn't see eye to eye on breaking aesthetics. I delved deeper into what constituted "real" breaking and hip-hop sensibilities. Our tastes deviated further from one another as a result. Adidas sneakers and pants ended up in my closet. I got into old funk music but also into golden age rap music like A Tribe Called Quest. One of their songs, "Scenario," was super hype and played on clip after clip on the internet. In fact, two of the first CDs I bought of my own voli-tion were albums by the nineties rap group. When I say "of my own voli-tion," I mean bought from outside the shadow of my brother and sister. This wasn't a purchase I made because I found the group rummaging through Johnny's gangsta rap records. This wasn't music Nancy bumped while she cruised around with her friends. This was something I could call my own. Danny put up with my weird new music, as long as we could also put on his raving music that the older guys played at the trailer park. Around then Danny changed his hair, getting with the times and switching his bowl cut for a more contemporary look. His hair was nice and faded, with gel that made his bangs look crispy in tips at the front. A look resembling that of the Midwest Breakaz.

While this fissure developed between my new friend and me, a letter from an old friend reached my mailbox. It had been months since I last saw Ruben, so it came as a shock when my dad brought in the bills and junk mail and handed me an envelope. To not have to think about it, I turned over the letter and ripped it open as fast as I could. The paper in-side was a single sheet of computer printer paper. I recognized Ruben's handwriting immediately, compact and uniform, like mine but more methodical. I could tell he had taken his time to get down his thoughts. Ruben wrote the following:

> Chuy. Man first off I'm sorry. For everything. For all the stupid shit that I said that night. You had every right to get mad at me and I shouldn't have came at you like that. Some people said I should forget it. Forget you. But I can't and I don't want to. You're my best friend. More than that you're like a brother to me. You're family. I know that I've never said that. I guess it's hard for me to say how I feel but I'm trying now. We miss you and when we would all hang. But more than that I miss you. I love you.
> —Ruben

The first thought that ran through my head was how much it took for him to write this out. This was potential evidence. I could show it to anyone. The thought of Ruben not caring about that did it. Teardrops pricked the letter. Each spot bled the ink and seeped into the page as they accumulated on the paper. It was all too much. I walked back to my room while folding the letter. I folded it as many times as I could, until it became thick and impossible to fold anymore.

Alone in my room, I continued to fight my swelling emotions. It was the first time anyone outside of my family told me they loved me. Hell, my family doesn't even say it that much. I didn't know what else to do, so I played music on my computer and danced. I had cleared enough room to work on toprock by my bed. It wasn't a lot of space but enough to work on my grooves and rhythm. I danced nonstop until my lungs burned and my feet ached. The letter was a lump on the corner of my computer desk. My gaze kept coming back to it as I rested between songs. While I danced, it unraveled from its last fold, like a plant on a time-lapse in a nature documentary.

I'm not sure how long I danced. It felt like hours or minutes. Time does funny things when I dance. All I knew is my mom surprised me with a harsh knock at my bedroom door. "Chuy!" she called from the other side. "Tu amigo está aquí." There was something in her voice when she said it. A kind of sadness or precaution. When I asked her who it was, she hesitated like she didn't want to say. It was Ruben. My mom had made her feelings known about Ruben and his dad before. But she knew how much being away from him tore at me. I went downstairs to greet the person I used to call my friend.

Outside on our side porch was Ruben shuffling from foot to foot. I shut the door behind me to buy myself some time. It was strange. Here was a person I had called my best friend since I was little, yet we didn't know how to greet each other on the cold cement of my porch. I noted the wind.

Ruben was the first to speak. "You get my letter?" he asked. His voice, usually so confident, came off guarded and measured.

"Yeah, I read it a couple of times. I don't have it with me now, but yeah. Yeah, I read it." The wind picked up and whistled through the gravel road beside my house. At that point in the season the days were short. By 5 p.m. it was pitch black and colder than you can imagine.

"I meant everything I wrote, Chuy. I didn't know how else to say it. It took me a couple of drafts. You know me, I'm not so good with saying stuff like that. Stuff that matters." Ruben's eyes were cast down. I followed his gaze to our feet. We stood in front of one another in a long silence as we tried to convey the emotional weight of a conversation neither of us knew the language for. "I'm sorry," Ruben said. His voice cracked as he said it and he looked away.

I don't think I apologized or accepted his apology. There was nothing confrontational in our encounter, no animosity or bad blood. But I made it known that I was not going to rekindle our friendship. I wasn't ready to forgive him. There was an anger and stubbornness that flickered at the sight of my old friend, but another part of it I didn't realize until much later. It was that I thought I needed to make a choice between my new life as a dancer and my old one with the gang at the Shack. I wanted to be a b-boy. I couldn't see how Ruben fit into that lifestyle.

Our conversation sputtered on my porch as the day became night and the wind cracked at our faces. The wind caused the corners of my eyes to sting and well up. They were the closest thing to tears that I would let Ruben see before he gave a half-hearted goodbye and walked home. I knew I was letting our friendship dissipate. The door was closing on what we knew as our relationship. I watched him walk away from my house. His figure receded as he walked along the sidewalk, until I couldn't make out his silhouette for the swaying trees along the street. The leaves trembling in the wind sounded like how I imagined waves on a beach would sound.

———————

January brought relief that the mass extinction event known as Y2K was all hype. I met the new millennium with a greater resolve to continue dancing. Dance was a refuge, a way to both process and escape my emotions. If a terrible day at school pissed me off, I could come home and take my frustration out on the dance floor. If I was in a good mood from a day gone right, I could celebrate with a good practice in my garage. I tried not to think about my last encounter with Ruben on my porch. We'd see each other in the classes we shared at school and were amicable but didn't talk much to one another, the way you regard an old friend at the grocery store where you both nod and walk by rather than stop and catch up. Dance was a way to distract myself from the fact that I had chosen to leave my old friends behind.

Luckily, I had some new characters in my garage. Tony and Marc Frausto were popping into our practice sessions after school. Tony and Marc seemed like brothers, the way they goofed off and bickered. One second they'd be laughing while trying to create a routine and the next they'd be at each other's throats. When they weren't acting a fool, they would also talk about their frequent trips to The Edge, the all-ages nightclub in Muscatine. My ears perked up whenever they mentioned it. The way they talked about it, it sounded like some type of haven for dancers. Like there were more dancers than nondancers. Like each night they went was constant battles and circles.

I wasn't close enough to the Fraustos to tag along when Tony's mom drove them on Saturday nights. There was also a hint of embarrassment in going because Ruben and the guys used to always make fun of Muscatine. They joked that it was this scuzzy place, full of scurvs and ghetto Mexicans. But my old friends couldn't judge me for asking Tony and Marc about the dancers at The Edge in the safety of my garage. Danny never seemed as interested in their long-winded accounts of the place. He would tune them out and continue to work on the cardboard while I grilled them for more details.

One Monday session Tony busted into the garage with uncharacteristic energy. He usually played it cool but was acting like his cousin at the moment. Turned out the Fraustos were a two-way channel of communication on The Edge. The way they told us about the dancers at the club, they had told them about us. That was when I understood that the work we were putting into the dance was paying off. Tony and Marc had been bragging about these two skilled guys in their hometown. Tony was breathless as he got to the point of his story. "I was telling these two breakers, Tyson and Josh, about you two. 'Cause Tyson and Josh are partners. They're a duo like you guys. And I told them how you and Danny were dope. They asked if they could take you in a battle."

That got our attention.

"Well, what'd they say to that?" I asked, excitement in my words.

"I mean—I told them how you guys don't come out to The Edge. And they said fuck it, if they're scared of coming to us, then we'll come to them. So I told them I'd talk to you guys about it. If you're down to battle, then it's a battle."

The excitement I was feeling mixed with fear and anxiety. Besides goofing off and play-battling Jerry a few times, I hadn't gotten into a real battle before. This was the Wild West and Tony was the messenger on horseback, informing us that we were to battle at high noon. We couldn't say no. I looked over at Danny, who was warming up with increased vigor. "Well, we better start training extra hard," he said, looking back at me.

"Tell those Muscatine guys Dizzy D and Jazzy J are down to battle whenever," I announced to the room. Tony smiled wide and said he'd tell them on MSN Messenger that night.

Now's as good a time as any to answer the question, "What the heck is a battle?" There are a lot of misconceptions about battles due to cheesy hip-hop dance movies like *You Got Served* and *Step Up*. They portray battles as lavishly choreographed group routines for big sums of money. *Real* battles are different. They're less sparkly and more gritty, in sweaty gyms or dingy clubs. Sure, there were big crowds at the events I watched. But they were the best of the best. The majority of dancers battled in front of a few dozen peers. Besides being smaller, battles were usually more individual than the routines on TV. Even in a crew or two-on-two situation, battles happened in individual rounds, where one person from each opposing crew took turns dancing. One side sent a person out, then the other side responded. When we're talking a real battle, to settle a beef, it's more about stacking each side's accumulated solo skills against each other.

The general outline of a battle is as follows. First off, we'll determine if we're going by rounds or by time. If it's by rounds, then that's usually predetermined by both sides. It could be something like, "Okay, let's settle this, five rounds? Five rounds, let's go!"

So we're set to go five rounds in a two-on-two battle. One person goes from their side onto the middle of the floor for their round. During their round, they bust out their set, the complete package of their movements from beginning to end. If you're well-rounded, your set will have something like a beginning, middle, and end, with good transitions from toprock to groundwork and whatever freezes, power moves, blowups, or signatures you want to throw in. A blowup is your massive exclamation-point moves. A signature is any move you've created that becomes associated with you as an individual. After you finish your set, in whatever way you deem necessary, you walk back to your crew's side of the floor. From there an individual from the other side does their set in response for their round. Sets and rounds aren't interchangeable. The set refers to the dance-movement package someone does, while a round refers to the unit of measurement of the battle. For example, someone could do one set, get up to talk shit, and immediately go down to do another set in the same round.

The driveway setting of our first battle.

While training for our upcoming battle, I was apprehensive about what was to come. It was nerve-racking to think that this could be an accumulation of everything I had been working for. The night before the scheduled battle, I couldn't sleep. I ran through possible worst-case scenarios while I tossed and turned. *What if I crash my air freezes and fall on my head? Hell, what if I try to walk out into the circle, trip on my untied shoelace, and fall on my head before I even get to dancing? I better be sure to tie my shoelaces tight before we start.* And so on and so forth. Every possible scenario ran through my head. Which I took as a good sign: it meant I actually cared about it.

The two dancers from Muscatine came right on time. It was a sunny Saturday afternoon in late March, which meant we could put the cardboard floor on the driveway for all to see. Funny, because our only witnesses for the battle were Tony and Marc, plus the random people passing by on the street. The cousins Frausto sat on the trunk and hood of my dad's lowrider. Their feet dangled over the side of the car as they watched, becoming impromptu commentators and audience members.

Tyson and Josh pulled up in a battered pickup truck with a muffler that needed service. They were both lanky white dudes. Tyson had a shaved head while Josh had shaggy blond hair and a goatee. They were sure in their movements as they got out of the truck. As they approached,

I realized they were a few years older than us. They looked like they were seniors or right out of high school.

"X. Stringz. Good to see you," Josh said as he one-arm hugged Tony and Marc on the lowrider. X and Stringz were their respective dancer names. "Yo, what up, we're the Wild Styles Crew," Josh said to me while shaking my hand. He had heavy eyelids and looked like he was a smoker. We gripped each other's hands in a firm handshake. I hoped he couldn't tell my palm was sweaty while he shook it. Danny gave them a slight nod from his corner of the floor, already deep into his warm-up routine.

From behind Josh, his partner Tyson came up. There seemed to be a hint of a smile on his face as he addressed us. "So, you're the guys X was talking about, eh? We had to come to see y'all ourselves. Well, should we get right down to it?"

"Hell yeah, you guys should," Marc said as he hopped off the hood of the lowrider to start up my old CD player. Marc had recently gotten a CD burned with music from one of the guys he danced with at The Edge. "I'll be the DJ. You guys are gonna get hype to this shit, let's go!"

Danny walked over to me while he rolled his wrists and got the kinks out of his neck. "Are you ready, man?" he asked while turning his body toward me and away from the others.

"Shit, I don't know. It feels like my heart's going to explode outta my chest. These guys look good," I replied.

Marc cupped his hands over his mouth and shouted like a boxing ring announcer, "Alright, we got the Wild Styles Crew all the way out of Muscatine versus the hometown squad Dizzy D and Jazzy J. Let's go!" He then hit play on the CD player and blasted the soundtrack to our battle. Tony let out a Mexican grito from the trunk of the lowrider while slapping the side of the car.

"Organ Donor" by DJ Shadow emanated from the boom box. Marc gave me a knowing look. This was one of the songs I loved from the *Freestyle Session 5* tape. The guys at The Edge must have got down to it too. The intro blasted while everyone paced on their respective sides of the cardboard. This is a thing that happens in the beginning of the battle. There is both a sizing up of the other side and a not wanting to be the first person to go out. It's like if you're the first person to go out, then you're giving the other crew something to retaliate against. Danny and I walked around each other while Josh and Tyson did the same.

They reminded me of sharks in the water. I kept wiping my palms on the front of my jeans but more sweat accumulated. It reminded me of one time as a kid when I fell onto a cactus plant in Mexico. My palms were full of cactus needles. My brother plucked out the needles and afterward I wiped my hands on my pants, not realizing there were more needles on the fabric. My brother had to yell at me to stop wiping my pants and getting more needles on my palms. *Wait.* What the heck was I thinking about? While pacing back and forth, I was finding refuge in a lost memory. Anything to curb the fear that battling these guys brought me.

Tony and Marc kept calling out from the car, "Whoever wants it the most goes first! Whoever is hungrier, take it to the floor!" These were all things they heard emcees on breaking tapes bark out in the beginning of battles. Finally Tony went out into the middle of the floor and took off his shoe. "Alright, whatever side the front points to goes first," he said, tossing the shoe in a twist. It spun in the air and landed with a plop, pointing between Danny and me. *Crap*, I thought. Here goes nothing and everything.

There was no more time to think. It was time to close my eyes and dive off into the abyss. *Okay, Chuy. Let the music guide you.*

My set was a blur. From the moment I began toprocking to the part where I was up and walking back to Danny was a time jump, as if I had time-traveled the moments I took up dancing. Danny smiled and patted my back, which indicated I had done good enough.

Tyson was the first to go. Josh clapped along to the beat as his partner danced. From the outset we could see he had been dancing longer than us. His movements were confident as he topped along to the music. His set revolved around swipes, an intermediate move where you rotate your body on your hands and feet. You scoop through the air and rotate, or "swipe," back onto your feet. Neither Danny nor I could do swipes. We couldn't grasp the mechanics of keeping our hips up high enough to keep the move going. After Tyson's fourth swipe in a row something happened, though. He faltered and didn't quite land on both feet. He did a mini tumble out of the move and salvaged it with a half-hearted freeze. Emulating the clips I'd seen on the internet, I slapped at the ground with my hand repeatedly. This gesture signifies that you think the other person has "crashed" or messed up his move. Tyson hadn't quite crashed, but it was enough of a flub that I thought it deserved the crash gesture, plus I knew it was a good way to get into someone's head.

After Tyson got up, it was Danny's turn. I slapped my partner's back and yelled at him to get hype. Danny rubbed his hands together and immediately launched into a flare. He did one clean flare and stood up to toprock some more. From there he went into windmills into a nice long backspin. As Tony and Marc shouted to the backspin, I pantomimed like I was fanning myself off from the wind of Danny's move.

It was then that I realized something important about the battle. That I was having fun. That I didn't want to be anywhere else doing anything else. This was home. Then I saw the look on the face opposite of me. It was Josh, and he was eager for Danny to finish his set so he could retaliate. One of the Fraustos shouted out, "Oh shit, let's see how Wild Style is going to answer that!"

Josh dove into the middle of the floor, got up, then busted out a clean and difficult power combo. Danny and I stood motionless as we lay witness to flares into nutcracker windmills then a backspin *back* to flares. That last transition was a particularly impressive one. Tony and Marc sprang from their seats on the lowrider. They jumped up and down as Josh brushed off his shoulder and gave us the biggest smirk I ever saw. *Crap, crap, crap.* I couldn't answer that. I wasn't even the power guy. Even if I could do power, my power wouldn't be of that caliber. I froze to the spot.

Luckily, while Josh was flaunting, the song on the boom box was changing over. Enough time to stall and act like these guys didn't have me shook. The song switched over to "Freestyler" by a group called Bomfunk MC's. I hadn't heard the song, but word was that it was a huge song for all the dancers at The Edge.

Okay, I got to focus on this one. As the music picked up, I decided to get into my toprock. So far everyone was toprocking for a few seconds before getting down to the rest of the set. I forced myself to groove to the music. Marc yelled out, "Holy shit, Chuy is killing those tops!" I could see from our opponents that they thought the same thing. From there I went into every footwork move and tech I could smush together. My feet were furious as they rained down on the floor.

To finish it off, I planned on going back to one of my early signatures: go up and hit my L-kick on one side, then stand up and quick hit on my right arm. It was the same double freeze that got me respect at Jerry's house. But I messed up on the transition to the second hand. My alignment misguided and my legs vaulted over my hips. I was going to crash. This wasn't going to be a minor stumble like Tyson had done earlier. This was going to be a big land-on-my-face-in-front-of-everyone-then-crawl-into-a-hole-and-die type of crash. Things went into slow motion again. Momentum was sending me down to the thin cardboard above hard, unforgiving cement. In my panic I did the only thing I could think of. I repositioned the hand I was doing my freeze on to land on my forearm.

The sound of my entire body crunching over my forearm and elbow took me by surprise. It was a loud, dull thunk of a noise. I was so preoccupied with the noise that I didn't realize I was currently suspended, frozen on my one forearm. My body had stacked itself. I had fallen into a new daring move, a one-handed handstand that fell down to a forearm freeze *and* was on beat.

Everyone erupted as I stood up in a daze. Even Tyson and Jerry were giving me props—meaning they were giving me the universal breaking props symbol, when you put one hand in front of yourself and shake it up and down as if quickly bouncing an imaginary basketball. The antithesis of the crash symbol I was expecting to get in the beginning of my freeze journey.

The next stretch of the battle was even. Danny and I were getting comfortable and had shaken off our nerves. Although Tyson and Josh were more technical than us, they hadn't seen moves like ours. They were used to the styles of the Muscatine scene. Since Danny and I worked in the seclusion of West Liberty, we had a style all our own. We went back and forth for the better part of ten minutes at a steady pace.

That is, until the end of the battle. To explain how Danny ended the battle, I have to explain a concept one of the members of Style Elements talks about. This member goes by B-boy Remind, and he happens to be my favorite dancer of all time. One of the concepts he pushes in breaking is "text." It's this idea of how you can have all these separate smaller moves that you can put together like text in language. With this approach you can put together dense poetic phrases of disparate movements. This is different than a lot of sets that amateur dancers like us were doing at the time. Our sets were showcases of repetitive moves.

If somebody had one good move, they would do it ad nauseam, to the point where people could chant out the number of moves in a row like the Laotians did during their flare competitions.

This whole concept of text is why the way Danny ended the battle was so dope. I still remember the set to this day. It was an example of what Remind would call good usage of text. Danny did this combo where he went from one move right into the next. Any one of these moves would have been the thesis of a lesser breaker's entire set. For the breakers reading this, here's exactly what he busted out: a front handspring to a bronco straight to apple jack (or V-kicks, as the kids are calling them nowadays) to a front flip that landed in a big ole suicide on the ground. In breaking terms, a suicide is any move that ends with coming down from a great height flat onto your back. The best-known suicide is by an OG b-boy named Frosty Freeze of the Rock Steady Crew. At the end of the eighties dance movie *Flashdance*, the Rock Steady Crew is dancing in the alley to "It's Just Begun" by the Jimmy Castor Bunch. Frosty Freeze does the purest example of a suicide. He launches himself in the air to come down on to his back. To a layperson, a breaking suicide can look like a crash, but if you do it correctly, it's like a pratfall in theater. It's all about how flat your back is when you land. If there's any bend in your back, you're in for a bad time. Well, Danny pulled out his suicide from a front flip, meaning he flipped forward to land on his back. I had never seen him do that before, and none of us had seen such an impressive finisher to a set in real life.

Tony, Marc, and I celebrated and showered Danny with praise at the top of our lungs. Tyson looked over at Josh, who gave him back a shrug. "I don't think we can top that!" he said, and he came over to forfeit the rest of the battle.

We had won. It was one of the greatest feelings I had felt in my life. Like winning all the football games at the field by my house at once. Danny and I hugged and shook our competition's hands. Looking back at the battle, and this goes without saying for any breaker who knows the moves I've described, it was rudimentary. We were all newbies. The dancers in the videos we watched could dance circles around our basic sets. But that didn't matter. To us it felt like we were on top of the world.

I thought nothing could bring me down from the high of winning that battle. The only problem was, no one besides the dancers were around to see it. It almost felt like I was leading a double life. People would know a different me on the dance floor than the Chuy at school. Schemes ran through my head the following Monday, ways I could tell my classmates about the feat that Danny and I had achieved.

But in the hallways the next morning there was a feeling thick in the air. It made the hair stand up on the back of my neck. Walking to my locker, I saw a group of girls consoling a girl in the middle. I recognized her thick black hair and backpack. Making my way through the people in the halls, I saw it was Veronica Galvan, tears streaking across her face. It echoed through the halls, that her older brother died in the night after a brief stay in the hospital. It was Arnie. It felt like everything was sucked out of me as my thoughts all rushed toward one person.

Ruben stood in line a few people away from me at Arnie's funeral. His family buried him in the West Liberty cemetery by the mobile court, behind the racetrack. We were in line to walk down the wet grass that ran down the middle of rows of metal chairs. Arnie was in his casket before the chairs, with his family in the front row. A priest I didn't recognize got up and said a few words. Formalities and ritual. The adults among us nodded their heads to different things he said. It seemed to be on cue, the spots in which they knew to acknowledge the pauses in his sermon.

After the funeral a lot of us went over to Arnie's parents' house. I had been there a few times before with Ruben as he hung out with the older kids. We ate barbecue and reminisced with our parents at long tables adorned with thin plastic. We all stayed a long time as more and more of the town congregated in the Galvan backyard. As the day turned to night, Arnie's friends cracked open beers and drank. It was the first of many nights of partying in their friend's honor.

While the adults grumbled about their kids not mourning properly, I stumbled across Ruben and Eric. Crying in an embrace. I felt so bad then. I wasn't supposed to be there—or rather, I should have been there all along. I should have been there for my friend before this went down. If we all weren't so stubborn, if we hadn't had these emotional blocks in place, we would have been there for each other when it all went to shit. I left my friends alone and started my way back home in the night. The drizzle that had been in the air all day turned hard and unforgiving as the sky mourned with my friends.

My defense mechanism, my refuge, was dance. It was there for me whenever I needed to process these complicated emotions I couldn't handle. Give me a clear floor and some music and I could make sense of it all. But there were other complications the weeks after Arnie's funeral. The big realization setting in was that Danny and I were also drifting apart. The fault line was growing, and I could see we were on different sides of the widening crack.

Our first battle as Dizzy D and Jazzy J was also the last. In learning more about the dance scene at large, we found out those names were already taken. It was a punch in the gut when a clip surfaced with a legendary Jazzy J from a crew called the Renegades. And there were at least two other Dizzys. We had to retire the names for fear of people calling us biters. To bite something means to steal or copy it without credit. There's more than one hand gesture for biting, that's how serious it is. The most used one is when you make your arms like an alligator chomping at something. To be a biter in the breaking world is to be the lowest of the low. We didn't want our names, our very identities, to be biting these more established dancers.

But more than our ill-fated choice of names, the differences in what the dance meant to us created this drifting apart. We couldn't reconcile what we were using dance to connect with. The bigger breaking scene in Muscatine that Tony and Marc promised enticed me. My tastes were expanding away from what Danny recognized as the reason why he started dancing in the first place. Like it was for Jerry, dancing was always a way for Danny to connect with his friends and cousins in town. Danny started to get more and more into raving and cars. Once Jerry and Danny were old enough to drive, they would go to Chicago for an event called Hot Import Nights. Danny even started to get into DJing electronic music. Over time we both could feel that our friendship was heading in different directions. My last friendship had exploded in a fury over stubbornness and ideological differences. Danny and I didn't so much as explode as drift by one another. Our journeys intersected for a brief time, only for them to diverge when the time was right.

With Danny gone, and not knowing who else to turn to, I made what I considered to be a social sacrifice. I started to hang out with Tony and

Marc. When they came over to my garage to practice with Danny and me, they were like the little brothers we tolerated. But I saw they liked the music that turned Danny off so much. They were into the Muscatine scene and unafraid of what people thought of them if they embraced it. It seems such a trivial thing, but as a high schooler, hanging out with two kids from junior high was closing a lot of doors on my social life. But the dance was still the beacon, so if choosing dance meant foregoing popularity, so be it.

I hung out with X and Stringz, or Tony and Marc, at Tony's house. We would practice in Tony's bedroom, where he had a small piece of linoleum and a three-piece CD player. X was short for Xplicito. Tony found the definition for explicit in the dictionary and thought it fit his dance style. He wanted to keep it raw on the dance floor.

To break down Marc's name, Stringz, you have to know the difference between breaking and popping. People unfamiliar with the different hip-hop and funk dance styles think they are interchangeable. Popping is part of the funk umbrella of dance styles. These styles formed on the West Coast. It's what people think of when they think of Michael Jackson doing a back glide, or lockers dancing on *Soul Train*, or someone doing the robot and waves. It's more of an upright dance with its own history and terminology. The BPMs of funk styles are slower—think less James Brown and more "Flashlight" by Parliament-Funkadelic. Although there is cross-pollination, these are all different types of dance. Part of the misconception comes from the eighties movies *Breakin'* and *Breakin' 2: Electric Boogaloo*, which treat popping, locking, and breaking as one and the same. This is because the two main actors, Shabba-Doo and Boogaloo Shrimp, were mainly poppers. Anyway, Tony and Marc realized that Marc's heftier, stiffer frame lent itself better to popping. Someone gave Marc the name Stringz because he could move like a puppet held up by strings.

Marc is the one who came up with my name, or rather the replacement of the now defunct Jazzy J moniker. He was watching me dance and swearing that he had never seen anyone hit the beats like I did. "That's what we should call you, man. Beats!"

"What about Original Beats?" I asked Marc. He agreed it fit, and that was my dancer name from then on. It still is. There are people who only know me as Beats in this world. It reminds me of a Russian novel, the way everyone has names on names on names. Depending on who you are, you can call me Jesus, Chuy, or Original Beats.

With my new name, it was finally time to do something I should have done a long time ago. Tony's mom picked me up in a red minivan and I joined Tony and Marc in the back. We were set to make the half-hour drive to Muscatine. It was time to see what The Edge was all about.

Tony's mom dropped us off at the parking lot by a rundown square building. I could feel the excitement build as we walked across the parking lot toward the entrance. It was hard not to get caught up in that feeling after hearing Tony and Marc talk about the place for so long. We paid the five-dollar entrance fee and walked down a long, dark hallway that opened up into a hall filled to the brim with teens. An explosion of bass rattled from towers of speakers lining the wall. Through the mass of people dancing and hanging around I could see graffiti plastered on one of the walls. Opposite this wall was a huge DJ booth overlooking the room. You had to walk up a small flight of stairs to get to the booth. Marc yelled into my ear that the DJ at the moment was a member of the crew that ran things here, KWC. "That's B-Boy Skippy. From the Killa Weapons Crew. Wait a little bit, when the circle forms he's gonna kill it."

Flanking both sides of the DJ booth were two raised circular platforms. Right away I could see there were people breaking on the platforms. There were people breaking all night. They would showcase their moves or settle scores and battle on those platforms. I gravitated to the platform farthest from the entrance, with a crowd whooping for two dancers battling it out in a heated exchange. The crowd was alive, pulsing against the music and resisting my efforts to get closer to see as much of the battle as I could.

From my spot by the platform, I saw there was a whole other section of the venue, an extra room where people could play pool and take a break from the musical onslaught in the main room. This was also the area where people would dip into the shadows and partake in various illicit drugs. Smoking, dropping, huffing, whatever they could manage low-key in the shadows.

While taking everything in, I could see there were factions present at The Edge. You had the breakers, poppers, and various other people into that scene. Then there was a juxtaposition of JNCO-pant-wearing, black-clad goths. There was a gradient from goths to agro metalheads to

Insane Clown Posse juggalos. But I wasn't well-versed enough in those subcultures to know where one stopped and the other started. Most of the kids in that room were from poorer socioeconomic backgrounds. The people at The Edge didn't fit into the norm of small-town Iowa lifestyles. And I was one of those people. I looked over at Tony and Marc, who both had big grins on their faces, like they had tried to tell me.

"Chuy, dude, one of the dopest breakers here is right next to you. Over your left shoulder. It's Krash," Tony said to me over the music. I noted the reverence in his voice as he talked. "He's the leader of KWC." Krash had on a green cutoff T-shirt with the words "The Edge" emblazoned across the back. The members of KWC owned the joint. Or rather, they worked at it. Krash was a bouncer and Skippy was a DJ. They knew and got paid by the owner of the club, a middle-aged guy with a son who was into dance. His son was actually in the crew as well. They called him "The Kid" as he was about eleven years old.

From his pulpit above us, Skippy announced on a microphone that it was about that time. The speakers were only a few feet from where I was and I could feel the bass in my bones. All the breakers gravitated toward the middle of the room for the main showcase of the night. Skippy ran down to meet with Krash as they posted up at the top of the cypher, or the circle formed by the crowd. More and more dancers came out of the woodwork to bust a set in the cypher. Tony egged me on to bust it out, but I got gun-shy. I wanted to see what this crew that owned the place had to show.

Skippy was the first from KWC to enter the circle. He was a small, wiry guy. Even though he was skinny, you could tell he was muscular. He had on a tight-fitting black T-shirt and jeans with pristine white shoes. Skippy was Mexican with a tight fade and style. He had a crooked nose that I assumed was the result of some childhood fight. While doing his toprock, he clicked his heels together in a jump. *Ah. Skippy. Gotcha*, I thought to myself. As he danced, a contingent of the crowd yelled louder. I noted there were a number of girls calling out for him, which he seemed to revel in. He definitely had charisma. Then he danced.

I didn't want to turn around and look at the faces Marc and Tony were making. For sure they'd have even bigger grins. They'd tried to tell me that these guys were the real deal. Skippy was light-years ahead of everyone else I had seen dance so far. He was better than Tyson and

Josh, and he was definitely better than I was. He ended his set with the fastest backspin I had ever seen. Then he proceeded to *hop* his backspin. He kept his momentum while he bounced on the ground like an errant top. I had to keep my jaw from going slack in wide-mouthed wonder.

Before I could completely formulate the thought that no one could top that, Krash ran out after his crewmate. Krash's physique was fuller than his counterpart's. His cutoff T-shirt exposed the musculature on his arms. He was mixed race, Vietnamese and white, and a good-looking guy. Krash was a football star in high school who had graduated and started dancing. His athleticism on the field translated to skills on the floor. He one-upped Skippy and everyone else in a fifty-mile radius. It was like a joke. Oh, you think you've seen the best? Wait, there's more!

Krash ended his set with an invert freeze out of a 1990, a move I couldn't comprehend, let alone attempt. Think of a dancer doing a pirouette. Now think of that pirouette upside down on one hand. Think of the skin of your palm peeling off from the centrifugal force of a move that seems to defy the laws of physics. That's how crazy it was to see Krash do a 1990 like it was second nature. The one time I attempted that move in my garage, it was a catastrophic failure. My body was a heap on the concrete with a lump on the top of my head from crashing straight onto the cement.

There was no holding it back anymore. I turned around to Tony and Marc, a huge smile plastered on my face. "I should have came here a long time ago, huh?" I yelled at them. They didn't even say "I told you so." They laughed and shook their heads before we all turned our attention back to the circle. To see what the next thing would be that blew our minds.

The night ended with Skippy turning on the lights and announcing, "We didn't need to go home, but we got to get the hell out of here." My ears rang as Tony and Marc said goodbye to various dancers. We walked under the fluorescent lights down the hallway. The wind felt like a splash of cold water after being in a haze. Tony spotted his mom's minivan and we joined the exodus of other misfit teens back to their cars. It was clear on that walk to the van while the tinnitus in my ears squealed and the wind caused my sweaty body to shiver: this place was going to be home, and I was going to get good enough to join KWC.

Tony and Marc had the same true north that I had. They had the same yearning for belonging when they saw Krash and Skippy owning The Edge. Our weekend trips to the club increased, and in making our faces known to the scene we got invited to a weekly practice. This practice happened at The Edge on Wednesday evenings. It was invite-only and the place where various crews that got down on the weekends would hone their skills. We jumped at the chance to practice with the groups we were so desperate to belong with. It was weird seeing the venue during the day. The bright fluorescent lights were all turned on, exposing the dirt and dilapidation of the place. I always knew The Edge wasn't the most pristine venue, but seeing it in the light put it all out there. But it didn't matter. What mattered was that we could dance in a noncompetitive, nonperformative space. It was in these weekly practice sessions that I got to know the other members of the group and learn Krash and Skippy's real names.

Jose Zamora was Skippy. Krash's real name was Jeff Nguyen. In these practices it became clear that Jeff was the leader of KWC. Not only was he the best dancer but he called the shots. When he talked, Jose and the other guys listened. Even people in the other crews that practiced there listened. We all did. The way Jeff was the leader reminded me of how Da was the leader of the Laotians back home. Or how Ruben and I both angled for the title, even if we never said as much out loud. Is it the nature of men and boys to filter themselves into followers and leaders? Jeff would make suggestions on what moves folks should keep and which ones to throw away. He would give pointers on moves to anyone who asked. Meaning he could already do all the moves we were struggling with.

We practiced at every Wednesday session we could get to that summer. As one practice was winding down, Jeff came over to us. "All you guys have style. What do they got in the water in West Liberty, huh? Keep it up and we might have to add some members to Killa Weapons!" Jeff had this way of talking like every statement he made was a declaration to the masses. His voice carried with confidence that he was making statements on behalf of the other members of his crew.

Jeff hinting that we could be the next members of KWC would have been the main point of discussion on the minivan ride back to West Liberty. It was for a bit, until it shifted toward *why* Jeff was the leader of KWC. Marc straightened up to tell the story. "Oh yeah, it's crazy. Jeff isn't just the leader of the crew. KWC is his baby."

I nodded at this bit of information. "So he got the best guys in Muscatine and formed the group?"

Marc reveled in the fact that I didn't know the whole story. "Nah, nah, nah. It's more than that. To know the whole story, you got to know about the story behind the story. The story behind the *backstory*. Listen up, boys and girls," he said in a hushed tone. Then he leaned in close and told me about the infamous rivalry between KWC and TFU. It went like this.

Jeff was actually in TFU, or The Flava Unit, before he created KWC. Hell, that's why he created Killa Weapons, because of the disrespect he felt from his old crew. TFU was the premiere crew in a crowd of good crews in Davenport. Davenport is one of the Quad Cities—two cities in Iowa and two in Illinois all clustered together. It's about a half-hour drive from Muscatine. The Flava Unit was an elite squad of dancers led by a guy named TermiNate, real name Nate. Nate saw potential in the younger, less experienced Jeff and joined him into the crew.

Thing was, Jeff started to get this suspicious feeling like he was being played a fool. Nate relegated him to unofficial lackey. Jeff would get everyone else waters and hold the camera while the others vanquished their rivals. After a year of that, Jeff quit the crew and swore two things: that he would amass a crew better than any in Iowa, and that they would forever be rivals with his old nemesis. He would get revenge on the group that disrespected him for so long.

We trained for that chance to join KWC all summer at Tony's. We had practice sessions where the torturous Iowa humidity drenched our shirts. Sometimes the day was one long session that started in the afternoon and stretched on until the lightning bugs were signals in the night. There were times when I got home and couldn't move my body I was so sore. It wasn't the training that kept me going. I liked Tony and Marc. Tony was girl crazy and talked a big game about his suaveness, and Marc had all manner of undiagnosed ADHD energy. But as we got better, we got closer. We called ourselves the Mexican Breaking Beans.

The summer going into my sophomore year was one of unbridled op-portunity. I had friends and purpose.

But, whenever you are on a path toward purpose, there are road-blocks. My roadblock was looming with the end of summer. Going into my sophomore year meant going back to playing football. The sport seemed so long ago, both in time and in my shifting interests. But I couldn't shake the status quo. The expectations of my old friends and classmates proved too strong. My training regimen stalled as the West Liberty Comets started brutal two-a-day practices.

I went on to play the entire season. I was a decent player. But my heart wasn't in it like before. That connection with the school and the town wasn't there anymore. It ate at me that I was too sore to go over to Tony's to practice after our coaches put us through our paces on the football field.

If ever there was a sign that my football days were behind me, it was the rude awakening our team got when we played Washington. The Washington players already towered over us as freshmen. As sopho-mores they were giants among men. It was a bloodbath. The worst thing was, you know how I mentioned all the times teams were racist toward us? Washington was the opposite of that. They were downright cordial on the field. They would knock our blocks off and *help us up* off the ground. The racism we faced was like a magic pill, blood drops for pi-ranhas, fueling our passion to retaliate on the field. The Washington players were too nice for us to tap into that rage, and we didn't stand a chance against the behemoths. One of them hit me so hard I got con-cussed and had to go to the hospital. A corn-fed monster smacking some sense into me. *Maybe it's time you put all your efforts into dancing, eh?*

I was born anew when football season was over. Tony and Marc wel-comed me with open arms as we got back to the Killa Weapons end-game. The silver lining of all that football was that it was good for my athleticism. And since I wasn't destroying my body every week, I could funnel my physicality to my dance.

It was late in October of my sophomore year in 2001 when we got into KWC. One practice Jeff turned off the music and made the announce-ment: Tony and I would battle into KWC right then and there. Marc had gotten into KWC a few months before us—as the designated popper of the group, he was a shoo-in. Tony and I partnered up and had to go round and round with all the other members of the group. There was no round or time limit. It was a test of our wills and tenacity. The concept of getting battled in a crew goes way back. You'd hear stories about how one person had to go thirty rounds to prove his worth.

Tony and I, with Marc at our side, battled until it felt like our guts would spill out. It was everything we had been working for this last year. Nothing was going to stand in our way. Not judgment from my old friends for trekking to Muscatine. Not the fact that the football coaches heard I wasn't coming back next year and used me as an example of *how not to regard your self-worth*. Eric told me the coaches made a big speech during practice. They said I was letting the team down to pursue silly fads. Fuck them. My perseverance had steeled itself in the last months. Going round for round with KWC, until my eyesight was blurry and my throat burned, was one last manifestation of that resolve. Tony and I collapsed after Jeff called the battle. "Congrats, you two. You're Killa Weapons family." We smiled from our spots on the floor. That set the next few years in motion, how I would inherit the bad blood with The Flava Unit, Jeff's old crew. And how Nate, the leader of our rival, would forever change my life.

TFU was better than KWC. This was the reason why Jeff added the Mexican Breaking Beans cohort into KWC. He saw the potential and talent in us. We were to be the new blood to rally the older, more experienced members of the crew. After we were joined in, Jeff and The Kid's dad organized a statewide competition. They even bought radio ads the same way that Night Storm, a bigger all-ages club in Davenport, advertised. Jeff knew that Nate would be chomping at the bit to win a tournament on KWC home turf, at the competition that Jeff himself organized. To add to the desperation, Jeff would have his hands full hosting and emceeing the event. Our leader and best dancer wouldn't be able to compete. Getting added to the crew was a chess move to mitigate the possibility of TFU steamrolling the Muscatine natives.

Jeff called his competition Circle of Skills. It was a three-on-three tournament, so Tony, Marc, and I would battle as Mexican Breaking Beans. The rest of KWC split straws and assembled in various cohorts. It was my first real tournament competition, where one had to battle through the ranks of opponents.

In getting to the venue it was clear that the vibe was different than regular Saturdays at The Edge. This was about who was the best—no time to sit back and socialize. The different crews and regions sequestered themselves in different circles. We sized up our opponents from the corners of our eyes. I noted how the different cities had different styles and aesthetics. Because we were all siloed from each other, our methods of dancing had slight variations. Des Moines looked different from Iowa City, which looked different from Nichols. This has dissipated with the prevalence of social media and the internet. Nowadays whole countries look like one another. Everyone is hip to how everyone else dances. A livestream of the next hot battle in the Ukraine is a click away from dancers in Wisconsin. Back in the day if you were a half hour away from another crew, it was months before you saw what next styles they were on.

That phenomenon was why I was so impressed by the skills developed by Triangulum Tribe. I hadn't seen Keven, Clemente, and Nicky for months. Turns out they had been hitting the lab and getting good. The thing was, they were still so young and small. Nicky had on a yellow hoodie that swallowed him up whole. But he was doing moves no one else could hit. Keven showed a sophistication in his style all the more impressive for his young age. Clemente had one of the big blowups of the night, when he did a handstand and curled his legs to touch his head like a contortionist. The three friends in essence got best in show and cutest dancers of the night. People swooned over the diminutive kids holding their own against people five to ten years older. I made a mental note to do a better job of watching the progress of these kids who went to the same school as me.

No matter how impressive Triangulum Tribe was, nothing compared to the inevitability of The Flava Unit. When Nate and his crew entered The Edge, it was like an aura descended upon the room. People talked about them in hushed tones. Their reputation preceded them, and they set out to exceed those expectations. They came through with multiple three-person squads. It was like they were trying to overload the brackets with their members. How big of a statement would that be if it were TFU versus TFU in the finals? The members of the group followed Nate's cues and didn't dance until Jeff called them up to battle in the tournament.

Worry crept up as I watched each of my rival's battles. There was a level of complexity to their movements that I hadn't seen in real life.

It was like the difference in text between Danny's set and the guys we faced in my driveway. Only it was these guys that we had beef with that were more complex than us. Older members of our crew whispered to us new guys who was who in TFU. They were the ones flanking Nate as he prowled the circles, like Isaiah, a power head and Nate's best friend. They also had a b-girl named Deja. She was one of the first b-girls I had seen and definitely the only one to compete. It's only in the last decade or so where gender barriers for b-girls have broken wide. For the longest time there would be one woman for a dozen b-boys. Now there are whole scenes with b-girls who are as good as, if not better than, their male counterparts.

But I was most interested in Nate's skills. I had heard so many stories of this cocky guy who had disrespected our crew so much that I had to see what he was like. In his first battle of the night, Nate affirmed all the tall tales I had heard about him. He was more than just cocky. Most breakers are cocky; it comes with the territory. But TermiNate was down-right arrogant. He wasn't afraid to talk trash and diss his opponents to their face, with all manner of gestures to coincide with his verbal barbs. An anger grew in me. I wanted to beat this guy so bad and prove my worth to my crew. The thing was, Nate could back up all the smack talk he did with pure style. He was a style head and footwork executioner. Like me. He played with and responded to the music the way I did. In the way that granted me my name. It wasn't that Nate was good; it was that he was good at doing the stuff *I* was good at. We had to beat him.

Nate's viciousness on the floor took people out before they knew what had happened. After he roasted someone he would do this gesture I had seen on our breaking videos. It was an aggressive and lewd gesture that has a special name in the breaking community. It's when you panto-mime holding a phallus and shoving it toward someone. This can cor-respond with the other hand holding your crotch. The community calls this action "cocking someone" or "throwing the cock." There's even a b-girl equivalent where you make both hands into a diamond shape and throw that at people. Over time the cock gesture has become so prevalent that it's lost some of its bite. Dancers dismiss it as a throwaway battle tactic. But it used to be never-forgive action. Something you would do to your worst enemy, like a slap across the face. The fact that Nate was throwing cocks was more fuel to the fire. I had to serve this clown some act right. The question was if the Mexican Breaking Beans were good enough to serve that justice.

One by one our KWC brethren got knocked out of the tournament. Skippy's group lost a particularly heated battle. After it was over, he left the venue in a rage. Then it happened in the blink of an eye: we were facing off against Nate's crew in the finals of the tournament. It felt at once surreal and something preordained. Like the plot of a sports movie, the stories and drama of the night distilled into one final confrontation, for all the marbles.

All I could see were the whites of Nate's eyes as he paced back and forth. His nostrils flared in anticipation to start the battle. My knees felt weak, like they were going to cramp up at any moment. Marc snapped me out of my stupor. "Alright, Chuy, this is everything we've been training for. Lead the way and we'll take these fools out." He said it with such conviction, the idea that I was leading them. If Marc and Tony believed we could beat these guys, if they believed in me, then I had to believe it too. Marc's words gave me the confidence I needed, and I walked out into the circle before anyone else could. I didn't want to wait until Jeff asked who was hungrier and for someone to spin a bottle to make someone go out. No, I had to show Nate I wasn't afraid of him.

Before I went down for my set, I looked Nate square in the face and pointed that I was going to take him out. It was like a basketball player calling his shot before making his way across the court. If I were going to go down, it would be in a blaze of glory. Nate and I each threw down a round, and I'd say we were even. We could do this. Tony and Marc followed my lead and we took it to our rivals for the entirety of the battle. After the dust settled and the battle was over, the judges went to a corner and deliberated.

It was out of my hands now. The three judges handed Jeff slips of paper. He did a good job of hiding his emotion as he walked in the middle of the circle. "Alright, guys, without further ado, we got the winners of the battle. Give it up for your Circle of Skills winners . . . Mexican Breaking Beans!"

We jumped up and down like we'd won the lottery. I jumped into Marc's arms at one point. The rest of KWC joined in our celebrations as Jeff remained neutral. He did slip a smile when I looked at him for approval though. It felt like the first time I had achieved something of my own accord. All the training and discipline was by our own hands. There were no coaches or peer pressure; in fact, our classmates were making fun of us for devoting ourselves to this. All that self-guided work led us to that actualization. To that feeling, that knowing it was all worth it.

I looked over at a stunned Nate, who had fire in his eyes. I could see it then, that I had officially inherited Jeff's old beef and created a new rival. Things were personal. Soon enough Nate would be clamoring for a rematch.

The outcome of Circle of Skills was controversial. There were lots of threads on message boards with people airing their grievances about how a KWC crew won a jam thrown by one of their own members. It was so prevalent that I brought up the topic with Jeff the next time we saw him. I asked if he was reading the message board complaints, from TFU and others, about favoritism. Jeff sensed my insecurities and assured me the judges weren't biased. But I couldn't shake the comments and creeping feeling that favoritism had come into play. No matter how much Jeff tried to allay my doubts about our win, the comments were plentiful and hard to argue. When the dust settled, the consensus was overwhelming. We needed to battle TFU again to prove it wasn't a fluke.

A curious thing happened in anticipation of what would be our final battle. In the next few months to a year, this grand inevitability descended on our crew. It was what I call the law of diminishing returns in breaking. Like how Danny had moved on from the dance before this, one by one the older members of KWC quit the scene. It wasn't limited to my crewmates, either. The scene itself was starting to dismantle at its seams.

The downfall began when The Edge closed. It was becoming too much of a financial burden on The Kid's dad. At first he tried cost-saving measures like cutting back on marketing and staff. Then he tried to clean up the club's image by banning certain types of clothing and types of kids. One time when we were in line to get in the venue, security turned away the goth kids in front of us at the door. That was a misstep. It meant The Edge was turning away a big part of its clientele without any groups to take its place. The goal was to attract shiny preppy kids who wouldn't want to associate with the misfits. That wasn't going to happen because the rest of us at the club were misfits too. The "popular" kids didn't want to be around a bunch of sweaty, stinky breakers. The Edge closed and a big percentage of the breakers stopped with it. To them, breaking was synonymous with that place. They wanted to leave their memories of the dance with the place they held so dear.

The generations in breaking last about four years. Some of that is because it's so taxing on your body. The older you get, the harder it is to keep up with the young'uns. It's easier to devote yourself to four-hour training sessions when you're a teenager. Once you're out of school and have to worry about jobs and responsibilities, it gets so much harder. But the passage of time and getting older weren't the only reasons dancers were quitting. Some of it echoed Danny's transition into different cultures. When his dad closed down The Edge, The Kid got into skateboarding. We saw less and less of him as he devoted himself to his new passion.

In addition to the hiatuses, the moving away and the moving on, there was the way life doled out tragedy. Looking back at this phase in the crew is like looking at a slow-moving car wreck. One by one, we lost crewmates to misfortune, from either bad luck or stupid choices.

Skippy started to date a girl he met at the clubs. Turns out she was underage. He kept on dating her and her family found out. They pressed charges against him and he skipped town. He left so fast we didn't have a chance to say goodbye. It was as if he vanished into thin air.

The most tragic case was a crewmate named Gumby. With the closing of The Edge, he started selling weed. It was small amounts but enough to help with funds. One of those deals went bad, with the cops pouncing on all involved. Gumby wasn't even selling that time—he was the lookout. The tragedy of it was that, unbeknownst to Gumby, the deal he was looking out for had more than weed exchanging hands. The dealer slipped some meth into the equation at the last minute. At the time meth use was a blight in Iowa and other midwestern states. It still is. States throw around the moniker of "Meth Capital of the World" like the worst game of hot potato. The state adopted a zero-tolerance policy on any drug deal involving meth. Gumby didn't stand a chance against the political machinations of Iowa trying to save face. He went to jail for the better part of a decade and I haven't seen him since.

By the time I was sixteen years old and in my junior year of high school, KWC was a shell of its former self. We looked around and the only members left were Marc, Tony, Jeff, and me. Which was crazy because it meant Jeff was the only original member of KWC still kicking. Was that the way things worked? You work so hard to become part of something bigger than yourself and it disintegrates after you get it?

On top of it all, I had this suspicion that Jeff was ready to call it, too. He was a leader with nothing to lead. All the friends he started dancing with had quit, skipped town, or gone to jail. Jeff was vocal about getting older. About how his body couldn't quite take it the way it used to. He'd say, "I tell you what, as I get older it's times like this I wish I didn't have the name Krash, 'cause I'm feeling it, boy." Jeff started talking about his dancing and crew involvement in the past tense. I knew then that our final battle with TFU would be our last battle with Jeff.

In this sorry state of KWC affairs, TermiNate was getting vocal about our long-awaited rematch. He'd wax poetic on the message boards that we had dodged TFU long enough; it was time to settle the score. By the end of my junior year, I had saved enough funds to throw my own jam in West Liberty. Even though KWC was hobbling along with only four members, we agreed to battle at my competition. Nate's messages were getting under my skin, and in a fit of hubris and annoyance, I agreed that we'd battle. To say no was to admit that we were chicken, or worse yet, to admit that our crew wasn't a crew at all anymore.

In Jeff's absence from our group, it was up to me to prepare us for that final confrontation with The Flava Unit. It called for drastic measures, and I took it upon myself to implement them. In an act that echoed the past, I injected new lifeblood into the group. Our secret weapon would be Triangulum Tribe, the young kids who had proved themselves at Circle of Skills. They were getting even better than their showing at the battle. I started to pick up Nicky, Keven, and Clemente to go practice at the Field House, a rec center in Iowa City. In discussions with Tony and Marc, we all agreed that getting the kids to join up to battle TFU was the best foot forward. I don't remember if I asked Jeff's blessing. But even though Jeff's passion for the craft was waning, he still had the rivalry with Nate. He knew it was the only way to save face and take it to the group that did him dirty for so long.

An odd thing happened in the lead-up to our last battle. In accepting the grudge-match offer, I got Nate's MSN Messenger handle and talked to him about the details. We worked together in hashing out the format of the battle. Not wanting any more controversies or hearsay after the fact, I proposed that our battle shouldn't be judged. Whatever happened, happened, and people could decide for themselves who won. Nate liked that idea. He also liked that I got judges from a prestigious Chicago crew for the official competition. Nate messaged me, saying, "No lie, I'm impressed that you got those judges. It shows you're thinking about keeping things legit."

A tinge of cognitive dissonance was brewing in my head. My conversations with Nate increased in frequency in the lead-up to the battle. They were the complete opposite of what I had expected. Things were amicable and not at all like the shit-talking I expected when we first started messaging each other. Who was this person I had hated for so long? What was the purpose of this grudge I inherited from a group of dancers who weren't even dancing anymore? If anything, Nate and I were more similar than different. We were both Mexican dancers who loved style and were holding up our crews. Our conversations put me at odds with myself and my motivation in settling this beef. But we were at escape velocity. Our final match was at hand.

By all accounts the jam was a success. Since we had been traveling to different midwestern cities to compete, they in turn came to West Liberty. The quality of dance was at an all-time high with dancers from Minnesota, Kansas, and Illinois coming in strong. One of the judges, B-boy Check-It, said it was impressive I was able to throw a jam of that caliber at sixteen years old. Looking back at it now, it was pretty crazy. I wasn't particularly enthused by high school. I was a solid C student. But the success of my jam proved that I could handle a big event. That I could put in the work that I couldn't muster up in academics.

About that battle. Although it was a pivotal battle in the Iowa record books, it wasn't as heated as the year's buildup suggested it would be. So much had changed. KWC had a brand new roster, with only one original member. Nate and I had gotten to know each other, and in the process developed a mutual respect between us.

The entire night Jeff had a camera and was documenting as much as he could. He interviewed Nate and me after the battle. We went outside the community center into the evening air. Jeff asked us who we thought took it.

Nate started. "You know, even though we got to talk about how this is home court, I have to say I thought you squeezed the win over us."

When it came my turn to reply, a revelation hit me. "You know what? I don't think it matters who won. 'Cause we had crews from all over the Midwest come and Iowa put on a show, right? What this showed me is that it's time that we squashed this beef." The words came out of me before I even knew what I was saying. The only thing more surprising was Nate's reaction.

"That's exactly what I was thinking. Shit, man, we could all join forces and take it to these other states. Got to keep showing 'em what Iowa has to offer!"

Nate and I propped an arm around one another while we talked at the camera. It was a bold statement to squash the beef on behalf of KWC while Jeff videotaped us. But it was one I needed to make. I realized that the entire time I'd been looking for leadership from so many people, from Ruben when I was a little kid all the way up to Jeff and this crew. But I was the one who assembled this new squad and threw this event on my own. I was the one who organized this battle and coordinated with Nate. It felt like I was in charge of my own actions on a grander scale. There was no reason to keep up a beef with someone I had no real animosity toward.

Nate and I continued to make plans after the camera stopped filming. "Shit, yo, I didn't realize Davenport was so close to West Liberty. You guys should come down to the studio that we session at," Nate said as we walked back into the venue. I jumped at Nate's offer. He was right. Davenport was less than an hour away.

Like I expected, Jeff was the last original member of KWC. He left and faded away from our lives. He never officially quit, but we stopped trying to get him to dance. Instead, we focused on this new coalition with these younger kids and our alliance with Nate's crew. We kept on dancing with Triangulum Tribe, and one day Nicky and I had a talk. Nicky was the best dancer in his group and we saw eye to eye. He laid it out. "Look, we want to keep dancing with you guys, but dancing as KWC doesn't really make sense, right? We're half and half Triangulum Tribe and Killa Weapons. That calls for a new crew."

I agreed and we set out to create a new group from the ashes of our former groups. We thought of the name together. Every time we went out to these big cities, people had no clue who we were. The biggest crew in Chicago was the Brickheadz, and one of their members, C. J., nodded with approval after he saw us dance in a circle once. "You guys said you were from Iowa? Out of nowhere, huh? You guys got some shit, though." Nicky and I talked about this interaction and inspiration hit. We were the nobodies from Iowa making a name for ourselves. The Nobodies! Yeah, yeah, but we needed to show that we were making that name. We ended up as The Distinctive Nobodies, and a completely new chapter of breaking turned its page.

It was a chapter I was determined to include Nate and TFU in. They represented access to a whole Davenport scene that we had cut ourselves off from. We took Nate up on his offer and drove up to the studio. We sessioned with members of TFU that we had only ever battled against. It was a good practice, full of possibility and wonder at how we had denied ourselves the chance at joining forces for so long. There was lots of talk after practice subsided, when we sat on the floor and stretched, drenched in sweat. We talked about all the events we could hit together and ways to help each other out with moves. Nate told us about a jam in Minneapolis happening the next week, that we should all hit it up, together, for the first time. The Distinctive Nobodies and The Flava Unit could show the Midwest what Iowa had to offer.

That practice was on a Saturday. The following Friday one of Nate's crewmates called Marc on his phone. We were all at Tony's kicking it after school, making plans for the weekend trip to the Twin Cities. Marc's voice cut through carefree atmosphere. "Wait, wait, Brandon, you're kidding, right. You're serious?" Tony and I pressed Marc for an answer after his face turned to shock and disbelief. "Nate got in a car crash. He's dead." With one phone call we got the news that would change the Iowa breaking scene forever.

POSTSCRIPT

Nathan Sierra died on Thursday, September 26, 2002. He was twenty-five years old. His death was a black hole of a tragedy. Nate was the linchpin that held the Davenport scene together. With a brutal efficiency, TFU and the Davenport scene dissipated in his absence. I talked to Nate's best friend and crew partner, Isaiah, afterward. He said he couldn't even walk into the studio Nate taught at, let alone try to practice without his best friend. His knees would get shaky and his grief would overwhelm him. Breaking in Davenport was synonymous with Nate. When he died, the scene died with him.

Tony, Marc, and I still went to the jam with Brandon that weekend. After much tear-filled discussion, we said that's what Nate would have wanted. We danced in his honor and then went to his visitation the following Monday. We skipped school to go to the visitation and funeral. Before they lowered his casket into its final resting place, I slipped a flyer into the crack of the casket. I nestled it between the roses other people left in respect. The flyer was for the next breaking jam happening in Kansas City the following week. A jam we would have gone to together.

Nate's funeral was over by noon. After driving back to West Liberty, Tony and Marc went home. For reasons not clear to me, I went back to school. Maybe it was because I didn't want to be alone with my thoughts and guilt at home. Nate's death tore at me. It was a crystallization of all the lessons I had learned, about following an unnecessary grudge and feeding into the tribalism of competing groups. But I had already learned that lesson. I made my own choices and extended the olive branch to Nate. We were going to change the scene together. In a moment, that was all gone. It was a cautionary tale of how life doesn't always follow the narratives you see in the movies or read in the books. It can be senseless and brutal.

Years after this saga I heard rumblings of new dancers in Davenport. The Distinctive Nobodies had made a name for themselves around Iowa and the midwestern scene. When new dancers researched who to look up in Iowa, the signs pointed to us. One of these dancers from Davenport reached out to me and said his crew wanted to connect. His name was Hai and his crew was Funktastic. They were a group of Vietnamese and Chinese American kids. Immigrants or the kids of immigrants. They reminded me of the Laotians I first started dancing with. After a few notes sent back and forth through Facebook, I went up to their practice spot.

It didn't hit me at first, that I had been here before. It took a few moments to realize the déjà vu was because of a real reason. Hai and the members of Funktastic practiced at a studio called Dance Works. It was the same studio where we practiced with Nate the week before he died. A chill ran up my spine as I realized how quickly time creates distance in your life. I exclaimed aloud in the middle of practice, "Oh shit, guys, I've been here before. I've practiced in this very spot. With an old friend before he passed."

Hai replied, "Oh, that's what the studio owner was talking about. That there used to be breakers here before us. Is that what the bench is about?" We went outside the studio and he showed me a bench dedicated to Nate. "I never put the two together. That this studio dedicated this bench to a b-boy. I didn't even know there was that big of a scene," Hai said as we looked at Nate's bench. Hai and Funktastic started dancing only a few years after the Davenport scene imploded with Nate's passing. It was enough time that no recollections of the past scene were around for them to hear. How quickly our history can vanish if we are not there to tell it.

I smiled as I remembered our battles. "Let me tell you about it," I said as the sun reflected light off the bench. "To talk about Nate is to talk about the beef between his crew, TFU, and my crew, KWC. To talk about KWC, I got to tell you about how I first got into the crew. But to talk about *that* is to talk about the crazy shit I was doing before I started dancing."

Hai didn't hesitate. "Yeah, man, let's hear it."

And we reflected on the past after dancing in the present.

PART FOUR

WHAT BONDS US TOGETHER

MY EYES SQUINTED AT the fluorescent lights as I entered the Casey's gas station and convenience store. My red work shirt was a wrinkled tapestry. I forgot to do my laundry and had to scrounge up the least dirty shirt from the hamper. The store was awash in artificial colors and smells. Day-old doughnuts sat behind veneers of glass. Wafts of long-stale coffee emanated from dollar dispensers. By the time I started my shift, the only ones still buying the stuff were truckers on their third-shift treks across the county. Candies and gums and pops lined the walls. Big League Chew, Jolly Ranchers, Starbursts, Pepsi, Mountain Dew, RC Cola.

I said hello to Peggy, the sole cashier and one of my former high school classmates. Peggy was the reason I'd gotten this job at the end of fall. She put in the word with Cindy, the manager, saying she'd graduated with me and I was capable of working in the back. So that was that, and I became the Casey's designated pizza maker and fried-food peddler.

I inspected the state of the rotating warmers while making my way to the back food station. "It's been pretty busy. Folks cleared out the warmers 'bout an hour ago. Well, except the Canadian bacon," Peggy said over the shoulder of a guy inspecting the wall of cigarettes behind the counter, his eyes darting around to find the right pack he was in the mood for. People never cleared out the Canadian bacon pizza. I didn't know why the lunch person kept making them when a regular pepperoni would fly off the rotating shelves. I made a mental note on how many pizzas I had to make to fill the warmers before the evening dinner rush hit.

I'd been working at the Casey's General Store in West Liberty for a couple of months by then. It wasn't going well. I graduated from high school in the spring of 2003 and it was now about a year later in the winter of 2004. I was the only food employee working from Wednesday through Sunday evening, meaning for the most part I was alone making pizzas for the town in a small, confined room over the weekends. It was at once busy and boring.

I took the job because I needed help paying for community college. My grades weren't good enough to get into the University of Iowa like I wanted. Most of my friends got into Iowa. Ruben and Eric's grades and ACT scores were good enough to get in, no problem. Ruben actually got a scholarship with the wrestling program so he was in clutch. My laissez-faire attitude toward school came back to bite me in the ass. I had to get my associate's degree at Kirkwood Community College before I could transfer to the U of I—that is, if I passed my classes, which I wasn't.

I was lonely. My week consisted of flunking through classes at Kirkwood at the beginning of the week then working at Casey's during the latter half. Working the evening shift on the weekends killed my social life. While I was fretting about the correct time to put popcorn chicken into the fryer while a taco pizza went through the conveyer oven, my friends were living it up on campus. That's how it felt to me anyway.

Truth is, I hadn't seen my old friends in a long time. Ruben and I reconciled our friendship after all the business with Nate and Arnie dying, but it never got to the same levels of camaraderie as before. We were friendly, but we were never quite ride-or-die friends again. Not like it was with the Pu-Tang Clan. Like it was during the Party Shack days. The best way to sum it up is, Ruben and I had our graduation parties on the same night last spring. It wasn't done on purpose. Our timelines fell like that and neither of us could change them. Ruben had his party at the Party Shack while I had mine in my garage. Our classmates went to one and then the other so as not to show favoritism. Josh Gingerich said that the carne asada Ruben's dad was cooking was good, but it didn't hold anything to my mom's mole sauce. But they did have kegs at the Shack, while my party was dry. That was a thing to consider when picking out which party to hit up in which order.

That all felt like ancient history, though, as I got out a memo pad to jot down the different ingredients and buckets of dough I needed to get from the storage room. I scribbled "2 dough, 1 black olive, 2 bags chips, tomato sauce" on the memo pad as I thought about my old friends. There's a thing that happens when you graduate from high school in a small town. Everyone moving on and getting displaced cuts short the relationships you thought were lifelong. The realization hits that things are so much bigger than what you thought they were in your little town. It's a social entropy as you drift away from the life you thought you knew in West Liberty to the one you were currently traversing full of the unknown. Full of the absence of the people you'd known for your whole life.

And, in my situation, full of dough getting stuck in the roller machine and angry calls when I didn't get some family's order right. "No, no. I meant one half sausage and pepperoni and the other half all pepperoni. Not half sausage, half pepperoni!" an angry caller might say. It wasn't a bad job in and of itself. In the grand scale of menial jobs I've acquired in my life, I'd skew it toward decent. Nowhere near as backbreaking as roofing or as sketchy as janitorial jobs at the mall. No, the actual job was fine. It was the amount of time I had to devote to it and the loneliness of it all that was getting to me. I kept asking my supervisor if we could hire anyone else to split my hours. She replied that it would cost too much to hire and train someone new. So I split being a full-time student at Kirkwood and working full time through my weekend hours at Casey's.

Casey's General Store. That was the official name. There's a spoken-word artist/author/rapper named Watsky who name-drops Casey's in his book *How to Ruin Everything*. In it he says, "I learn Casey's General Store is not a general store, it's just a gas station that sells shitty pizza." The first time I heard that line I got defensive, like you get defensive when someone makes fun of a sibling you don't get along with. Like whoa, whoa. I have a complicated relationship with that place, but as an Iowan that prick of defense manifests. Who is this guy from the coast talking shit about our institutions? Because if you talk to any Iowan they'll know what you're talking about when you talk about Casey's. Part of it is good marketing. There's a saying, part of our shared experience that I can't pinpoint the origin of: "How do you find the town's baseball field? Turn right at the Casey's and sooner or later you'll be there." It makes me think of this idealized version of Iowa. The version that people who've never been to Iowa picture when they close their eyes. *Field of Dreams*. Corn on the cob. Casey's after you catch a fly ball at a T-ball game.

So besides being a gas station with a carry-out pizza section, what made Casey's different? There are a few things of note. One was their coupon policy. Back in the day every pizza box had a coupon you could tear out. Save twenty of those bad boys and you got yourself a free pizza. Many a junk drawer accumulated grease-speckled cardboard coupons. Much to the dismay of my friends and family, Casey's discontinued the box coupons a couple of years ago. One time I visited home and my mom relayed how she was trying to cash in all her coupons before she couldn't do it anymore. A last hurrah of a bygone era.

There are another two reasons why Casey's was and still is special. First, it's the home of the breakfast pizza, or as their current marketing says, "bizza," although we never called it that. An internet forum asked Mila Kunis, famous actress and wife of Iowa native Ashton Kutcher, what her favorite gas station food was. She replied, "It's a place called Casey's, and they're all over Iowa, and they do a delicious breakfast pizza."

A breakfast pizza is easy to imagine. It's eggs, bacon, and cheese with a sausage gravy sauce. Taco pizza, the second thing that makes Casey's stand out, is a little harder for outside folks to wrap their heads around. Casey's taco pizza consists of ground beef, lettuce, and tomato on a crust lined with a bean dip spread. The pièce de résistance is the crushed tortillas chips that cake the top of the pie. I would go heavy on the chips for the West Liberty patrons I served, because I knew how much I liked those chips when I ate taco pizza. I threw in a couple extra hot sauce packets because you could never have enough.

Why does this matter? In the grand scheme of things, it doesn't. But it speaks to that small-town pride in cultural things. It's like Chicago deep dish or Cincinnati and its history with goetta. If someone from outside the Midwest comes around, the conversation with Iowans will inevitably lead to, "What? You haven't tried Casey's taco pizza? We got to order it sometime for you to try it out."

The other reason why this all matters is more complicated. In many ways my family and I were at our lowest point when I was working at Casey's. For a long time I attributed working there to a personal downward spiral, one that coincided with the near dissolution of my parents' relationship. When I picture taco pizza, pork tenderloins, and mozzarella sticks rotating on platters, I think of the hole I found myself in the year after I graduated high school. Fair warning. This is a horror story.

Let's look at the end of a typical shift after I'd been working at Casey's for a few months, when it was well into winter and the outside air stung when you breathed. We would stop taking orders at 10 p.m. A few people always managed to call right up to the deadline or just after, which meant I'd finish the last pizzas around 10:30. By this time my head was fuzzy and my stomach was in knots because I hadn't eaten an ounce of food all day. I remember it being hard to take orders by the end of a shift, the hunger was so real. But as it got close to 11 p.m., the official closing time, my spirits were up. The saliva glands in my mouth were a Pavlovian exercise. My classical conditioning was the hours-old food in the warmers. If there were any errant pizza slices or onion rings or cheese spuds in the warmers at closing time, they were mine to take. Management told us to throw it away while we dumped out the old grease traps, but no one cared if you took food home. Something like excitement or yearning enveloped me as I snatched up food items and put them in their respective baggies and clamshells.

Peggy hollered over from the cash register as I packed up my food. "I can't believe you don't gain any weight from all that food you take home. You share it with your family or something?"

It took me a second to process that Peggy was waiting for a response. By this point it had been about twenty-four hours since I'd last eaten anything. My stomach was cramping up, I was so hungry. "No, yeah. Yeah, my family eats it with me when I bring it home," I said. A lie that warranted turning my face from Peggy. It was only after I finished packing up the last of the food that I realized Peggy hadn't registered that I answered in the first place. It was a question born out of boredom, out of the need to fill the air with social niceties. I finished sweeping and mopping. We turned off the lights and I sped across town to binge on as much food as I could before I burst.

When I got home, I did my best to get to my room as fast as I could, even though it was late enough that my parents were already asleep. I didn't want to risk them finding the bag of food at my side. I didn't share any of the food with my family. They didn't even know it existed. They couldn't know about the food because I couldn't let them suspect what I did after.

After I finished eating, it was all endorphins and adrenaline. It was like a drug, how powerful this act was for me. I ate until I couldn't eat anymore. Scraps of food wrappers crinkled in the larger bag I carried them in. As soon as I finished eating, I stood up. By this time it was routine. A predetermined set of patterns I could rely on. I had trained my body to be as efficient as I could with what I was going to do next. While I went to Kirkwood it was my parents and I living at home, my brother and sister having long since moved out. I had the bedroom downstairs opposite the bathroom. My parents slept in the main bedroom upstairs, the bedroom where Nancy chucked the battery at me when we were younger, where we had our fight to end all fights.

Since the bathroom was so close, it was only a few seconds before I was looking at myself in the mirror. My hands steadied themselves on the corners of the laminate countertop. Its white edges cut into my palms as my face looked back at me. By this point my breathing slowed and there was another feeling washing over. A counterpoint to the feeling that enveloped me while I gorged on my food. I turned on the bathroom faucet and cupped water in my hands. I don't know why I did it this way instead of getting a cup. Maybe it was so I could be flexible if I found myself in a public bathroom where I didn't have access to a cup or glass. I would slurp up a few handfuls of faucet water. Enough to feel uncomfortable.

There would be a moment of reckoning, of clarity, when I wiped the water from my chin and took a long look at myself in the mirror. It was at this point that pangs of shame would creep up on me. Like tendrils of a weed overcoming a garden. I had worked on this. All it took were a couple of hard swallows. It used to be that I had to stick my finger down my throat, like in the movies. But I could do it now without any physical obstructions. I could will it to be. After a few more swallows, I could feel that feeling in my throat. It's in the same place where you feel you're coming down with something. In your lymph nodes. Then it was happening. The toilet seat was already up and ready. I knew enough to make it that way. I bent over the toilet as I purged everything I had eaten a few moments ago.

It was violence. Calling it a purge is the best way to get at the truth of it. The undigested food slapped the water of the toilet as my throat burned from the force. It didn't take long. It never did. I flushed once, got some toilet paper to clean the rim of the seat, making sure to get under the rim as well, then flushed again. I surveyed my face as I looked in the mirror while I washed my hands. My skin was flushed and my eyes bloodshot. The capillaries jagged and angry. *Breathe a bit, Chuy. Let it come down.*

This is when the third and most lasting feeling overcame me. It's hard to put into words for those who don't know. It's something like a deep satisfaction. Like how I imagine a sculptor looks at a finished piece. Like you finally got what you deserved at the end of a long shift. Or like you have a secret all to yourself and keeping control of that secret gives you power.

I finished washing my hands and leaned forward, inches away from the mirror. I turned my face to the right and brandished the top row of teeth. My fingers came up to inspect one tooth. The week before, after vomiting at my friend's house in Iowa City, I went to the sink and a chunk of this tooth fell out. I didn't know it at the time, but the bile and acid were messing me up. Corroding the enamel of my teeth. It was like something in a body horror movie. Like something an early Sam Raimi would direct. This didn't stop me though. That feeling I felt while eating too much and puking it all up was too alluring. I wrung my hands out on a towel and walked out, feelings of power and secrecy flooding my body like the chemicals they are.

––––––––––

This feels like a confession. Before now only a handful of people knew about this period of my life, when the physical manifestations of bulimia nervosa took hold. I phrase it like that because, like how alcoholics talk about their relationship with the drink, you never get over it. It lives with you. The best you can do is hope to manage the physical act of the affliction and not revert or succumb to the urges.

The physical habit of throwing up food lasted for a couple of years. In talking to therapists, I've parsed out different ideas on the why of it all. At the time I thought it was cut and dried. After the first few months working at Casey's, I gained a few pounds from eating the end-of-shift food. The loneliness of my life and access to copious amount of junk food led to this inevitability. But gaining weight came at odds with my identity as a dancer.

There it is. Things start to click when I bring that up. I, like a lot of other b-boys, have something of an obsession with being light. We call it being skinny-buff. Like Bruce Lee. I remember fretting over the fact that I was gaining weight. *This is going to make it harder for me to dance. To move my body the way I want to.* I'm not sure when it first happened. I imagine it was the natural progression of eating too much and feeling guilty and ashamed. It felt like I wasn't passionate enough as a dancer because I didn't even have the discipline to regulate my food intake. In the back of my head I thought that purging everything out was its own type of discipline. It showed that I cared about the dance.

This is, of course, bullshit. The dangerous thinking of someone suffering from things bigger than themselves. But in talking about this episode I have to be real with how I regarded the demons I lived with. It took me a long time to look at the bigger picture. To realize that in many ways I was at the nadir of something. That all these factors—school, work, and family—were making me feel a type of way that caused me to lash out. But instead of lashing out at those around me, I directed it inward. This was a penance for a punishment I couldn't comprehend. One that woke me up every morning I lived with my parents that winter.

The morning after that shift, my mom woke me up. Her repeated cries came muffled from the bathroom I had thrown up in the night before. She did this every morning. A good cry that ramped up with time. Involuntary sobs that broke like a levee into one long, sustained wail. This was my alarm clock as of late. Every morning I'd wake up staring at the ceiling, listening to the cries of my mother.

There was no way around it: my parents' relationship was in shambles. I can't get too much into it, for a couple of reasons. One, my parents are still together and have moved on from this point in their relationship. They got help like I got help and their own individual actions are theirs to live with and tell. Two, they still live in West Liberty. And West Liberty is a lot of things, but in the end it is still a small town with folks who like to talk. There is gossip in backyards and in hushed tones outside the Dollar General. There are little old Mexican ladies talking shit in their living rooms.

So here's what I can say. My parents' relationship was a wreck. It was real bad. By any traditional American white-person metric, they should have gotten a divorce a long time ago. But my parents, like me, are stubborn. Their strict Roman Catholic upbringing forbade any talk of divorce. They took their vows seriously and would have rather lived with the animus then separate. So that's what they did. It is not a coincidence that both of the Joshes came from families with divorced parents, while I didn't know of any Mexicans or Laotians with parents who split up. In fact, the only Mexican adult I knew who was divorced was one of my tías. She split from her husband because he beat her. But even then it was a crisis of conscience for her to break her matrimonial vows.

My parents were long past their breaking point and still together. My dad would leave the house for hours. He wasn't coming home after his job anymore to work in the garage before dinner. Sometimes he wouldn't get home until after midnight. My mom would meet the absence of my father with various emotions. Despair, anger, flippancy. We weren't dealing with any of these problems, mind you. We let them accumulate and fester in us, like a vessel filling with an unknown substance, expanding until the walls began to crack under the pressure.

By the time I was dressed and out of my room, my mom was alone at the kitchen table. Her malaise followed her from room to room. She spoke aloud, not to me but loud enough that I could hear it. "Ay, Dios. Por favor ayúdame. Ayuda a toda mi familia." She prayed like this often, full of desperation and angst. The first few months, when I thought my parents were going through a regular tiff, I would talk to my mom. See if she was okay. If there was anything I could say to make it better. But nothing worked.

The last time I said anything, I messed up. I said, "Ama, maybe you should leave if neither of you are happy and you can't make it better. That's what people do." My mom bolted upright as she scolded me. She told me that the devil was in me for saying such things. It was sacrilegious to even bring that up.

As she got up, the kitchen chair clattered. "Dios, este chamaco no sabe que está haciendo. Ayuda a este niño también." She said it like a prayer, but it felt like a scolding. I walked away from my mother and the kitchen table. Holding in what I wanted to say. I didn't need any help. That's what I thought at the time.

My mom muttering to herself and crying was a daily occurrence. One I grew calloused toward. My dad wouldn't talk anything out. He didn't want to communicate. And my mom wanted nothing more than to let everything out. She was a torrent of emotion. They couldn't make the two pieces fit, and my stance was that they needed to separate. With that not being an option, we were in purgatory. Every day was the same dream of barely contained rage from my mother and cold indifference from my father.

Sobs filled the kitchen as I tried my best to ignore them and get a Red Bull out of the fridge. It was late in the morning and I would be getting hungry soon. On workdays it seemed like I had only a few hours before I had to get back to Casey's to sling pizzas. I wanted to make the most of my afternoon and fend off the hunger pangs that would come. My breakfast was a single Red Bull that I drank on the way to Iowa City. I would dance at the Field House for a few hours by myself, practicing my b-boy moves on the main deck to a tinny boom box I kept in my car.

I practiced by myself because my crewmates were all working or at school in the mornings. Training hours were weekday evenings, which meant I could hit up crew practices during the early week. But my work schedule prevented more than a few. So if I wanted to keep on training, I had to go by myself in the afternoons. I didn't mind it. Breaking felt like the only time I was in full control. It was the outlet I thought I needed to sort through the mess that my family was in. That I was in. I would drill combinations and battle through the creeping hunger. I was always hungry. In a way, the hunger reminded me that I was on the right track. That I was making the necessary sacrifices to become a better dancer.

The insidious thing about my outlook on breaking is that I regarded it as my savior. It felt like the only thing keeping me moving forward. But in reality it was one of the catalysts that sparked my eating disorder. Looking back it's easier to see the harm I was doing to myself. How this striving toward a certain body type descended into an obsession.

Body dysmorphic traits can run through all forms of dance, including the predominately male world of breaking. But the preconceived notion is that it affects women. When you think of a dancer with an eating disorder, what type of dancer comes to mind? If you Google it, what comes up? B-boys and hip-hop dancers should show up in the search results with the ballet and classically trained dancers, but they don't. The guys in their b-boy stances are as likely to feel the same pressures as the bun heads at the barre. I know I'm not the only breaker who had an unhealthy obsession with being skinny-buff. I'm willing to bet I'm not the only one who lives with an eating disorder. The tricky thing is, it's such a new, niche dance that there's a lack of studies. And the macho aesthetic of breaking runs counter to admitting you have a disorder. So it goes under the radar and the assumptions get levied at other dancers.

There is a picture of me around this time. I am lying by the side of a pool in blue swim trunks. I am emaciated. My skin sticks to my ribs and my cheeks are hollow. When I played football in high school, I was a skinny dude. At the most, at around seventeen years old, I weighed about 150 pounds. At the time of the photo by the pool, at the height of my bulimia, I weighed 105 pounds. That photo is seared into my brain because when I first saw it I remember thinking I was overweight. That's how bad it can get. How firmly your demons take hold of you.

Nobody knew what I was up to, but they noticed a change in my physique. They inadvertently showered me with toxic praise. I sought out those words from unassuming folks. "Oh wow, Chuy, you look good! You must be dancing all the time, huh?" I got so many compliments on my physique and work ethic. It became this feedback loop of praise and affliction. They said I looked great, and I convinced myself that it also meant I was in control.

I latched onto those words of encouragement and fueled my practices with them. I regarded the hunger pangs like I did b-boy burns and bruises. It was all a badge of honor to show how much I was embodying the dance. After practice I would drive home to shower before work. If my hunger was too great to ignore, I would have a bowl of cereal or a small side salad. This was the only real sustenance I allowed myself. Meaning it was the only thing like a meal I would eat without purging it from my body immediately after.

Driving back to West Liberty from practice was a meditation. I took Highway 6 back and forth from West Lib to Iowa City. I've must have driven this road thousands of times. It's the road I think of when I think of home. When I was driving back that winter, the landscape was barren. Cold, hard fields zoomed past as I drove home in silence. All I could think was that I hoped my parents weren't home. That I would have a reprieve from their fighting. Or their nonfighting, which was somehow even worse. If no one was home, I could have my daily snack, shower, and take off for Casey's.

It was with relief that I pulled up to our house and saw there were no other cars in the gravel driveway. That relief was short lived after I showered and was getting ready in my room. My room shared a wall with the living room, and I could hear the sound of the entrance door opening. If what followed was the footfalls of my dad's heavy work shoes, I'd be in the clear. He would ignore me like I did him. We'd pass each other without an acknowledgment. I cursed to myself when I heard the scuffle of multiple people entering our house. It was my mom joined with other hushed tones—my tías Nelle, Irma, and Berta. Here to offer support in her time of need. I thought about my reaction to my mom earlier that morning, when I told her she should leave. My tías would do a much better job of showing their condolences, of being there for my mother.

Before I knew what happened, their voices mixed together into a wail. It was a chorus of anguish. My mom's sisters joined their eldest sister in her peril. The hairs on my arms stood on end as the sound pierced through the wall. There was something about that explosion of emotion. I couldn't handle it. The way the sound hit was more like a plea to a higher power than cries of empathy for a sister. Like the base prayer from the bottom of your gut. *Please, please. Por favor. Save this marriage. Help these poor souls find their peace.*

Quickly, so as not to draw any attention from my tías in the living room, I grabbed my keys and walked through the kitchen and to the refuge outside. The door closed off their cries like I had sealed off their torment from my heart. I got in my car and drove around town until it was time to start my shift at Casey's. My gut in knots as I tried to ignore the hunger pangs. My thoughts preoccupied with food on warmers, rotating in their stagnant heat.

Our supervisor, Cindy, joined Peggy in the fluorescence of the store. Cindy was a middle-aged woman with feathered blonde hair like she used to be a rocker in the eighties. She chain-smoked and took frequent breaks, grabbing a pack of cigs from the wall behind the counter and smoking by the dumpsters. Cindy was gruff but fair. She stood up for me when a customer came in after they got their pizza saying I messed up their order and wanting a refund. She asked them why they ate it all if they didn't like it and wanted their money back.

Cindy greeted me after the jingle of the front door subsided. "Back for another glorious shift, eh?" she asked, deadpan. I smiled and gave her the laugh I give white employers when they want me to laugh at something. Her tone shifted as she tapped her finger on an open newspaper on the counter. "Hey, before I forget. Don't you know this kid in today's paper? Peggy says you two went to school with him, right? It's a shame—" her voice descended into gravelly enunciations as she muttered to herself. I couldn't catch what she said because I'd just seen who she was talking about in the paper.

His name was in bold in the police blotter. University of Iowa wrestler arrested. It was Ruben. They used a photo he took for the wrestling team. You could make out that he was wearing a suit with an askew black-and-gold tie. It was a small blurb so it got right into it. "UI wrestler arrested for the following: interference with official acts, providing alcohol to minors, possession of alcohol under the legal age, driving while barred."

"Damn, Ruben," I almost caught myself saying before I said to Cindy, "Yeah, he was my friend growing up. We don't hang out anymore though." Cindy shrugged and flipped the pages of the newspaper, muttering something to herself about kids these days.

It had been a while since I'd thought of my old friends. Most of them were going to the U of I so I rarely saw them. Seeing Ruben's profile in the paper confirmed my suspicion that my old friends were still drinking and living that life on campus. When I split with them because of breaking, because of the drifting apart of our lives, I quit drinking. This would not be the last time Ruben's name was emblazoned in newspaper headlines. Each time it happened the papers added to the rap sheet, accompanying the same team photo of my friend in his school tie. Seeing the very public downfall of my old friend was a reminder that we all have our demons. I was able to escape the drink but got caught in an eating disorder. Our traumas manifested themselves in different ways, but we were fighting them all the same.

The last time I'd talked to the guys was a few months back. Eric asked me if I wanted to go out to the bars with them. I told them I had to work that night, like I did every weekend. Eric, after fighting his height all his life, finally hit a growth spurt in college. It took him until he was almost in his twenties. He's taller than I am now. The people he met in college had no clue he'd been the runt of the litter all his life.

I don't know if I would have gone out with them if I hadn't had to work my shift at Casey's. The bars weren't my scene, and it seemed like they were going out for a singular purpose: to get drunk. It did feel frustrating to have my work dictate another aspect of my social life. It felt like a loneliness time loop. Get up to the sound of my mom crying, go practice, go to work, puke until I could taste bile, go to sleep, repeat. I don't know why I didn't quit. I needed the money, sure, but it was like I couldn't separate myself from the cycle of pathos. It was like I woke from a dream but couldn't move from the bed. An observer of my own undoing. Death by popcorn chicken and specialty pizzas.

Eric popped into my head as I went through the beginning shift check. There was something else about Ruben and Eric that was getting at me. About my old friends and the way we grew up. Like there was an unresolved story. Snippets of a night from long ago snapped into focus. One thought cascaded into many, until I was no longer in a Casey's measuring out dough for pizzas but back with my old friends. The night we almost killed Eric.

In a lot of ways, West Liberty messed us up. As somebody who grew up there and champions my hometown, it's a controversial statement. We like to extoll the virtues of the state's first majority Hispanic town. We highlight the good times. The diversity and uniqueness of it all. But, there are other sides of it, the unspoken sides of small towns. The racism, the violence, the misogyny, the alcoholism. Those things shaped my childhood as much as the Kimberly Park pool and Wapsi Creek fields. Seeing my friend in the police blotter reminded me how much the pursuit of the drink molded us as kids.

One night my parents were on vacation to Mexico and my brother threw a party. I had my friends over and we were all hanging out upstairs playing video games while my older brother and his friends drank downstairs. We were around twelve or thirteen years old. Josh Gingerich and Ruben went downstairs and snuck some beers for us. We drank the drink of our older siblings while we played *Tenchu: Stealth Assassins* on my brother's PlayStation. We were content with siphoning off the older kids' beers for the rest of the night, but a knock on the door interrupted our game session. One of my brother's friends opened the door. *Oh crap*, we all thought.

"Hey, what's going on in here?" the guy asked as we tried to hide our contraband. Remember, my brother is around ten years older than me, so this dude would have been in his early twenties. "Wait, are you little kids drinking in here?" None of us knew what to say. Eric tried to stammer out a response, but the guy threw us a curveball. "That's awesome! I wish I was as cool as you when I was your age." And that was that. We kept on drinking, emboldened by the proud words of a man who stumbled up the stairs and congratulated a bunch of kids for underage drinking.

I can't predict who will read these words. Depending on who you are, the previous story may mortify you, or you might not see what the big deal is. If you grew up in a town like West Liberty, then it's nothing out of the ordinary. It feels almost trivial to put it on paper because I can hear the echoes of my hometown asking, what's the problem? We were to be men, and men drink. That was the natural order of things as laid out to us as children. That's what my friends were battling while I battled my demons at Casey's.

The night we almost killed Eric happened at the Party Shack. Of course it did. That rundown garage was our childhood into teenage years. Its unassuming physicality hid an edifice that towered over our developing lives. I had my first sexual encounter at the Shack, with a girl after a quinceañera practice. We walked from the community center at the fairgrounds and I told her we could hide away in a spot I knew. We found ourselves in the stuffy garage, hidden from the oversaturated daylight and brutal summer heat.

This particular night was in that transition period before high school. Before Ruben and I had our big blowout. This was when we were stealing our parents' liquor and taking our spoils to the Shack. That night we found the motherlode. Gingerich had made friends with a kid in our grade and somehow convinced him to steal two full bottles of his dad's liquor for us. The good stuff, though we couldn't differentiate between what was good and not. Weird thing was, that kid didn't even hang out with us. He stole his dad's alcohol and put it inside their grill for us to take. Jerry and I procured the goods in a clandestine mission. We clutched the bottles as we ran across town back to Ruben's, unsheathing them for our friends in the safety of the Shack's walls.

What followed was a case study in taking things too far. Because we had worked so hard to get the bottles. Because we didn't understand the concept of limits. I mean, how much should kids who weighed less than a hundred pounds drink? Who was there to teach us about pacing ourselves? That sharing two full bottles of alcohol between six skinny kids was playing with fire?

Actually, there was an extra kid with us. Joining Ruben, Jerry, Josh Gingerich, Eric, and me was Eric's brother Pepe. Pepe was a year younger than Eric and got the funny gene of the Maldonado boys. He made us laugh and we enjoyed having him around. Sometimes he would get into it with Eric and that was funny to us too. Pepe was even smaller than Eric. Smaller but rounder. That was something we joked with the Maldonados about, that all the boys looked like their dad, like the same person, only with different variants in place. Pepe was the chubbier little-brother version of Eric the way that Sergio was the oldest and biggest model. At the end of the previous school year, after a junior high dance, we set it up so Pepe would fight this kid in our grade. The kid was small for our class, which meant he was the same size as Pepe. They scrapped for a few seconds before the kid's dad pulled into the parking lot and broke it up. He yelled at us to get away. When Pepe talked back, the old guy said with thinly veiled racism, "Okay, that's enough out of you, Pedro," knowing damn well that wasn't his name. We crowded around Pepe and congratulated him on holding his own while the man walked away with his bruised son.

In the Shack we did that thing West Liberty kids do. We pushed ourselves to see who could drink the most. Who could tolerate the fire going down their throat with the most machismo. I made a production of not showing any reaction at all when downing a gulp from the bottle. Ruben and Jerry hollered and patted me on the back as I gave a little shrug and passed the bottle to Josh. Josh tried to do the same but couldn't help contorting his face and sucking in his breath in reaction to the liquor. But it was Eric, tiny little Eric, who drank the most that night. He was trying to show Pepe the ropes. Trying to prove something to his little brother. He gulped from the bottle until he couldn't see or stand straight.

It wasn't long into the night when we realized that something was wrong. That Eric had drank until he was out of his senses. He stumbled among the four walls of the Shack, growing more belligerent and nonsensical as the alcohol took root in his gut. Pepe was the one to first call it out. "Hey, is my brother okay, guys? He doesn't seem like he's okay. Hey. Eric," Pepe called out his older brother's name again and again.

The festive atmosphere of the Shack dissipated as Eric's inebriation solidified. It wasn't that he was drunk. It was that he was blacking out and unintelligible. Panic crept up as the rest of us looked to one another for how to best deal with our drunk friend.

Jerry tried to dismiss it at first. "Ah, it's no worries, guys. I've seen folks at parties get like that. Let's cut him off and get him some water." We all agreed and attempted to talk to Eric.

At this point Eric was emotional. His slurred enunciations became these primal, guttural yells. Like he was so drunk he couldn't make sense of his emotions, like they were all coming out at once. He began to cry and holler. We just needed him to sober up a bit, that's all. He'd drink some water and snap out of it.

But his cries worsened and he was refusing to drink any water. There was panic in Pepe's voice as he tried to get through to his older brother. "Hey. Hey Eric, man, come on, drink some water, bro." We echoed Pepe's pleas but to no avail. Us crowding around Eric and trying to calm him down made things worse. He started to get mad and lash out at us in his drunken stupor. Somehow, after much coaxing and pleading from the group, we got him onto the mattress in the corner of the Shack. After repeated attempts to get up and say he was fine, Eric slumped onto the bed.

The rest of us had sobered up by then, from the fear of not knowing what to do. We went outside into the night air to get some space between us and our drunk friend. Pepe stayed by his brother's side, keeping an eye on him. We all agreed that we didn't know what to do. "As long as he stays asleep, we should be good," I said. Ruben nodded and posted up against the entrance of the Shack.

"I don't know, man. Him out like that makes me nervous," Josh said. We stood around in a huddle outside the Shack, adding a thought here or there. Acting like we knew what the hell we were doing. After a bit it seemed like everything would be okay. We began to joke and say that we were never going to let Eric hear the last of this. Then Pepe hollered for us from inside.

Eric had pissed himself on the mattress. He had come to and was even more distraught than before. Pepe was wrestling with Eric, who was stumbling off the mattress and outside the Shack. "Yo, Eric, chill out, man. Get back inside!" Ruben hissed as we all met our friend at the doorway. Eric was full-on crying now. He was a confused little boy, crying out into the sky. He lost his footing and fell down from the doorway, spilling out into Ruben's backyard. His cry grew shrill from the ground. Jerry and Josh joined Ruben as they scolded Eric to calm down and get back into the Shack. That's all he had to do. Get back in and away from the outside world.

Eric's cries echoed into the night, getting louder and louder. He began to cry for his mother. We scrambled and talked over one another as we tried to get our friend back inside the garage. "Dude, what do we do? He's going to wake people up. We're fucked." I kept glancing at Ruben's house across the backyard. His parents' bedroom was far enough from the Shack that we could get in all sorts of trouble without them knowing, but not when we were outside. Not when one of us was crying and hollering from the backyard.

What followed was an act of desperation. It was an attempt to put a stop to the noise and crying. To regain control of a situation that had long ago spiraled away from us. I don't know who did it first. As far as I know, we all started at the same time. Our pleas of desperation turned to anger. Our scrambling and clawing at Eric to get up turned into something else. We circled around our friend and began to kick and strike him. "Shut up. Yo. Shut up!" we repeated at Eric as he continued to cry.

"Hey, what are you guys doing, stop it! That's my brother," said Pepe as he got on his hands and knees and attempted to shield our blows. We cursed at him to get out of the way as we rained blows down on our friend. It was an act of violence that has stayed with me forever. It was the act of a bunch of kids, terrified that their friend would get them in trouble. That his cries would notify the town. We resorted to the only means we knew to get him to stop. His cries subsided as he gasped for air and reeled from our strikes. Pepe and Ruben picked up the heap of Eric's body and dragged him back into the Shack. The rest of us followed and closed the wooden door behind us. The door scraped against the floor as we pushed our whole weight against the wood, closing it tight.

After we got Eric back into the Shack, he passed out on the urine-stained mattress. We all stayed up and took shifts watching him. We knew enough to lay him on his side so he didn't choke on his own vomit. When the sun broke through the night, Eric was still drunk. He came to and didn't remember anything. I don't know if he recalls what we did to him.

It being Sunday morning, Pepe argued that they needed to get home. We tried to talk him out of it so Eric could sober up with us. But Sunday service was coming up. Pepe said, "Believe me, it will be a hell of a lot worse if we're not back to go to church. You guys don't know how my parents get." We got mad and continued to put up a fuss, but Pepe was adamant. He stood close to a stumbling Eric as they made the walk back to their house.

The rest of the story of the Maldonados I heard secondhand. The story went that Pepe asked his older brothers to help. They secured Eric in a bedroom to buy some time. But their parents were God-fearing, church-going Mexicans, and they'd be damned if one of their boys wasn't going to church with them. That's when they found out their boy was hungover in his bedroom. They got mad. And scared. There was talk of taking Eric to get his stomach pumped. But there was some quick thinking. One of the brothers brought up that if their parents took this kid to the hospital, they would have to explain to some white doctors what had happened. Would they even be able to articulate it in English? Who would those people blame? Those white people didn't know how it worked in West Liberty.

So they left Eric home to sober up, but not before his mom called all the other Mexican moms she knew. We were caught. And in deep shit. When I realized the adults in our life knew about that night, a pinprick of realization hit me: we jumped Eric outside the Shack for nothing. There was no time to dwell on that though. We were catastrophizing all the horrible punishments we would get. And you want to know what we were most scared of? That somehow word would get back to our eighth-grade football coaches and we wouldn't get to play come fall. Which didn't even happen. That might be the most messed up bit of this whole story. I got into more trouble the time I talked back to one of my tíos than I ever did for our drinking escapades. We got slapped on the wrist—remember, boys will be men, and men drink.

Back at the Casey's my stomach lurched thinking back on that night. The memory is one of those that hits me when I least expect it. Like lightning. The memory of us attacking Eric on the ground as he cried for help. Whenever it resurfaces, it feels like a lifetime ago. Like we were different people. Stupid kids showing the depravity of humanity. Like a *Lord of the Flies* scene played out in the humid night of a midwestern town. While corroborating stories for this book, I chatted with Gingerich via Facebook. We went down memory lane. We went over some of the greatest hits. Things that made it into this book, like rummaging through my brother's things in the garage. Things that didn't make the cut, like the night we swear we heard a ghost at a cemetery. But it was Gingerich who mentioned it first, "The night we almost killed Eric . . . "

So why do I bring this up? Why does it come creeping back into my thoughts? The whole process of telling these stories has been an unburdening. I want to get at the truth of our childhoods. It was like walking a tightrope. Lots of bad things happened to us. We did lots of bad things to other people. Shit, we did lots of bad things to ourselves. There are two questions I ruminate on in my passing age. One is whether I had a "good" childhood. Which is such a complicated question for anyone, but for us growing up the way we did in West Lib, it's all compounded. We had a unique, celebratory, maddening, surreal, horrific childhood— often all at once.

The other question is whether or not I am a good person. Writing it here brings up a spark of anxiety, because I want to excuse all the bad things I've done. I want to scream out about all the horrible things that have happened to me. I want to convey what it was like to be a little kid and have a grown-up call me a "wetback" and a "spic." But in that same breath I need to also scream out about Eric. It would be easy to let the incriminating stuff fall by the wayside, to paint this picture of utopia in small-town form. Or to color ourselves as forever victims. We were the scrappy kids fighting against boredom and racists. That's one way I pitched this book. We were the *Stranger Things* kids, but instead of fighting Demogorgons we were fighting racist kids at recess. But that's not the whole truth, right? We were also fighting against innocence. We were fighting against ourselves. And in that fight we hurt a lot of people.

During the writing of this book I received a letter. An anonymous letter in my work mailbox, addressed to me with no return address. A week or so before I got this letter, I made some social media posts about how I was trying to get a full picture of what it was like for us growing up in

West Liberty. I also did another post detailing this time we went to Perkins with the Laosthas. I got sick after eating a Tremendous Twelve and it's been a silly, fun West Liberty legend since.

Back to this letter. I figured it was something boring, work related, but when I opened it up, it proved to be something far different. Here's a highlight of what it said:

Dear Mr. Renteria, I hope this letter finds you well,
First of all, I want to thank you from the bottom of my heart that you are writing a book about our town that we grew up in. I am a graduate of West Liberty and as you will find in this letter a terrible writer.

You talk about racism but do you talk about prejudice? How it sucked not being one of the "popular" Mexicans or Laotians or Asians or Central Americans or even Anglos. What did it feel like being a true first-generation Mexican in high school and looking at the cool Mexicans hanging out with the cool Anglos and realizing "I'm never going to be part of that group," you would think it would suck right?

How it felt getting bullied in the trailer courts and being scared to death to ride your bike because the "cool Laotians" would want to beat you up for God knows what reason. Ask certain people how it felt like getting picked on by Ruben Chavez and Eric Maldonado and nobody doing a damn thing to stop it. Ask the less popular girls how it felt not getting to wear a jersey on Fridays for football. Ask on how within your own team there were tensions and fights and bullying and cliques within.

If you want the true story of West Liberty I believe you will take this advice and put it to good use because you are a good person. Like I said before I am not a writer like you I am nowhere near it. All I have is my West Liberty education below my belt. It's going to be hard but at least the people who never got noticed will get noticed by you. I look forward to reading your book as much as I looked forward to reading the last one.
Sincerely,
A former West Liberty citizen and graduate

His words caused me to think of the accumulated anger and trauma we both experienced and caused. It's the same panic I felt at the Casey's when I thought back on that night with Eric. It's the same thing I feel in the pit of my stomach as I detail the same story on these pages. What makes a person good? Or a town bad? Is it an accumulation of the good deeds against the burden of the bad things that happen? I don't know. That's the thing, I don't know. Alone in the back of a gas station, this was the feeling that corresponded with my every action. The anonymous letter said that I was a good person. I don't know if I agree.

————————

Every Casey's shift was the same. Try to deal with all these complicated emotions about my family, about my friends, about our hometown. Get through the shift. Call after call. Pizza after pizza. While the ever-present hunger grows and all worries dissipate. The hunger would get so all-consuming that it overpowered these existential questions of goodness. By the time I was packing the end-of-shift food, it was all I could think of and I was grateful. Every other worry recessed into the fringes of my attention. Bingeing and purging was all that mattered. I dumped as much food as I could stuff into Casey's branded baggies and said good-bye to Peggy and Cindy on the way out. They, too, were gone from my attention as I sped across town. The smells from the fried food in the passenger seat contributed to this lapse in object permanence. Nothing else mattered.

My dad in the kitchen interrupted my singular purpose of bingeing. He was sitting by himself at the kitchen table, alone and quiet. Like he always seemed to be as of late. It looked like he had gotten in before me. Or rather it felt like he'd just gotten in. I held the bag of warm food behind me as I greeted him. The warmth of the plastic bag radiated against my low back. My father had lost weight. Not a significant amount. But enough. Lately he was trimming his mustache and goatee with care. And I could have sworn his facial hair used to be less vibrant. Cheryl, the girl who broke up with me and inadvertently jump-started my dance career, talked about it once. Cheryl and I got back together throughout high school. It was a miserable affair. We thought that, as high school sweethearts, we should belong together. We both were too scared to end it first. After high school the relationship came to its natural end. At the tail end of it, she noticed my dad was getting fitter, dressing nicer. "You know what that means, right?" she asked me once. "When a man isn't around as much and starts taking care of himself?" I refused to answer her. Refused to look at the truth she spoke in the guise of questions.

My dad nodded at me as he thumbed his keys on the kitchen table. I nodded back, trying not to engage in conversation. Trying not to notice anything about my dad I didn't want to face. He asked me about work. That's something we did as family. As father and son. We avoided the real conversations and instead asked about work. "¿Y la trabajo, cómo está?"

"It was the same. Long. By myself the whole time," I said as I stood with my back to the wall. This seemed like a formality. Like we had crossed paths and the powers that be dictated that we must now make small talk. I knew our talk wouldn't last long. My dad, already a quiet man, had been even more stoic lately. He wasn't engaging with anyone. It was like he was a ghost that existed through the motions he performed throughout the house. Wake up. Go to work. Come home late in the night. Ignore the festering divide growing in the house.

I realized something as our brief conversation sputtered to a stop, after I finished mumbling specifics about how many calls I took that night, about the people who came to say hi after getting gas. I was breathing out of my mouth. It was a reflex. Like how I was keeping the bag away from my dad's eye level so he wouldn't notice how much food I was going to eat. I was breathing through my mouth so I wouldn't accidentally smell the unfamiliar perfume on my dad.

I don't know how to make it any clearer without feeling like I'm throwing a bomb back at my hometown. Read between the lines and feel how much this episode in my life messed me up. It's not enough to say that my parents were fighting. It's to say that they were at the end of the line and refusing to go over. My dad finished his pleasantries with me and got back to doing nothing sitting at the kitchen table. I avoided his eyes and made it to my room. Happy to not have to think anymore. To have the food encompass my being. This was a primal physical thing. To eat until it hurt and purge in the bathroom until it hurt even more. When I finished, my throat was on fire. In the bathroom by myself was when I finally felt in control.

Some would say that my bingeing and purging was a sin. I know my religious grandma would have said that. It's one of the seven deadly sins. Gluttony. It's interesting to think about this time in my life from that perspective. In a lot of ways it felt like what I was doing was penance. It was a manifestation of how ineffectual I felt in dealing with my family's problems. The sins of my father when he left our home. The wrath building up in my mother. It felt like it wasn't my place to force them to deal with their problems, plus my mom said it was blasphemous to encourage them to separate. So we were in purgatory. My dad wouldn't leave. My mom wouldn't leave. No one would talk. We were in this house destined to live the same quiet fury. So I purged. Because I didn't know what else to do. Because deep down I knew it was hurting me, and that seemed like something I deserved.

————————

Weeks of rising familial tensions went by. All buildup and no release. There were small moments amplified by the tension of the last few months. A word unsaid. A plea to stay home ignored. I kept on working, kept on purging. I started to puke outside the safety of our bathroom more and more. I would vomit in public restrooms after eating too much at a restaurant. Or excuse myself at a friend's house after they splurged on a pizza for us to eat. I became a master of cleaning up and hiding my messes. The efficiency of my purging improved. I developed a pride in how fast I could go from expelling to washing up in a sink and back to polite society. It was like a game. Improve my times, improve the efficacy of my charade. I used to pretend I was going to the bathroom. Now I was so fast I could say that I was freshening up. Just a little piss and washing of hands before we leave. No one ever caught me. No one ever knew unless I told them. And I didn't tell anybody what was going on.

There were a few close calls. One of the hardest things to keep under wraps is the smell. Vomit can have a very distinct smell that people are hip to. One time I threw up dinner in my bathroom while my friend and crewmate Keven was visiting. As I opened the door to leave, he was right there trying to get in. That usually didn't happen. Usually people wait a bit before entering after you use the restroom. It's a bit of awkward social etiquette that I used to my advantage, but Keven was too comfortable with our friendship. He needed to go. I balked at his presence before me. Sure enough, as he entered the bathroom he blurted out, "Dude, it smells in here."

"Yeah, yeah. I just went to the bathroom, man," I said with more panic than was necessary. I said it in a way that conveyed he was stepping over the line, how rude it was of him to bring that up. In actuality his barging in terrified me. I wouldn't know what to say if anyone found out about my eating disorder.

"No, but it smells messed up. It smells like puke in here," he said, oblivious. I managed a laugh. Played it off like he was crazy and his senses were betraying him. A necessary gaslighting to keep him away. I don't know if he ever knew. I don't think so. I don't think he even suspected it. When it came to my friends and my crew, I projected an aura of leadership. I was the glue holding our dance group together. I was the one who was rational and in charge. I protected that image at all costs. No, I'm certain no one knew what I was doing.

One night while heading into a work shift at Casey's, I bumped into Eric. He was walking out of the store after getting gas. We exchanged pleasantries outside in the parking lot. It was too cold to sit and talk for long, but we shivered and hopped from foot to foot while we caught up. I apologized for not being able to go out to downtown Iowa City the time he invited me. "Oh man, I forgot about that! No, it's actually good that you didn't go out, man. That night was messed up. Freaking Ruben, man. You know how he gets. He got drunk at the bar, and he can't stop. So he keeps on drinking and eventually he starts to steal people's drinks around us. Straight up stumbling around trying to find whatever glass he can and pounding it."

I opened my eyes wide at Eric's story. It was tough to hear. Tough to think about my old friend acting like that. A few months later I would experience it myself. I went out with the guys and Ruben did the same thing Eric detailed. For Ruben, going out was no longer about getting some drinks with friends. It was about getting as drunk as possible in the shortest amount of time. I left the bar before it got any worse, shook at the sight of my old friend stumbling around and invading people's space to siphon off their drinks.

I also left because I knew it meant trouble. I knew I was seeing a repeat of the story Eric told me in the parking lot of Casey's. "So he's going around stealing people's drinks and he comes across the wrong table and gets into it. And no one will back down so we take it outside."

"Shit," I replied, picturing the scene. "And you guys went outside with him?"

"What else could we do? We had to have his back, right?" I nodded, unable to articulate a response that would please someone from West Liberty. "Let me tell you, Chuy, if we didn't get set up by these guys. They had all their friends waiting around the corner. We got our asses kicked."

Eric proceeded to go into the gory details and to talk about honor and how it wasn't like how it was in our town. *Honor?* the thought came to me. *Was it honorable when your own friends jumped you, Eric? Were we honorable then?*

I couldn't help but see the parallels between that night and the night we jumped Eric. Couldn't help but feel we were on a natural progression from that messed-up night so long ago. Ruben needed to keep up our drinking that we started when we were young. He needed to drink so bad it threw his world into chaos. A part of me connected with that feeling. Where my bingeing and purging vice was all done in secrecy, Ruben's was out in the open, with ramifications across friend groups and towns.

Eric's story dwindled to a close. I muttered that I was going to be late for my shift before we embraced and went our separate ways. I walked into the fluorescence of the gas station, to start another shift that would end like all the other ones before it.

One of those mornings started like all the others and ended with me messing up. I woke up to the sound of my mom crying yet again. This time seemed worse than the countless mornings before it, if that was even possible. When her cries in the kitchen woke me up, something in me snapped. At the futility of our situation. At the fact that my parents wouldn't end their suffering. My suffering.

I walked out of my bedroom and confronted my mother. I cut short her cries that were even more amped up than when I was in bed. I wanted those shrieks to end. My voice was husky, still transitioning from my sleep. "Ama," I called out in a fury, "ya. No más. You need to leave. You guys need to be fucking done. I don't care. I don't care about you crying anymore. Because you're not going to do anything. Either of you. It's going to keep on happening and I can't care anymore. Crying over it is not going to help!" I was too angry to try to translate to Spanish for my mom. The words flew out of my mouth in English that bled together in a scattershot. As my anger grew, the words turned into something like a sustained yell. A scolding of my mother for withstanding the sins of my father. For not cutting the ties we so desperately needed her to.

My mom erupted at my callousness. "No, pinche chamaco. Es la planta. La West Liberty Food." There'd been some type of accident at the turkey plant where my dad worked. Something like a gas leak or a warning of an impending explosion. The plant evacuated all the workers. There was chaos as word rippled through the town that something was up. The anger drained from me as I reeled at the news. I stood caught in the kitchen not knowing how to react.

Now it was my mom's turn to get mad. She laid into me and called out to the heavens to forgive me for my indifference to her plight. I felt like a fool. Like a little boy who lashed out at things I couldn't comprehend. Everything ended up okay at the plant that day, though the story did make the local news. The real damage happened to the already deteriorating relationship I had with my mother. In trying to stop my mother's anguish, I showed my hand. She knew then that if things got worse, I wouldn't be empathetic. She knew that I couldn't find it in my heart to stick with her through the dissolution of their relationship. That when things reached the absolute bottom, she would be all alone. That morning was one of many factors that played into the night when our purgatory of silent resentment and anger finally burst.

———————

It happened late one night. It was at the start of the week because I didn't have work that day. My dad had stayed out again after work. Didn't come home until nine or so, doing God knows what. I arrived home from a late practice with my crew at the Field House. When I got there, my parents were arguing in the living room again. Well, it was as close to an argument as my parents got, meaning my dad gave little to no response to the continued fury of my mom. I made it a point to walk straight from the kitchen door to my bedroom. My mom's questions resonated as I tried to move as quickly as possible to the safety of my bedroom. *Where were you? Why won't you tell me? What do you expect me to do here all alone? What happened to us?* Each question asked without a response.

The wall between the living room and my bedroom muffled my mom's sustained confrontation. I put on headphones and played music on my computer to further distance myself from the routine. It wasn't the first time my mother had confronted my father, and I thought at the time that it wouldn't be the last, either. It was always the same. My dad would be aloof. They would skirt around the real issues tearing at their relationship. They would exhaust themselves without coming to a resolution, only to pick it up the next night. I turned up my music and distracted myself with message boards on dance tutorials. The computer was a gateway for me to escape this never-ending loop of a confrontation. Its fuzzy monitor reflected the extreme gauntness my face now possessed. I would have been hungry by then, as it was late enough that my binge-and-purge session was due. I would have to wait for my parents to tire themselves out before I put myself through the paces of eating until I couldn't eat anymore.

A loud crack and scuffle in the living room next door changed everything. It was so loud that it cut through the music blasting through my headphones. It was a fight. It was my parents fighting. There was another crash that I could feel in the floor of the house followed by a muffled yelp. I ripped my headphones off and bolted out of my chair. I don't know why, but I thought my dad had snapped. Maybe it was because I was so used to seeing men express themselves through anger and violence. Or because I suspected that's what I would have done, kept it all bottled up for too long only to let it out in a flurry of emotion.

I ran through the dark hallway and skidded to a stop in front of the living room. I was half right. I am my mother's son. I get my anger and passion from her, and I'll never forget that fact after this night. Before me was my dad with his arms outstretched, his work shirt tangled, a few buttons popped off. He was silent as he held my mom at bay. The noises I heard, the crashes and scuffles, were coming from her. She was hitting my dad and shouting curses. She said to him in Spanish, "Why? Why won't you say anything? Why won't you do anything? Eh? ¿Por qué?" It was the end. The end of her trying to talk anything out of my father. Now she would try to hit and claw it out of him. But it didn't work. He deflected her blows, standing silent in the middle of the living room.

My voice came out, and it was one of two small details I will never forget about this night. A voice and a scent. The voice was mine. I called out to my mom to stop. For the whole situation to stop. But when I spoke, I sounded different. I didn't recognize the fear and desperation in my own voice. It sounded like a kid going through puberty. Cracking and faltering. It was a high-pitched plea for normalcy. "¡Ama! ¡Ama! What are you doing? Stop!"

But the situation was too far gone. The woman before me knew she was alone in her despair as my father deflected her blows but still refused to engage. She pushed him back and they stood there for a second, both of them breathing and looking at each other. I stood in the living room hallway thinking it might be over. Then came the second detail I remember from that night, the smell of my mom's perfume as she pushed past me into the kitchen. It was the everyday perfume my mom had worn since I was a kid. Something she got at a department store, JCPenney or Younkers. But she'd worn it long enough that it smelled like my mom. There was a dissonance as I inhaled that forever-associated scent of my mother as she went into the kitchen and got a knife from the drawer.

"Whoa! Whoa, Mom. Mom. Jesus Christ, what the fuck?" I yelled out as my mom started walking with the knife. Her eyes were all wide, white bulbs, and they revealed something to me, something about how she didn't care anymore, how this was pure adrenaline and reaction. I was full-on crying now. My voice was an alien entity. I noticed it then, that as my words cascaded out of me, they sounded like someone else's. It felt like I was someone else completely. Like I had disassociated from reality and the only thing tethering me to the room was the fact that I knew my voice was different. "¡Ama! ¡Por favor!" I cried out like I was a little boy on a playground everyone else had abandoned, like I needed to scream at the top of my lungs to be found. While doing so, I jumped in front of her, putting my hands up and blocking her forward momentum from my dad. I cried so loud and moved so fast it snapped something out of my mom. She dropped the knife and shook her head as she looked at me, then at her husband. He left then, going out the entrance opposite from us. I remember walking to my mother and hugging her as she let it out. The sweet smell of that perfume hung on her as her nails dug into my arms and she cried.

———————

That night after everything settled and my father left, my mom retreated to the upstairs bedroom and I was alone. I had saved my dad's life, or at the very least had saved him from serious harm from my mother. I sat in the same room where it happened. I was alone at the kitchen table with cans of my father's beer splayed out in front of me, going over the look on my mother's face. The knife in her hand. My voice. I couldn't even bring myself to eat after that. Couldn't bring myself to gorge myself and then purge as a display of control over something. I wasn't in control. Although I had saved my father and stopped my mother, that wasn't control. None of us were in control anymore. It was all reactionary, all hidden feelings and unresolved conflict leading us to the night's events.

Disillusioned by the idea of being in control, I decided to run hard the other way. I would be out of control. I didn't want to feel any way about this situation. I didn't want to have to think or act out or process stopping my mom from stabbing my dad. So there I was at the kitchen table observing the condensation on the cans of beer lined up before me. With a flair for the dramatic, I decided my best course of action to oblivion was to get drunker than I ever had before. As drunk as Eric that night in the Shack. As drunk as I thought my friends were getting, living that college life. I would forgo my unspoken demons for the demons of my friends. Bulimia wouldn't cut it this time; binge drinking myself into a stupor seemed a more appropriate penance. With a sharp inhale I cracked open the first beer and drank it as fast as I could. I didn't let my momentum stop. As soon as I clanged the empty can on the table, I cracked open the second one and downed it. And so on and so on.

I'm not sure how many I drank in those few minutes. I was a light-weight, sure, due to my eating disorder but also due to not drinking much in a long time. All I know is things started getting dim before I finished. And still I kept at it. There's a competitive eater who talks about how his body shuts down as he gets far into a competition. It's physically taxing to consume that much food in such a short time. His words reminded me of how I felt that night, my belly distended from drinking so much. It hurt to swallow the liquid, but I continued to gulp it down. It wasn't long before the room was spinning and hazy. With my goal complete, I stumbled to my bedroom, trying hard not to puke. *No, don't puke this time, Chuy. This time keep it all in. This is the opposite of control. The more drink you keep in, the more numb you'll feel to it all. Keep that shit in.* I came to my knees at the foot of my bed, and that's the last thing I remember before it all went dark.

That was the low point. The moment when I knew I had a problem. In my reaction to my parents' fight, I was able to admit that I was not okay. It's hard to convey what I mean by this. I mean, I knew bingeing and purging wasn't okay. But there was something about it I could excuse. Not as normal behavior but as something I did that I could stop. It was something like an addiction or a coping mechanism that I didn't quite realize was a coping mechanism. Getting drunk alone in my kitchen so I couldn't feel the emotions of the night was a reckoning. I was not okay. My family was not okay.

Slowly and with more ups and downs than I can fit here, we started our journey back from our lowest point. I have to stress that it took years for my parents to mend their relationship. It took decades for me to come to terms with the fact that I have an eating disorder. Just now, before changing it, I typed "had" an eating disorder. The repercussions of this episode in our lives are still felt. It took real-life small steps to put ourselves back together, not a sweeping gesture. I didn't have a sit-down with my parents after that night where we hugged and cried. I didn't climb to the top of a mountain and swear that I would never binge and purge again.

No, it happened through years of messy work. My parents went to therapy, no doubt one of the hardest things for two old-school Mexicans to do. "Mental health and counseling? ¿Qué es eso?" They worked through their problems and discussed the root of things.

It's a similar story with the physical manifestations of my bulimia nervosa. It took a long time for me to stop getting up after meals and retching. Years. But there were a couple of big things that happened after the knife incident that further opened my eyes.

The first was on a national level. In 2005 Terri Schiavo died. Her death was national news and one of the endless examples of political bickering between talking heads. Terri Schiavo was on life support and certain people thought it wasn't right to pull the plug, even though she was in an irreversible vegetative state. George W. Bush got involved. It was a mess. After seven years, she died in 2005. A year or so after the knife incident with my parents. Through all the political discourse, there was an underlying point lost on the masses. Terri Schiavo had an eating disorder that doctors say led to brain damage and cardiac arrest. It was the reason she died. Through all the bickering about the right to die and quality of life, all I could think about was how I could have been her. That I could be doing major, irreversible damage to my body. It was a cautionary tale but also something more. It helped me to realize that my eating disorder wasn't simply about wanting to stay fit and light for dancing. It wasn't about looking good. It was about trauma and not knowing how else to process that trauma.

The other thing that helped me come to this realization was a bizarre tidbit of pop culture. There was a show called *Mad TV*. It was something like a competitor to *Saturday Night Live* in the late nineties and early aughts. I grew up watching *SNL* but also appreciated the edgier skits on *Mad TV*. I also liked that *Mad TV* had more performers of color who looked like me. I could relate to them more than the all-white casts of *SNL*. Much like the epiphany of sharing the same eating disorder with Terri Schiavo, *Mad TV* aired something that struck me upside the head. It was a parody of a QVC infomercial, "Call this number now to make three easy payments of $19.99" style. The product they were hawking? A mouth guard that protected your teeth while you vomited. It was meant to be a product for models and dancers. Now this is of course in bad taste and a sketch with no real punch line. But when I happened upon this sketch, it clicked. I remembered my broken tooth. The sketch talked about the bile and acid in your stomach dissolving your teeth. This stupid, crass show actually connected the dots for me. And much like Terri Schiavo forced me to look at the mental harm I'd gone through, this sketch made me look at the physical damage I had already done.

One of the steps to recovery was severing the ties with my job at Casey's. I want to be careful here. For the longest time I blamed Casey's and my access to their food as the cause of my eating disorder rather than it being an unfortunate set of circumstances that aligned to enable me. But at the time, I viewed Casey's as a manifestation of the loneliness and spinning of wheels that I felt my life was. It also didn't help that my supervisors weren't giving me the time off I needed.

Finally, things came to a head one shift. Some of my crew talked about going to a breaking event in Chicago the coming weekend. Keven almost asked me if I wanted to go but stopped himself, remembering I worked every weekend. *Screw that*, I thought, *I deserve to do the thing I love*. I asked for the weekend off, only for Cindy to turn me down yet again. "I know, I know, Chuy. But like I said before, we really don't have anyone else to cover the shifts."

The night before the jam I decided would be my last shift at Casey's. I wrote a note to my boss and left it on the counter saying that I needed to focus on other things in my life and that I quit. At ten o'clock that night, I made my last pizza for a caller. They wanted a supreme. I proceeded to make the best supreme pizza one could possibly make, loaded with twice the normal amount of toppings. I made a point to run the pizza through the conveyor-belt oven twice to make sure I cooked it perfectly with all those ingredients. I handed the family their pizza with something like pride, hoping they would be taken aback when they lifted the box. After cleaning the work area and looking over my "I quit" note, I walked past the empty warmers. Without any bags of food in my hand this time.

In the grand scheme of my recovery, quitting like that was a symbolic gesture. It still took years and many more actions to deal with and process my eating disorder. I would seek professional help. Therapy and medication. But at the time, quitting Casey's felt like self-love. It felt like I was in control of my life for the first time in a long time.

EPILOGUE

IN 2008 A GROUP FROM West Liberty went out to a bar in Coralville. At the end of a long night of drinking, they attempted to drive home. It was one of the West Liberty Laotians at the helm of the car, transporting a squad of people while he was drunk out of his mind. He tried to get on the interstate but ended up getting turned around and merging into the turnoff. He was going the wrong way on the interstate and didn't know it. It wasn't long before the car, going full speed, came across a semi. The man driving the car would go to jail for a long time. The fact that he refused to plead guilty to manslaughter sent ripples through the Laotian community in West Liberty, dividing his family from others who looked at his plea as a slap in the face.

Jerry Sayabeth's wife was in the car. She survived, but it took years of physical therapy to recover from the damage the crash had done. I remember talking to Jerry after it happened, and it was hard. I always regarded Jerry as this class clown, larger-than-life character. But there was nothing funny about this situation, and his somberness reflected the tragedy.

Another person in the car didn't make it. Kelly Oseguera died on the interstate that night. I used to work with Kelly, at my first job at Subway. She was a shorty. I had to help her reach the plastic bins we kept vegetables in during storage. Kelly was also Ruben Chavez's high school girlfriend. They dated for years in a tumultuous relationship that ended before the crash. Even though they were no longer together, I can't fathom the pain and stress that would put on someone.

This was yet another case in a long line of instances where the drink consumed folks from West Liberty. I was thinking of tragedies like that when I lined up all those beers on the table. The demons of the town that I talk about. That incident showed the fragility of life and the interconnectedness of life in a town where everyone knows each other. It also, no doubt, led to trauma and pain for my friends Jerry and Ruben.

Ruben eventually lost his wrestling scholarship. He got into too much trouble downtown. Had too big of an arrest record. Every story I heard down the pipeline was yet another tale of him getting into trouble. Further descending into the drink.

There has always been this unspoken connection between Ruben and me. Our lives paralleled each other in a lot of ways. One of these parallels is how much we struggled with our college education. It took me four and a half years to get my two-year associate degree from Kirkwood Community College. After that I transferred to the University of Iowa and was immediately put on academic probation for poor grades in my first semester. It would be another three years before I graduated with a degree in dance. It took Ruben a little longer. He oscillated between majors, but I'd wager that trying to go to school and socialize the way he did made it that much harder to get through it.

Another parallel concerns our parents, who are all around the same age and entering their twilight years. They're getting old and health issues are increasing in frequency and severity. A couple of years ago Ruben's parents both went through cancer scares. This was a wake-up call. An impetus to reflect on the way things were going in my old friend's life. At the time we hadn't hung out in years. We saw each other sometimes while hanging out with mutual friends. By a turn of fate, his parents' health scares coincided with my old crewmate Nicky moving in with me in an apartment in Iowa City. Ruben was hanging out with Nicky while shucking his old habits. Slowly and gingerly, Ruben and I began hanging out again. I had quit drinking a long time ago. I don't consider myself a teetotaler, but I know too well the ramifications of the drink and generally stay away. Ruben saw that in me, that I could be something of a role model or a rock to lean on.

Around that time I scored a job at the newly rebuilt Hancher Auditorium, a performing arts center at the University of Iowa. This was in addition to a teaching gig I had with the university. I was still breaking for fun with Nicky in our apartment and at practice spots with younger college kids. But teaching hip-hop dance to university students was where I was actually getting decent paychecks.

This is all to say that I was figuring things out in my life. Ruben saw that and let it influence him. My old friend started declining drinks at the poker table. He started working out and getting fit. He got a job as an assistant wrestling coach at a nearby high school. Darcy, my girlfriend at the time, said, "You know, your friend Ruben seems like a real good guy. Why haven't we hung out with him before?" She didn't know about his struggles. She didn't know how belligerent he would get at the bars. I alluded to these struggles but instead focused on how Ruben seemed to be in a better place. He graduated college and got a job. He started therapy like I had. Things went well for a few years. It felt good to have my friend back. To have someone who knew about the way we grew up. Darcy noted how Ruben made me laugh, that I seemed to be at ease with him in a way she hadn't seen before. "It's like you're home with him," she said.

Then he slipped into old habits. I don't need to get into specifics. I'm wary of exploiting another person's struggles. But there is a lesson we can provide to others like us. Other Mexican men. Other kids from West Liberty.

We are still friends. We always will be. Ruben was there when I proposed to Darcy. He was a groomsman at my wedding, the only one from our old friend group to get the honor. But once again, things are different. The rift between us is always there. A reminder of the trauma we are too afraid to parse through.

I thought of you, Ruben, as I wrote these stories. I reflected on our ups and downs, remembered and reminisced about all the crazy things we did as kids. Winced at the atrocities we committed against one another. Laughed and cried and felt it deep down that we share this connection to each other and to the town we grew up in. I don't know if our childhood was good or if I can say that I am a good person. All I know is that I will always root for you, my friend. There is a love between us that is deeper than the trauma. You were the first person I remember saying you loved me, and that means something. You were one of the first people I told about my eating disorder. That means something too.

We were boys who grew up too fast and men who still have to process our upbringing. And like the town we grew up in, we are messy and complicated and vessels full of all that is good and all that is bad. But I'm connected to you and I mean every word I write. To quote something that no one else will get, it's like the end of *Pu-Tang: The Lost Empire*. When you and Jerry are dying on the yard gasping for air, Jerry rattles out in his death throes, "Pu-tang . . . forever." We were some weird, crazy kids, bro, but we got it right when we made that movie. Even if Jerry did slice me with that knife and the ending fight scenes were way too long.

Me, Ruben, Zane, and Eric.

Whether our childhoods were good or not becomes irrelevant when I think about how you and I got through it all. Yes, we heard and experienced it young. We saw shit we shouldn't have seen, did things no kids should think of doing. But it's up to us as aging men to not let that take over us. Even apart, when things get bad or we haven't seen each other in a bit, I know we'll always have each other. That what bonds us together isn't the hate and trauma we experienced or the hate and trauma we dealt out but that mutual love and respect we will always have. No one can take that away. I love you.

ACKNOWLEDGMENTS

DARCY, MY LOVE, it is no coincidence that I found the courage to tell my stories after I met you. Thank you for your forever honest and sincere support. Thank you to everyone at the University of Iowa Press for their guidance and openness in working with me. Special thanks to Meredith Stabel for your kindness and patience from beginning to end. Your insights were more than I could ask for. Shout out to Ranjit for starting the conversation and pointing me in the right direction. Our coffee sessions were a necessary preamble to all that came after. Thanks also to Keven Xayasene for your help with all my random questions on Laotian culture. I am grateful for everyone in my hometown who has shown me so much love and support. I am humbled at the chance to tell a piece of our story. My hope is to continue forward together. To echo the great André 3000: Wes Lib got something to say. Let's tell 'em.